No Easy Answers

NO EASY ANSWERS

The Learning Disabled Child at Home and at School

Revised Edition

SALLY L. SMITH

BANTAM BOOKS

NEW YORK TORONTO LONDON SYDNEY AUCKLAND

NO EASY ANSWERS

A Bantam Book

PRINTING HISTORY

Winthrop edition published June 1979
Bantam mass market edition published January 1981
Bantam trade paperback edition / March 1995

All rights reserved.
Copyright © 1979, 1980, 1995 by Sally L. Smith.
Cover design by One Plus One Studio.
Book design by Ellen Cipriano
No part of this book may be reproduced or transmitted
in any form or by any means, electronic or mechanical,
including photocopying, recording, or by any information
storage and retrieval system, without permission in
writing from the publisher.
For information address: Bantam Books.

Library of Congress Cataloging-in-Publication Data

Smith, Sally Liberman.
    No easy answers : the learning disabled child at home
and at school / Sally L. Smith. — Rev. ed., Bantam trade
pbk. ed.
       p.   cm.
    Includes bibliographical references and index.
    ISBN 0-553-35450-7
    1. Learning disabled children—Education.   2. Home
and school.
    I. Title.
LC4704.S625   1995   94-36478
                                     CIP

Published simultaneously in the United States and Canada

Bantam Books are published by Bantam Books, a division of Bantam
Doubleday Dell Publishing Group, Inc. Its trademark, consisting of the
words "Bantam Books" and the portrayal of a rooster, is Registered in
U.S. Patent and Trademark Office and in other countries. Marca
Registrada. Bantam Books, 1540 Broadway, New York, New York 10036.

PRINTED IN THE UNITED STATES OF AMERICA

BVG 0 9 8 7 6 5 4 3 2 1

To my son Gary,

who has been my finest teacher
and my hardest taskmaster.

He, who did not read until he was thirteen years old,
because of his severe learning disabilities, once said: "*Now* I
understand how people can read to themselves. They have
to share it with their brains!"

CONTENTS

Preface   ix
Preface to the First Edition   xii
Acknowledgments   xv
1 Have You Seen This Child?   1
2 Immaturity and the Need for Organization   10
3 No One Cause, No One Answer   20
4 Attention-Deficit/Hyperactivity Disorder (ADHD)   34
5 The Need to Learn How to Learn   54
6 Managing Space and Time   73
7 Learning the Three Rs   94
8 Teachers: Their Concerns and Feelings   122
9 Teaching Approaches   150
10 Teaching Through the Arts and the Academic Clubs   169
11 Parents: Their Concerns and Feelings   193
12 Parents and Teachers and the Individuals with
      Disabilities Education Act   220
13 Adolescence: Socialization and Organization   260
14 The Key Is Organization   290

Conclusion   Educating the Learning Disabled for the
                 Future   296
Appendix 1   Glossary   311
Appendix 2   Recommended Books   320
Appendix 3   Tapes and Videos   342
Appendix 4   Information Centers, Organizations, and
                 Research Centers   346
Appendix 5   Recommended Professional Journals   357
Appendix 6   Description and List of Tests Ordinarily Used to
                 Diagnose Learning Disabled Students   362
Appendix 7   The Lab School of Washington   384
Index   388

PREFACE

The first edition of *No Easy Answers: The Learning Disabled Child at Home and at School* was published by Bantam in 1981. More than a decade later Bantam is bringing out a new edition to help parents and teachers unlock the mysteries of learning disabilities. I wrote the book because I wished I had owned such a book in the 1960s when my son with severe learning disabilities (what's now called ADHD) was growing up. The insights of a desperate mother, dealing with the vital needs of a child crying out for assistance, were the passionate beginnings of my knowledge about learning disabilities. I read everything that was written on the subject, and in 1967 I had the audacity (and perhaps naïveté) to design and direct a school for my son, and others like him, when there was no such thing available.

No Easy Answers: The Learning Disabled Child at Home and at School is based on my own experience. As mother, teacher, school administrator, and university professor, I have lived with the problems of the learning disabled every day since the early 1960s. The thousands of children with severe learning disabilities who attended

The Lab School and an extraordinarily gifted faculty have been my teachers since 1967.

I was the Founder/Director of The Lab School, which was situated from 1967 to 1982 at the Kingsbury Center in Washington, DC. Twenty-eight years later I am still actively managing the school. In 1982, we became an independent body, The Lab School of Washington, with the same program, the same students and parents, and the same faculty. Independence allowed the school to expand from 80 students to 250 students spanning kindergarten through twelfth grade with an after-school arts and sports program. A diagnostic clinic with testing and tutoring services for the community and a training course for tutors began in 1983.

In 1984, The Night School for seventy-five to ninety adults with learning disabilities was added. A Wednesday-night lecture-discussion series began in 1985 to offer parents and those who aid them in the Washington metropolitan community a forum to explore feelings and problems related to raising a child or adolescent with learning disabilities. Large departments of occupational therapy, speech and language therapy, and psychotherapy grew to serve the wider Washington community as well as the school.

In 1985, to offer encouragement and motivation to our students and parents, The Lab School began giving Outstanding Learning Disabled Achiever Awards to celebrities with learning disabilities who had distinguished themselves in a particular field. A career- and college-counseling center specifically tailored for the learning disabled opened its doors in 1987. In 1993, the International Materials and Services Center was inaugurated in order to share Lab School materials, techniques, and methods with others in our country and abroad.

In 1975, I began teaching at The American University. In 1976, I became full-time faculty and associate professor in charge of the graduate program in special education: learning disabilities, and in 1982, I became professor. Now, in 1995, I am still teaching and in charge of the department of special education in The School of

Education. I have been forced to learn everything I can so that the graduate students will have access to the latest research and practices in the field, and children with learning disabilities will be better served.

This new edition of *No Easy Answers* contains all the original information with updates where necessary. I have added more material on the related disorders of Attention Deficit Disorder (ADD) and Attention-Deficit/Hyperactivity Disorder (ADHD), on the gifted child with learning disabilities, the nursery-school youngster who is at risk for learning disabilities, more on behavior management, a final chapter on "Educating the Learning Disabled for the Future," and a whole new Appendix of current resources.

Sally L. Smith
January 1995

PREFACE TO THE FIRST EDITION

As we enter the 1980s we are able to control many aspects of our lives by push buttons, levers, switches, computers, test tubes, and nuclear energy, but we still have to deal with many of the human issues over which we have little control. We each wrestle with feelings, relationships, and values daily, and the way in which we deal with them determines the quality of the life we lead. There are rarely easy answers, simple solutions, perfect ways to handle human problems. This is especially true with the learning problems of children. Not machines but the brains and hearts of human beings are needed to help children overcome these problems. Compassion is not enough, although it is always welcome. Knowledge in depth of the child, his particular learning problems, and the tasks we are asking him to do are needed in order to help a learning disabled child to function effectively in school and in society.

This book is an introduction to the world of the learning disabled child. It is about the intelligent youngster who has trouble learning, not about the retarded or the emotionally disturbed child. It is about the child whose nervous system is delayed in maturing. He looks typical for his age, but he does not learn as other children his age do because he has a hidden handicap. In some ways, this child is similar to a much younger child, although in other ways he functions at his own age level or above. His wide scattering of abilities and disabilities makes him into a very uneven, inconsistent, unpredictable child who puzzles the adults around him.

Disorder prevails in a child who is delayed in development. He is scattered in his attention, as well as in his growth. He lacks the tools to organize what he sees, hears, touches, feels, smells, and tastes to make sense of his environment. Normally by school age, a child develops a sense of order, which is the solid base on which future learning is built. The child with disorder does not have an organized base. He has a learning disorder.

Although disorder is the key characteristic of these children, the term *learning disabled* is appropriate, for they are indeed disabled by their disorder. It is the term educators prefer to describe the intelligent child who experiences much learning difficulty at school. Doctors most frequently use the term *minimal brain dysfunction.*

This book is concerned with the immaturity that causes this disorder and the forces that provide the order necessary to deal with it. It explains how the learning disabled youngster becomes defeated at school, how his movement, language, reading, writing, spelling, and arithmetic are affected by his disorder. It deals primarily with the child who has a severe learning disability, but it is equally applicable to the great number of mildly handicapped children who slide through school getting C's and D's when their potential is for solid A's.

The magnitude of the problem of learning disabilities was forced into national attention in the late 1970s, primarily through the efforts of concerned parents who banded together for action. Public Law 94-142 (effective in 1978) now mandates all states to provide proper educational services for these youngsters. Currently the media are publicizing the problems of these intelligent children who fail to learn properly and who frequently end up as school dropouts. The nation is finally becoming concerned about the wasted potential that ends up on the lines of the unemployed, in the courts, in jails, in guidance clinics and mental institutions. The time has come for us to spot these children early and give them what they need.

This book probes the multiple causes of learning disabilities and postulates that the learning disabled child's prime need is for help in organizing almost every area of his life. He needs explicit teaching of organization skills, along with the three Rs. *Teaching the learning disabled child the approach to a task is as important as teaching the task itself.* This book explores the feelings of the adults closest to the learning disabled child—the many stages and dimensions of their reactions to him. It registers the feelings of the learning disabled child and follows him into his adolescence and preparation for an independent life. Addressed both to professionals in the education field, in health care, day care, recreational and youth organizations, and to parents, the text outlines the problems and offers guidelines and practical approaches.

This book embodies what I have learned from The Lab School students, their parents, and the teachers and artists who have worked with the children. There are no easy answers. No one way works with every learning disabled child. There are, however, basic principles and approaches that do work. Learning disabled youngsters can learn how to learn. They can succeed!

ACKNOWLEDGMENTS

Elisabeth Benson Booz made this book a reality, not only through her constant talented assistance but through her determination that I write it. On every page of the manuscript "Ben's" sharp eye and quick and creative mind have provided useful criticism and editorial correction. She is a dear and close friend, whose love of life is infectious. I treasure the hours spent together and find no way to thank her adequately for all she has done.

To Dr. Edna Small for her valuable help on the psychological material;
To Dr. Grace Gabe for her consulting on the neurological material;
To Mary Mitchell, reading specialist, and Sue Hollis, former Lab School head teacher, for their expert advice on sections applying to reading;
To Helen Colson, who did so much for The Lab School in the early years;
To Sheila Weiss, Helen Levine, Peter Braun, Karen Vartanian, Neela Seldin, Noel Kerns, Diana Leonard Meltzer, and Barbara

Karayn of The Lab School for their continual support over many years;

To Karen Duncan of The Lab School, and Justine Maloney of LDA, great advocates for children with learning disabilities, for their help on current legislation;

To Dr. Luanne Knight, Head of Diagnostic and Psychological Services of The Lab School, for assistance on the testing materials appearing in appendix G;

To Ruth Switzer Pearl for substantial help in understanding PL 94-142, and her wicked sense of humor that kept me working on that chapter;

To Lois Meyer for her painstaking work in helping to update the appendixes and helping in general;

To Tina Kierzek for interpreting the purple scrawl so well!

MY GRATEFUL APPRECIATION

I want to thank my two older sons, Randall Alan Smith and Nicholas Lee Smith, who have lived much of this book with me, for their support, deep caring, rich humor, sensitivity, and ingenuity. They have helped their younger brother learn how to learn.

MY ADMIRATION AND LOVE

O N E

HAVE YOU SEEN THIS CHILD?

He reads *saw* for *was*.

He says a *b* is a *d*, and a *d* is a *p*.

He skips, omits, or adds words when he reads aloud.

She reads well but can hardly spell a word.

She writes 41 for 14.

He can do any mental arithmetic problem but can't write it down.

She doesn't know today the multiplication tables she knew yesterday.

He can talk about life on Mars but can't add 2 + 2.

He puts down the same answer to four different math problems.

He draws the same thing over and over again.

She asks endless questions but doesn't seem interested in the answers.

He is an expert strategist in checkers but doesn't understand simple riddles.

He has an adult vocabulary but avoids using the past tense.

She starts talking in the middle of an idea.

He calls breakfast *lunch* and confuses *yesterday* with *tomorrow*.

He can't tell you what has just been said.

She can talk about Homer but can't tell you the days of the week.

He discusses monsoons but does not know the order of the seasons.

He can remember the television ads but not his own telephone number.

She can remember what you say to her but not what she sees. She can't picture things in her mind.

She can't see the difference between Africa and South America on the map.

He doesn't see the difference between *pin, pan,* and *pun.*

She is a good child, quiet and polite, but she doesn't learn.

He prefers to play with children much younger than himself.

She says whatever pops into her head.

He rushes headlong into his work, is the first one finished, and does every problem wrong.

She has trouble lining up and can't keep her hands off the child in front of her.

He doesn't stop talking, giggles too much, and laughs the loudest and the longest.

He doesn't look where he's going, bumps into the door, swings his lunch box into the nearest leg, trips on his own feet, and doesn't look at the person who is talking to him.

He loses his homework, misplaces his book, forgets where he is to be.

She leaves a trail of her belongings behind her wherever she goes.

He acts like an absentminded professor (and has untied shoelaces as well).

She likes routines, is upset by changes, and is reluctant to try anything new.

He wants everything done the same way.

He doesn't follow directions.

She is distracted by the least little thing.

He doesn't pay attention.

He doesn't look.

She doesn't listen.

He doesn't remember.

She doesn't do what she's supposed to do.

HAVE YOU SEEN THIS CHILD?

Is this a bad child?

Willful?

Lazy?

Manipulative?

Spoiled?

Disturbed?

Probably not. This might be a very young child, or it could be a learning disabled child. It isn't that other children don't behave this way. They do! It is THE QUANTITY, INTENSITY, AND LONG DURATION OF IMMATURE BEHAVIOR that make the learning disabled child different. It is the uneven quality of this child which is confounding. He is demanding, bewildering, baffling, and consuming. One day he can do something, and the next he can't. Some of her talents are extraordinary, yet she cannot manage the simplest routines of daily existence. This erratic quality makes the adults around him and her feel insecure. What will happen next? Is he doing it on purpose? Does she do it to get me mad? These are typical questions asked by the adults who deal with the learning disabled child. They don't understand. His talents and successes give them hope. His distractibility, infantile responses, and disorganization exasperate them. They don't know what is going on. That, in itself, is exhausting. Teachers and parents find themselves feeling drained and inadequate. They want to do the very most and best they can for him, but they don't know what to do. When they are with such a child, adults who are otherwise competent often feel helpless and incompetent.

THEY FACE SO MANY DIFFICULTIES

Imagine yourself to be this child, such a patchwork quilt of "can dos" and "can't dos." Would you believe you are intelligent, as the adults say, when all your buddies can read and you can't? Wouldn't you wonder about yourself if you kept hearing all kinds of sounds but missed what the teacher said? Other kids could remember so much, but you couldn't. Wouldn't that bother you? Might you wonder if something were terribly wrong with you if you were always forgetting things or tripping over your own feet and your friends didn't? Have you ever wakened in an unfamiliar hotel room and tapped that terrible feeling of utter disorientation—"Where am I"? There is nothing familiar to hold on to, and for a brief moment your mind is blank. This is the way many learning disabled children feel in everyday space. And the lack of a sense of time and timing that they feel is comparable to your jet trip to Australia, where twenty hours later, without a watch, you have no sense of what time it is. Try threading a needle with a pair of extra-thick rubber gloves on, and you will come close to the feeling of the child whose hands don't work well for him when he tries to hold a pencil and write. Try it while someone is stating firmly that if you only tried harder, you could do it.

If you analyze the process of tying your shoelaces, you will realize how exceedingly complex an act it is. Now imagine trying to tie a bow when you cannot visualize what a loop looks like. It is the feeling of the lost driver who knows his destination but doesn't know where he is starting from, of the frantic mother who is being yelled at but can't locate her car keys anywhere. Frantic and overwhelmed—common feelings of the learning disabled child, who is confused, bewildered, doesn't know where to begin, what to do, how to go about doing a task, doesn't understand what's going on within him—this despairing child overwhelms the adults around him. Frequently he would rather be called "bad" than "dumb," so he will say, "I won't," when he means,

"I can't." Often she comes across as negative, hostile, or silly; she may be a loner, avoiding help, laughing at adults, sporting the "I don't care" attitude or saying, "I think this work is boring and stupid" when she can't do it. Sometimes he presents himself as sweet, kind, considerate, overly conscientious. Whatever the outside cover, the inside is hurting. Most adults feel that hurt, and when they don't know how to remove it, they feel helpless. Too often, the frightened child is forgotten along with the precious qualities that the child does have.

THEY ALSO DISPLAY A HEARTY ENTHUSIASM...

There is something extremely appealing about a wide-eyed, open-armed youngster with a beaming smile. "Look, the sun is smiling on us today!" he says as he hugs the world around him. "I'm glad Mr. Rain stayed away," an immature statement for an eleven-year-old but still a pleasure to hear.

There's a sheer joy—temporary though it may be—that many learning disabled children bring to life. Often they seem to embrace life with an enthusiasm and jauntiness that most of us lose with maturity. The spontaneous expression of feelings, the unedited comment, the untrampled-upon gesture are all trademarks of the impulsive child. There's a freshness that he conveys, perhaps because he doesn't see the whole picture, that turns our attention to experiences we have come to take for granted. In the midst of checking the route map, watching the road signs, estimating when the next gas stop must be made, our attention is suddenly diverted to an unexpected delight when the learning disabled child remarks, "How fresh and good the grass smells!"

Often overly sensitive to the feelings and relationships of the people around him, this is the child who slips her hand clumsily into the hand of a troubled adult and squeezes gently. The adult silently wonders, "How did that little girl know what I needed just at that time?" Many adults have commented that learning disabled children seem to have ESP, a certain profound knowledge of emotional states (even if the child can't apply it to himself).

Sometimes a learning disabled child is very shy and retiring, tending to back away from social situations, and especially unfamiliar ones. Often, however, he meets people easily, although he may have trouble maintaining those relationships. In one family of three children, it was always the learning disabled child who knew everyone at the unfamiliar swimming pool, had become a well-known figure in the hotel dining room, and had met every new neighbor within minutes of their arrival. He didn't remember their names but everyone knew his. "Oh, you're Joe's family!" people would say to the rest of them. His friendliness to strangers and his open, guileless remarks enchanted newcomers. In any new situation, this family found it was Joe who made everybody feel at home at once. His impulsiveness may have led him to wandering, but he did get the layout of a new place down pat—that is, if he found his way back to the appointed spot. He had a way of heading toward the men's room but along the way discovering all sorts of fascinating byways to share with his family. He was indiscriminate in his choice of companions. He was equally at ease with a beggar and a millionaire, both of whom introduced him to exciting new experiences. He would always come back from one of his jaunts (while the family was frantically looking for him) bearing a precious gift somebody had given him—a flower or a candy—or leading some embarrassed but friendly stranger back with him.

Not sufficiently afraid of the dangerous or the unknown, the learning disabled child frequently embarks on adventures that could fill a novel. She's the one who discovers the unbeaten path to the hermit's cottage and has tea with him, uncovers the nest of blue eggs, finds the attic closet filled with treasures (even though she may get locked inside it for a while). Walking along the beach picking up pebbles at random, he finds a half-dollar. He is the one who ducks under the barrier and gets to shake the governor's hand. Important people are treated like any other friends by this child, who is not famous for diplomacy and has no sense of priorities. He doesn't discriminate, to the point that it becomes poor judgment in social situations.

He is likely to be an asset at a party, where he genuinely welcomes people and puts others at ease. Trouble may come later if he meets with a frustration or misinterprets a remark. At school, he often takes on the welcoming role at the beginning of the term or in a new grouping.

...AND MANY OTHER SPECIAL QUALITIES

Some learning disabled youngsters are not hyperactive, impulsive, or outgoing, but they too have a quality about them that can make others feel good about themselves. Albert, quiet and resourceful, seems to gather children around him. They feel strength in him. They admire his athletic prowess. He seems to have a fund of resources, untried ways of doing things. The learning disabled youngster, because there is so much he can't seem to do like others, must call upon his own ingenuity and use a different perspective. Perhaps learning disabilities have been at the root of some of our most valued inventions. We know that Thomas Edison's learning disabilities brought him failure at school, but they also helped to bring us the lightbulb. Auguste Rodin, the magnificent sculptor, had difficulty learning to read and write; he was known as the worst student in his school. Albert Einstein's teachers found him to be a slow learner and socially awkward. And Hans Christian Andersen, who spun all those lovely fairy tales, was an extremely poor student and said to be very immature. Yet his naïveté and his eternal childlike qualities have brought pleasure to countless people.

The learning disabled youngster, along with all the heartache he feels and brings into his home, often touches the family with a freshness, a pure natural quality. When Harry laughed, it was such a full, resounding roar of delight that his family couldn't help but laugh with him. The unscreened pleasure he took in watching the antics of a litter of puppies permeated the whole house. Unfortunately that same loud laugh, and its duration, might send him to the principal's office at school.

Although the learning disabled child is not known for his humor and is often laughed at for his clumsiness of speech, action, or social behavior, many times he coins a phrase that is uproarious. Martin, after suffering along with a classmate who wouldn't stop talking about electricity, said, "That guy is so obsessed with electricity that someday he's going to go to the bathroom and a lightbulb will come out!"

Moodiness can bring bright moments too. Just as a young child is very distractible and often can be led out of a bad moment by his own distractibility, so it is with the learning disabled child. The perturbed girl with the storm clouds gathering around her can suddenly change into a sparkling delight if an adult strikes the right chord and provokes her to laugh by imitating her pouting. Within minutes her mood can change, often for the better. Her responsiveness lends itself to adult direction.

Courage is a quality we all admire. With the blind child, the deaf, the paralyzed, the public admires every effort. Such a large part of the learning disabled child's troubles goes unseen that she does not receive anything like the praise she so justly deserves. Imagine the effort it takes to operate within the disorder felt by this child. It takes an immense amount of effort every day for the learning disabled child to face the world of school with its meaningless symbols and confused instruction. Not only is she picking herself up literally much of the time, but she is also picking herself up from constant failures and disappointments and keeping going.

It is a wonder that so many learning disabled children have developed strong characters and unique personalities, but they have. True, some of them are quiet, very closed people, called eccentric, but more often than not they are respected for their difference and their specific talents. Many are free spirits, venturing into life with abandon. The brakes are not on enough. The maturity that builds good judgment is not working well enough. But there's a joy, a heartwarming quality that brings out all the good instincts in a person. Many brothers or sisters of learning disabled children (and a sprinkling of parents too) have felt a certain envy and admiration of the free spirit. One older brother said, "I'm so regulated by what I should do and what I have to do, I've lost sight of what I can do or want to do or like to do. And HE DOES IT ALL!"

Teachers often say that they can't get over how good-looking, appealing, and affectionate the learning disabled children in their classrooms are and how unusually creative so many of them are. The learning disabled child has to use other outlets when the switchboard of the brain doesn't make the proper connections; she has to travel new pathways. She has to use all the resources at her disposal to accomplish the simplest of tasks. She has to combat the disorder overwhelming her, making her easily fatigued. She has to work far harder than the rest of us, and still take the abuse of being called lazy.

Have you seen *this* child?

T W O

IMMATURITY AND THE NEED FOR ORGANIZATION

Organization is the lifeline, the safeguard, the medicine, and the key to learning for the child who is disabled by disorganization, or disorder. This intelligent child cannot filter out and organize the sensations that are coming to his brain from his eyes and his ears and through his body. He is overstimulated, bombarded by every sensation. He cannot sort out that which is relevant from that which is not. He lacks discrimination. The filtering mechanism of his brain is not working properly, and so the mass of sights, sounds, and feelings is coming in unscreened, causing DISORDER. Because the child registers fragments of what is coming in, what comes out is therefore fragmented, disorganized, irrelevant, disordered. He is indiscriminate in his reactions and often in his statements. Although at times he displays a very mature intellect and sensitivity, he is frequently scattered and inappropriate.

A two-year-old is both delightful and exhausting. She runs around a room touching everything in sight. She yells when she is denied a cookie. She rolls on the floor in delight. She spills her milk and breaks her mug. You can tell a home where there is a two-year-old because everything movable or breakable is out of her reach. Unless her environment is arranged to suit her two-year-old ways, she is a menace.

Her movements are random—hit or miss. She uses her whole body when one hand would do—everything in excess. Her attention, her aims, and her belongings are scattered. She is clumsy, unfocused, and inefficient in anything she does. Nobody expects her to be any other way because she is two. She is funny, her mispronounced words and inappropriate remarks are hilarious, and, although she keeps things hopping and may be exhausting, she is a joy.

But the same behavior in a seven-year-old is not charming. It is a cause of ever-growing anxiety to her parents, and it is not accepted or tolerated by others. The behavior itself is not abnormal, but it is inappropriate to the child's age. It is immature.

For children whose nervous systems develop normally, neural organization happens naturally. They sort out their world. They discriminate between essential and nonessential. They focus. They soon learn to judge distances and lapses of time accurately. They can place themselves and their belongings in their proper places. They can meet deadlines. By the third grade, they know half of everything they will ever know. Most of what follows will be regroupings, substitutions, refinements of categories, the creation of more sophisticated filing systems in their minds.

A child who develops normally learns to control his body and to concentrate with his mind; each new step in his growth lays a foundation for the next. What was random and undirected becomes focused and efficient. If you watch a four-year-old trying to throw a ball, you see him take an exaggerated stance with his feet wide apart, and his whole body, including his contorted face, goes into the act of throwing. He can't speak while he throws. It takes all his thought and energy to accomplish his throw, inefficient though it may be, and he can't possibly do another thing at the same time. A twelve-year-old throws the ball with accuracy and a neat economy of movement, while calling instructions to his teammates. Through trial and error, he has built up a body memory of what works, and he uses only the necessary muscles and energy. His body knows the relationship of its different parts, and his reactions are fast. The superfluous, random movements of the younger child have been replaced by automatic, accurate ones, and he can now do several things at once. Not so for the learning disabled child.

At The Lab School of Washington, the children's difficulty with integrating two or more things at once shows up typically in drama class. When Wayne was playing the part of a bus driver, he could not maintain his pantomime of holding the steering wheel and at the same time asking the passengers where they were going. He would either "drive" in silence or put his hands in his lap to ask the question. Similarly, at lunchtime, Linda could not talk and eat at the same time. Her sandwich remained uneaten because she could not organize herself to speak, take a bite while listening to the response, chew, swallow, and be ready to speak again. Such a child can concentrate on only one thing at a time, and often not for very long.

INDISCRIMINATE REACTIONS

Nobody expects a three-year-old to sit still for long with a picture book on her lap. In a very few minutes she will be up and exploring— looking, touching everything around her—and any loud noise will draw her to it. This same behavior in a seven-year-old is called *distractibility,* and it is one of the most easily recognized characteristics of a learning disabled child. She reacts indiscriminately to everything going on around her.

Maturity is achieved by separating out the parts from a whole, differentiating them, and integrating them back into an understand-able and usable unity, which produces organization. You can't pull things together properly until you can sort out the pieces. You have to know where the parts of your body are and what they can do before you can become coordinated, with all parts working together smoothly. A baby cannot move in a coordinated way, partly because he does not have sufficient awareness of his own body. Just as the infant must babble in a random way before he can speak, so move-ment begins in a random way before it becomes purposeful and specific. The preschool youngster learns to separate out one part of the body from another, left from right, before he can begin to unify and coordinate his body. Normally by the age of five or six, the child knows his right side from his left and can use the two together in actions when both are needed, as in opening a jar. He has freedom of action. The learning disabled child does not follow the normal pattern of maturing. A doctor would say that he suffers from neurological immaturity or minimal brain dysfunction. An educator would say that he has a learning disability. A parent would say, "Something is wrong; he's so inconsistent."

DISCRIMINATION

Separating out is at the root of the learning disabled child's problem. Because of the lag in his neural development, he is bombarded by too many sensations at once. Because of his immaturity, he reacts to too much with too much body and mind. He doesn't discriminate. His inability to separate out one idea from another, one sound, one symbol, is related to his difficulty in separating out body parts and one side from the other. This affects his judgment of space and explains why so many of these children spill their milk, drop their papers, and knock over objects by mistake. Physical activities have to be broken down and taught to them in sequence, step-by-step. Some learning disabled children appear very well coordinated in sports and dance but still have subtle spatial difficulties and cannot coordinate the eye and the hand to work smoothly together.

Random action cannot become coordinated and efficient until the body knows which parts to use. By separating out the functions of the parts, a child becomes aware of the limits of her whole body and herself as a separate entity in space. A baby's first big sorting job is separating herself out as an individual being from all around her. At first she tends to see everything as an extension of herself. Then she sees objects separate from herself. As she grows older, she sees relationships among objects, isolates them, learns to see their differences and also their similarities. From these she makes generalizations and creates abstract ideas. Her mind is going through the same process of development and control that her body followed earlier: separation, differentiation, integration.

The ultimate maturing occurs in the transition from adolescence to adulthood, when the young person sees herself both as a unique, differentiated part of a larger society and as a meaningful unit in her own right. The rest of her life will be spent discovering the infinite possibilities in her personhood and integrating them into wholeness.

At the very core of growth is this process of identifying differences and similarities and then pulling them together to give meaning to life. This is the very serious business of the preschooler, his prime developmental task. Through play, he is sorting out reality and fantasy, sights, sounds, and movements. All his exploring, touching, smelling, opening, closing, and tasting are organizing his environment. The preschooler is fully occupied as he discriminates one color from another, one shape from another, and identifies sounds, sizes, and sequences. Through play, he is sorting out one item from another; as one puts together a puzzle, he is putting together his world, making sense of it.

Usually the child with an intact nervous system is a well-organized human being by school age. He has sorted, classified, and categorized information into the proper compartments in his mind. He has achieved the maturation necessary to learn efficiently. By age six, most youngsters are ready for formal education (although some cultures believe they are not ready until seven). His equipment can handle it; he has the tools to do the job.

The learning disabled youngster is not ready for formal education on time. He is consumed by disorder and disorganization. He is immature. He doesn't have the internal organization necessary to pay attention. It's not just that he doesn't pay attention; he pays too much attention to too many things. The least little stimulus plays havoc with his concentration. Almost anything can distract this child. It is the creative and scientific challenge to his teacher to capture—and keep—the focus of this distractible child.

A CONFUSING ENVIRONMENT

Imagine how you might feel if you are in a boat on a rough sea and you see people on the shore waving to you, flags being waved at you, a loudspeaker saying something you can't understand, people in another boat nearby yelling to you—but all you can hear is the roar of the waves. The learning disabled youngster feels that desperation to understand what's going on but is swept up by the surrounding sensations. His immature brain can't automatically relegate these sensations to a subordinate place so that he can focus on the real purpose of the moment.

Have you ever been swept into a festival or a rally where you had no idea what was going on, what the point of it was, what the chanting and movement all around you was about? You couldn't make sense of the whole experience. Have you ever tried to find your way in a strange city following someone's directions that referred to streets you haven't seen—and with the noise of the traffic, screaming sirens, and people shouting all around you, making it harder to understand?

When you want to understand something and you can't filter out what's important, what's meaningful from what isn't, you probably feel overwhelmed, dumb, threatened, perhaps helpless, and then angry. It is frustrating to be unable to separate out the essential parts and pull them together into a meaningful whole. You can't make sense of your environment this way.

For learning disabled children, the ability to organize has somehow been short-circuited, and normal learning cannot follow. If a child cannot be sure what comes first, in the middle, or last, then getting dressed is an ordeal, the days of the week stay jumbled, counting or reciting the alphabet becomes a hopeless chore, and reading is an impossibility. Janet can't get down to work. She's busy putting her lunch away, hanging up her jacket, talking to her neighbor, tying her shoelace, which does not seem to be tight enough and has to be retied, noticing that Alfred didn't put his lunch away in the right spot and that there's a funny groove on the floor next to a crack in the linoleum, and then she's occupied chasing a fly, which she calls a bee. Finally she is led to her seat. Focused by her teacher, she puts on earphones and listens to a book. Soon it is time to stop. The teacher motions to her, taps her, finally removes the earphones from her, and Janet flies into a tantrum. This is a typical story of some children with learning disabilities. They can't get started, have a terrible time focusing, and then won't stop. They flit from activity to activity at home, not settling down, getting under everybody's feet, and then—usually near mealtime—becoming engrossed in something, and won't, almost *can't*, stop, no matter how many warnings are given. It's as though the activity has taken over the child, and the child can't get out from under it unless an adult does it for her. This behavior is called *perseveration*.

A child may draw one circle and continue to draw more all over her paper until the teacher takes the pencil out of her hand. Her drawing is an unthinking action, where the mind is seemingly separated from the hand that is circling. Sometimes it is the one activity that a child can do and be successful at. She may fear not being able to manage a new task.

To shift easily from one activity to another demands more flexibility and control than the learning disabled child seems to have. To the parent, it often seems like moving mountains, bringing as much of the mountain to Mohammed as possible. Rather than have Abba create a scene, his mother will bring the clothes to him (instead of insisting that he get the clothes himself) and practically dress him to help him end the activity and be ready to go out for the party on time.

ANIMISM

Frequently the immature child will give life and personality to objects. This is called *animism*—the failure to recognize the difference between animate and inanimate objects. A school-age learning disabled child may behave like a small child in the nursery who talks to his teddy bear, says that the car has "gone beddy-bye" when it is in the garage, or greets his breakfast with "Hello, Sugar Pops!" He will admonish his pencil, "Go on—write!" or see his Cuisenaire rods as having a fight: "You go in here before the yellow guy gets you. Okay, red guy, how are you going to get him?" This behavior is symbolic of an unawareness of himself as a person fully separate from what is around him—a person who occupies a distinct personal space with a precious individuality all his own.

DEFINING HIMSELF

Ordinarily the learning disabled child is highly egocentric. Like any very young child, he expects to be the center of attention and does not pay attention to others. He wants his parents to himself. Frequently he wants only one friend. Sharing is difficult, and just as he can handle only one thing at a time, so it is that very often he can manage best with just one other person. The learning disabled youngster of seven or eight is frequently similar in his social behavior to the two- or three-year-old. He craves center stage, not out of any base ambitions but because of immaturity. He has trouble defining who he is. He seems to need constant recognition of his existence long after the preschool years are over. Because of his many difficulties (such as being unable to read or write, to tie shoelaces, or to use language correctly to portray his needs and wants), he is dependent longer on the adults around him and must call for help over a longer period of time. The need for attention may equal the need for help, and many learning disabled youngsters have cleverly discovered that helplessness brings swift attention. Also there are many children who would so much rather receive negative attention than no attention that they will purposely get in trouble or act out to evoke an adult response. Some youngsters will provoke trouble with other children to make sure they are not ignored; they can then complain about being teased or picked on, but they have been the center of everyone's attention. This behavior happens frequently with learning disabled youngsters.

The preschool child spouts many unrealistic goals with all the confidence of a believer. "Next year I shall climb the highest mountain in the world," says four-year-old Les. Nine-year-old Hans, who has learning disabilities, also believes he can do it "next year." Many learning disabled youngsters continue to draw Superman as a representation of themselves (long after that stage has passed in most other children) because they are immature and also are looking for ways to feel more powerful and competent.

The chronological age of a youngster simply states how much time he has spent on earth. The developmental age tells us at what stage he is in his growth—physical, social, emotional, mental. The child with learning disabilities is immature in many phases of his development (although not all), and his developmental age is usually several years below his chronological age. He is lagging in parts of his development, but what he is doing is normal for an earlier phase of growth. His behavior is not abnormal, just delayed. We tend to make allowances for the immaturity of a child who looks immature for his age but often expect far too much from a thirteen-year-old who has suddenly become six feet tall. Yet, at the same time, we must remember that every learning disabled child's unevenness includes areas of strength, which we must build on, and not ask too little of him.

We have to teach the learning disabled child at his developmental level yet present the material in ways that satisfy his chronological age. His age and the special interests of his age group command respect. Sophisticated use of very primary materials is what is demanded of the teacher to help the learning disabled child acquire a foundation of organizational skills that will allow him to progress academically.

THREE

NO ONE CAUSE, NO ONE ANSWER

It is difficult to say how many learning disabled children there are because the experts disagree. Several believe that 10 to 20 percent of America's children have some form of learning disability and that 4 to 7 percent are severe enough to require special schooling. The U.S. Department of Education (1989) reported that 4.73 percent of all school-age children (over two million children) receive special educational services for learning disabilities as defined by Public Law 94-142. The Inter Agency Committee on Learning Disabilities mandated by Congress believes that 5 to 10 percent is a reasonable estimate. Some specialists in the field of learning disabilities disagree with that estimate. One says that one American child out of four has some problem in regard to learning. Another estimates that there are at least eight million youngsters in this category and the ACLD Foundation says that one out of six American families has to cope with learning disabilities in children and/or adults. Suffice it to say that many of our children have learning disorders and that there are at least a couple in any average classroom.

Learning disabled children range from the most severely handicapped, who cannot function even with a great deal of extra help in a normal classroom, to mild underachievers who get C's and D's when they have the capacity to get A's. They are children whose reading, spelling, and often arithmetic skills are considerably below (sometimes far below) the norms. Often their spoken language, thinking, and behavior are described as very immature for their age.

The United States government describes a specific learning disability as a "disorder in one or more of the basic psychological processes involved in understanding and using language, spoken or written, which may manifest itself in an imperfect ability to listen, think, speak, read, write, spell, and do mathematical calculations."

In 1989 the National Joint Committee on Learning Disabilities (NJCLD) offered a definition that included individuals of all ages and added a social component.

Learning Disabilities is a general term that refers to a heterogeneous group of disorders manifested by significant difficulties in the acquisition and use of listening, speaking, reading, writing, reasoning or mathematical abilities. These disorders are intrinsic to the individual, presumed to be due to central nervous system dysfunction and may occur across the life span. Problems in self-regulatory behaviors, social perception and social interaction may exist with learning disabilities but do not by themselves constitute a learning disability. Although learning disabilities may occur concomitantly with other handicapping conditions (for example, sensory impairment, mental retardation, serious emotional disturbance) or with extrinsic influences (such as cultural differences, insufficient or inappropriate instruction), they are not the result of those conditions or influences. (National Joint Committee on Learning Disabilities, 1989, p. 1)

Although *learning disabilities* is the preferred term among educators, many others are used. Some of these terms are used to refer to learning disabilities even though technically they may be describing related conditions.

Association deficit pathology
Attention deficit disorder
Attention-Deficit/Hyperactivity Disorder
Brain-injured child
Central-nervous-system disorder
Conceptually handicapped
Congenital alexia
Congenital strephosymbolia
Diffuse brain damage
Dyscalculia
Dysgraphia
Dyslexia
Educationally handicapped
Focused attention disorder
Hidden handicap
Hyperactivity
Hyperkinetic behavior syndrome
Hypoactivity
Hypokinetic behavior syndrome
Language disability
Language-disordered child
Maturation lag
Minimal brain damage
Minimal brain dysfunction
Minimal brain injury
Minimal cerebral dysfunction
Minimal cerebral palsy
Minimal chronic brain syndrome
Multisensory disorders
Neurological immaturity
Neurologically handicapped
Neurophrenia

Neurophysiological dysynchrony
Organic brain dysfunction
Organicity
Perceptually handicapped
Primary reading retardation
Psycholinguistic disabilities
Psychoneurological disorders
Reading disability
Specific dyslexia
Specific learning disabilities
Strephosymbolia
Strauss syndrome
The child with multisensory difficulties
The interjacent child
The invisibly handicapped child
The other child
Waysider
Word blindness

Learning disabled children for the most part are being educated in mainstream classrooms without much extra attention, and they experience much defeat and failure. Some spend the majority of their school time in the mainstream, with extra help from resource teachers and tutors. Others are largely kept in resource rooms and learning centers, going to the mainstream whenever possible. A relative few are in contained classrooms or special schools for the learning disabled.

MANY POSSIBLE CAUSES

How did they become learning disabled? Are they diseased, damaged, rejected children? Parents often worry that they did something wrong, they know not what, that produced these problems. They fear they gave the child too much love and attention, or too little.

Sometimes parents point to each other accusingly about family secrets—the unmentionable relative who may be retarded, emotionally disturbed, or an unlabeled deviate. Teachers often point to the parents as the cause, for spoiling the child or allowing him to be egocentric and lazy. Sometimes neighbors label the child as dull, undisciplined, and manipulative. If it is not the child's upbringing, parents and teachers may point to the child's diet and blame too many soft drinks, junk food snacks, or additives. Or they may blame some environmental element like air pollution or a nearby military radar installation.

What causes learning disabilities?
There is no single cause. . . .
There seem to be many causes. . . .

The following are conditions that have been identified as contributing to a child's having learning disabilities:

Before Birth

Maternal malnutrition
Bleeding in pregnancy
Poor placental attachment to the uterus
Toxemia in pregnancy
*Infectious disease of pregnant mother (German measles, a virus
    disease, influenza, or a chronic disease)*
Alcoholism during pregnancy
The taking of certain drugs during pregnancy
RH incompatibility

During Birth

*Long or difficult delivery producing anoxia (not enough oxygen in
    the brain)*
Prematurity
Breech delivery

Cord around neck
Poor position in the uterus (such as a left posterior position)
Dry birth (the water broke prematurely)
*Intracranial pressure at the time of birth due to forceps delivery or
    a narrow pelvic arch in the mother*
*Rapid delivery, exposing the infant too quickly to a new air pres-
    sure*

After Birth

*A long time to produce breathing after birth (often occurs with
    prematurity, difficult delivery, or twins)*
High fever at an early age
Sharp blow to head from fall or accident
Meningitis or encephalitis
Lead poisoning
Drug intoxication
*Oxygen deprivation due to suffocation, respiratory distress, or
    breath holding*
Severe nutritional deficiencies

Heredity seems to be a factor. In many families, reading disabilities can be traced through several generations. Usually the father, an uncle, or other relatives had the problem. Difficulties with spelling, math, or handwriting may also appear at various times in a family's history.

It is not worth agonizing over which of these factors produced the problems of a particular child. It might be something else not even mentioned here, not known yet. Placing blame, feeling overwhelmed with guilt, giving way to fear that some thoughtless action produced a child's learning problems have never been found to help parents help children with the problem. Sometimes it temporarily helps teachers (who feel frustrated by the learning disabled child) to blame parents, but that doesn't help the children either. Teachers, like parents, usually wish to do the best they can for each child and often seek an easy cause that can be remedied fast. The causes of learning disability are beyond teacher control as they are beyond parent control. Teachers waste time and energy looking for causes, valuable time needed for the study of each student in order to discover how he learns best. All races, religions, economic classes; fat, thin, tall, small parents; youthful parents, older parents have produced children with learning disorders. No one group in society produces more learning disabled children than any other.

In proportionately very few cases have doctors found evidence of actual brain damage. In fact, many brain-damaged children do not have learning disabilities. Scientists are working in the area of medical computer science to detect signs of brain damage or dysfunction that previously could not be monitored; these clinicians hope that by locating exact areas and types of dysfunction in the brain, more precise treatments will be possible. Some neurologists point out that stroke victims, adults who have suffered damage to their brains, and those with cerebral palsy show many impairments of language and thought similar to those of children with learning disorders. One theory is that learning disability is an extremely mild and narrowly selective form of cerebral palsy. The Lab School, which admits only intelligent children with learning disabilities, enrolls 250 children. A few of them have known brain damage, but 60 children act just like these few. Many others simply act in a very immature manner. So far, our knowledge of the brain is so limited that we do not know yet what else to look for or how to detect it.

We know only that there is a lag in the development of learning disabled children; their central nervous systems are delayed in maturing. Neurological examinations most often fail to reveal any medical evidence that would support a diagnosis of brain injury. The absence of clear signs of brain injury led the medical world to believe that the constellation of soft neurological signs had to be noted. This is what led up to such medical terms as *minimal cerebral dysfunction, minimal brain injury,* and *minimal brain dysfunction* (MBD). The soft signs include:

> *Persistence of some primitive reflexes of the central nervous sys-*
>   *tem, which should no longer be present after certain ages*
> *Distractibility (lack of concentration)*
> *Hyperactivity*
> *Impulsivity*
> *Perseveration*
> *Inconsistency*
> *Left-right confusion*
> *Irritability*
> *Talkativeness*
> *Awkwardness*
> *Poor speech*
> *Social immaturity*

Scientists, neurologists, and neurophysiologists are seeking answers to the causes of neurological immaturity to pinpoint the factors responsible for this maturational lag that we currently call *learning disabilities.*

Some specialists say that the cause doesn't matter; we must focus on educating the child. True, we must reach the child early and give him readiness. We must find ways to teach him to do the things he cannot do. We can do this, as educators, without knowing the causes. But other specialists say that the cause does matter; when we know the reason, we will be able to treat the child faster and more efficiently. It is possible within the next five to ten years that advances in neurochemistry and neurophysiology will identify the dysfunctioning parts of the brain. When more precise localization of brain anatomy is correlated with various thinking processes, masses of research will have to be done to determine which part of the brain responds best to what type of education. But at this point, there are no sudden cures or easy answers.

The learning disabled child needs more time to grow, more time to do his work, more time to learn. He must work hard. His parents and teachers must work hard with him and provide him with the support he needs in order to learn properly and to behave appropriately. Those are the only reliable cures at this point.

LARGE RECOGNITION OF THE PROBLEM

The study of learning disabilities, which did not become a recognized field that received government grants until the late 1960s and early 1970s, faces many unanswered questions about causes. Why is there so much more learning disability today than fifty years ago? Part of the explanation may lie in the fact that these children were categorized as mentally retarded or emotionally disturbed. Many learning disabled children are still being written off as culturally deprived. Disadvantaged conditions and poor schooling are cited as the causes of learning disabilities in inner-city children. Sometimes they are. However, high fevers, malnutrition, lead poisoning, maternal malnutrition, lack of proper prenatal care, and similar factors may contribute to learning disabilities, causing poor performance at school. In fact, there may not be more cases today, simply a better recognition of the problem. Some specialists claim that until the advent of miracle drugs and the widespread use of antibiotics, many learning disabled youngsters died of respiratory ailments before they ever reached school age. The Lab School experience is that our students seem to have more allergies, asthma, and respiratory problems than the regular population.

It is also possible that the one-room schoolhouse of yesteryear allowed for slow maturing. The heterogeneous groupings allowed a child to proceed at his or her own pace. In the early 1900s, as the frontier disappeared and Americans moved toward the cities, mass education took on a vast, new importance. Public school systems burgeoned, paralleled by the growth of public libraries and standard-ization of education at all levels. No longer could parents direct their children's education. The rise of modern industry required stan-dardized human components in its management, and our upwardly mobile society came to see education as a measurable step to individ-ual success and to a prosperous, enlightened nation. Only in a culture obsessed with the speed of education and measurable results would those who fail to meet these norms at school be considered disabled people. In fact, they are disabled learners and may be fine people.

Our national panic when Russia launched Sputnik in 1957 was merely the latest phenomenon in the trend to standardization, now seen on a worldwide scale. The American public, worried that the Russians were smarter, more educated, and more efficient, exerted pressure on educators. Out went a lot of the play in nursery schools and kindergartens; letters and numbers replaced motor activities in many preschools. It is possible that the children who needed more time and more sensory-motor activities were deprived of them, and their development lagged further.

As our population becomes more concentrated in cities and suburbs, our schoolrooms have become more crowded. We are sur-rounded by BIGNESS—the bigness of government, cities, buildings, supermarkets, jumbo eggs, and giant-sized aspirin. Bigness can be overwhelming. Individuality is not prized. Attention to each person's very special needs can become lost. The standardization of quantity rather than quality often determines our values: how much we own, how many high grades we have, how many correct answers we made.

A child cannot always conform within the given time period; if he does not, too often he is classed as a failure. Perhaps because of the uncertainty of our times, the rapid changes in lifestyles, the vanishing of accepted traditions, we have become more dependent on the right answer than before and less tolerant of individual differences. Under this pressure, the child with a learning disability may become so burdened with defeat and failure that he doesn't even learn at his own pace and thus widens the gap.

Some subscribe to the theory that our polluted air and rivers, excess noise, and our unclean environment have contributed to the increase in delayed development in our children. Some believe that insecticides and pesticides pollute our children's brains. None of this has been proven.

Boys seem to be affected with learning disabilities more frequently than girls are. Some theories hold that males are more vulnerable at birth and are more prone to injury since the infant mortality rate is much higher among boys than girls. Some claim that the male fetus is somewhat larger than the female and is thus more susceptible to injury at birth. One researcher believes that boys have more trouble exiting at the time of birth because male heads are larger. We really don't know.

In the late 1960s, there were fifteen boys to every girl at The Lab School. By the late 1970s, there were nine boys to every girl, even though suitable female candidates were put at the top of the waiting list. The ratio of boys to girls lowered to seven boys to one girl in the early 1980s and four boys to one girl in the early 1990s. It could be that a girl's education wasn't considered important until Women's Liberation took hold, and that accounted for the preponderance of males. The fact that so many more boys than girls were ADHD and difficult for teachers to manage could partially explain the ratio (but when they existed, the ADHD girls were often rougher and harder to handle than the boys). Many Lab School girls have been hypoactive, ADD daydreamers with speech and language problems. Some researchers at Yale went into an elementary school in Connecticut and tested everybody for reading problems (not necessarily learning disabilities); they discovered that there were an equal number of boys and girls in trouble. When I have spoken at local chapters of the Learning Disabilities Association of America (LDA) and discussed this question with parents, it has appeared that there are more boys than girls with this difficulty.

Why is the learning disabled child much harder to manage and teach in hot, humid weather, before storms, on very hazy days, and, some say, when there is a full moon? Educators have noted that weather and seasons affect their performance, but nobody knows why.

Is there a connection between hypoglycemia (low blood sugar) and learning disabilities? So far no substantive connection has been proven.

Doctors have noticed a significant relationship between allergic reactions and hyperactivity and learning disabilities. Some of them have treated the children with antihistamines, corticosteroids, and megavitamins. Some of those children experienced relief from allergies, and at the same time their hyperactivity decreased and their learning improved; some did not.

A few years ago some doctors felt that learning disabled children have vitamin deficiencies and prescribed large doses of vitamins with no significant success. There are always a few children who improve dramatically, but for any method to be considered a cure, it has to cure many. So far it hasn't.

A few specialists, convinced that learning disabled children are lacking in protein, recommend a high protein diet (much red meat, eggs, and soybeans). Although some youngsters have demonstrated more energy to learn because of this treatment, no known instant school successes have resulted. And some doctors state that high protein diets are dangerous, for they can cause metabolic imbalance.

Another theory is that food additives cause hyperactivity and many cases of learning disability. The affected child is put on a special diet, monitored constantly, and in a number of cases has improved. Still there is no definite proof of this connection and no clear evidence that food additives cause learning disabilities.

Some educators believe that learning disabilities do not exist— that there are simply unmotivated children. Others believe there are merely undisciplined students. Their remedies follow their interpretation of the causes. Every once in a while a child improves under their care, but these hard-liners do not have the answer for children with learning disabilities in general.

Today big money can be made by taking advantage of the prevalence and seriousness of learning disabilities. Along with excellent schools and treatment centers, a number of "instant remediation" parlors have opened. From pinching ears, to systematic yelling, to acupuncture, to transcendental meditation, to tactile treatments, to patterning of one sort or another, to helium experiences, parents are being promised substantive help by fly-by-night groups. All kinds of causes are enumerated, and these entrepreneurs usually make parents feel responsible for the problem, as well as for the success of the treatment.

In our culture, where speed is a supreme value, and where we prize the microwave dinners, the freeze-dried coffee, the soup can, we grab for the instant answer regarding learning disabilities. UNFORTUNATELY THERE IS NO ONE CAUSE. THERE IS NO EASY ANSWER.

FOCUS ON THE SYMPTOM, NOT THE CAUSE

Rather than focusing on the prime cause of learning disabilities, which may be one of the many mentioned above, teachers need to focus on the prime symptom—immaturity or delayed development—and the disorganization and disorder that accompany it. Each child is unique. His problems weave their own pattern. Each teacher must be a detective of sorts to determine how each child learns best, what modalities or channels of learning are a child's strongest ones, what interests can be built on, what specific disabilities are there to remediate. Each teacher needs to learn a multitude of approaches and methods of teaching and to learn the very special skill of being able to match the appropriate method or combination of methods to the individual child's specific needs. (For details about these approaches see chapters 9 and 10).

Most difficult to handle is the child who does not, *can* not, seem to pay attention to what is said. The teacher has to seek ways to entice the interest of the child, magnetize it, pull it along, and sustain it. Attention can be there one moment and be gone the next. The teacher cannot teach unless he can reach the child and lure the child into his realm, empowering her to focus, to take what he gives and act upon it.

F O U R

ATTENTION-DEFICIT/ HYPERACTIVITY DISORDER (ADHD)

In recent years the terms ADD and ADHD have come to occupy a prominent place in discussions of children with neurological disorders. The terms *Attention Deficit Disorder* (ADD) and *Attention-Deficit/Hyperactivity Disorder* (ADHD) have caused some confusion to the public, especially to parents.

Many professional and parent groups classify ADD and ADHD as conditions totally separate from learning disabilities. Others, myself included, see these conditions as closely associated, since many people with learning disabilities also suffer from attention disorders that stem from similar neurological dysfunctions, though they may originate in different parts of the brain. Not all people with attention disorders have learning disabilities, but many of them do.

Attention-Deficit/Hyperactivity Disorder (ADHD) is the official medical diagnostic label for a pattern of symptoms of inattention and/or hyperactivity and impulsivity. ADHD is listed in the standard psychiatric reference work, the *Diagnostic and Statistical Manual of Mental Disorders, 4th Edition* (DSM IV, 1994). Three subtypes of ADHD have been officially identified: ADHD, Predominantly Inattentive Type; ADHD, Predominantly Hyperactive-Impulsive Type; ADHD, Combined Type. The term "learning disabilities," which covers a cluster of learning problems stemming from a neurological base, does not appear in this reference book. Rather, what is commonly referred to as a learning disability would fall under the label "Learning Disorders" in DSM IV, with the specific subentries Reading Disorder, Mathematics Disorder, and Disorder of Written Expression. The DSM IV reports that there is a higher incidence of learning disorders in individuals with ADHD than in the general population.

The DSM IV is important because it is used as a communication tool between medical practitioners and insurance companies. Doctors use the term ADHD a great deal because the official status of terms like this makes it possible both to prescribe medication and apply to insurance companies for payment of services. It also allows for consistent diagnosis of the disorder, so that all the professionals talk about the same problem.

I have given examples throughout this book of attention-deficit/hyperactivity disorder. The Lab School always enrolls a large number of students with ADHD. My son is ADHD. I have not, for the most part, separated out the attention and impulse control problems from the learning disabilities since I believe they are all part of the same process involved in academic functioning and socialization. So, throughout this book you will often read about ADHD along with learning disabilities.

Youngsters who have ADHD without learning disabilities may need medical treatment, and they usually respond well to it. They often do not need special education. However, as a school head, I often have this telephone conversation with a desperate parent:

PARENT: My child has been diagnosed by the doctor as
ADHD. He has been put on medication, but he's still
failing at school. Do you deal with ADHD children?

ME: Yes, along with their learning disabilities, we do. Does
your child have reading, oral language, writing, spelling,
or math problems? How about his organizational skills?
Does he demonstrate memory problems? What about his
sense of time and timing, his coordination, and his judgment in space?

PARENT: He has trouble with all of those things except for
math.

ME: Has he been tested for learning disabilities?

PARENT: He doesn't have learning disabilities. He has
ADHD.

There is continuing disagreement and confusion among parents and
educators as to the relationship between ADHD and learning disabilities. I have added this chapter since children with ADHD are
eligible for special education and related services under federal law
when ADHD impairs their learning or educational performance.
ADHD has not been listed as a separate disability because those who
require special education and related services may be eligible for
services that already exist under Public Law IDEA (formerly PL
94-142), under *learning disabilities, other health impaired* (OHI), or
emotional disturbances. On September 16, 1991, the assistant secretary for the Office of Special Education and Related Services, the
assistant secretary for the Office of Civil Rights, and the assistant
secretary for the Office of Elementary and Secondary Education
issued a clarification of policy "to address the needs of children with
attention deficit disorder within general and/or special education."
The memorandum pointed out that the youngsters who do not meet
the criteria for services under IDEA may be eligible for services, such
as accommodations, under Section 504 of the Rehabilitation Act of

1973. For more information on IDEA see chapter 12. Section 504 is covered on page 283.

The history of ADHD can be traced back to its first report in medical literature, written by a Dr. Still in 1902, in which he described children having "morbid defects in moral control." The child with attention-deficit/hyperactivity disorder has been described over the years as a brain-injured child, a child with minimal brain dysfunction (MBD), or a hyperkinetic child.

ADHD seems to be a neurological dysfunction caused by a neurochemical deficiency. A landmark study done at the National Institute of Mental Health, headed by Dr. Alan Zametkin, points to differences in brain chemistry that cause this condition. Much more research needs to be done before scientists will conclude that there is one cause.

ATTENTION

ADHD, Predominantly Inattentive Type, is marked primarily by difficulties sustaining attention or persevering with tasks. As one faculty member at The Lab School said, "ADHD kids are those that need us standing over them every single minute or they get nothing done. They can't begin anything, stay focused, or switch to another activity without our doing it with them, and almost *for* them." Outside stimulation distracts them, particularly if what they're doing doesn't appeal to them. The child can't figure out what he receives through his senses, even though his eyes, ears, and other sense organs are intact. The messages he receives are jumbled and scattered. The pattern on the tablecloth and the food on his plate come through with equal intensity, so he cannot tell which is which. He gives importance to everything indiscriminately, establishing no priorities or order. He cannot focus on one thing to the exclusion of all others. He can't ignore the footsteps in the hall, the light tumbling in through the venetian blinds, or the movement of his classmate's pencil. The jangling earrings of his teacher cause him to lose track of what she is saying. Everything going on in the classroom distracts him from what he is there to do, which is to learn. Since his nervous system is late in developing, his immature brain is not yet equipped to automatically filter out the irrelevant and unnecessary material. The chances are good that his nervous system will mature in time; researchers say that about 50 percent of children with ADHD mature out of these characteristics by puberty, another 25 percent grow out of them by adolescence, leaving 25 percent as adults with ADHD.

HYPERACTIVITY-IMPULSIVITY

ADHD, Predominantly Hyperactive-Impulsive Type, is another category in DSM IV. You've seen this child blurting out answers before questions have been completed, having difficulty taking turns, interrupting everybody and everything. The clamor of stimuli on his nervous system, the overload that causes the child to switch his attention rapidly from one stimulus to another makes him appear distractible. His behavioral response to each stimulus that seizes his attention makes him appear impulsive. The child can't slow down in order to think ahead and plan the next step. His thoughts come tumbling straight out, and he says the first thing he thinks of without pausing to see if it is really all right to say it. For example, Jerry's mother and father were discussing how to seat their guests at a forthcoming dinner party and shared the impression that Mr. Brown was an old hypocrite. Jerry, whose vocabulary, at age twelve, was large in spite of his learning disabilities, was interested in this new word and asked what it meant. His parents explained that it meant somebody who says one thing and does another, and Jerry showed that he understood this idea by identifying a child in his class who displayed these same traits. His mother and father were very pleased at Jerry's quickness and turned back to planning the party. That evening, when Jerry greeted the guests before he went to bed, he met Mr. Brown, and said, with pure delight at his new knowledge: "Hello, Mr. Brown—so you're the old hypocrite!" Impulsively, Jerry said the first thing that came to his mind, which also demonstrated his lack of social judgment.

The child with hyperactivity-impulsivity is unable to inhibit behavior such as squirming or chattering when requested to do so. Impulsivity affects a child's ability to persist in a task. Impulsive behavior has been described earlier in this book. It is in the boy who rushes headlong through his work and is the first one finished but gets most of the answers wrong, the girl who pushes everyone aside to be first in line, the boy who can't wait his turn in a game of checkers and overturns the board, and the girl who starts an activity even before she knows what to do. This child can't wait for anything!

She speaks before she thinks, acts before she reasons, and leaps before she looks. Is it any wonder that she is often accident-prone? She follows her first impulse and becomes a victim of her impulsiveness. She sees a big, fat zipper on a woman's dress and pulls it down before anyone knows what's happening, and discovers the lady has on no underwear. She does not stop and think about it, weighing the consequences of whether such fun is worth it. The same child, on her way across the room to retrieve her sneakers, stops to play with a toy and forgets all about the sneakers. Not only is she distracted, but she cannot postpone what she feels like doing at that very instant.

Some ADHD youngsters can't stop what they are doing, as though the necessary energy and organization are more than they can muster. Their brakes don't work. They can't put their toys away, turn off the television, or stop coloring. They tend to need the help of an adult to take away the crayon or stand in front of the television. The adult assists the transition by monitoring the children and often physically helping them and verbally reminding, "We'll put the toys away now because we have to leave and go to the playground."

The impulsive child is irritable. Little things that don't bother other children his age make him blow up in a rage or dissolve in tears. He doesn't distinguish big from small issues or hard blows from mild criticism. People say he is high-strung or oversensitive. His moods are unpredictable. Within half an hour he may change from a tight-lipped, stubborn mule to a screaming demon, and then to a sweet and manageable child, full of regret about the scene he has just created.

The ADHD child usually feels terrible remorse after an impulsive act. "I didn't think—I'm sorry," he says sadly. It's as though he is completely gathered up and taken over by overwhelming impulses, helpless to do anything about them or to employ his reason to control himself until he calms down. He is known to have "emotional lability," mood swings, big ups and downs. He overreacts or underreacts, but rarely acts in proportion to the situation at hand.

It is not surprising that the ADHD child often has a low tolerance for frustration, which causes her either to withdraw or explode. This low frustration tolerance makes it difficult for her to stick to a task. So, combine learning disabilities with the inability to handle much frustration, and then you know why it is so difficult to teach these youngsters. The job of the teacher is to repeatedly tell these students, until they can say it to themselves, "Stop. Think. Plan. *Then act.*" This strategy is a crucial part of teaching an ADHD child; it is as important as substantive subject matter.

In this book I refer to the *Now Child,* the impulsive one who can't delay gratification and has no established boundaries, thus requiring the outside world to provide parameters. Clinicians often refer to the behavior of the Now Child as *poor regulation* and *disinhibited behavior.* Many American adults say they want to free their children from the inhibitions they grew up with, but parents of children with ADHD want nothing more than to inhibit their children!

Along with attention problems and impulsiveness, ADHD children often show excessive hyperactivity, especially of the body and mouth, general restlessness, and fidgety behavior. Stemming from an immature brain, hyperactivity is characterized by uncoordinated, random, unthinking, unfocused, and excessive movement. The hyperactive child is in constant motion—not necessarily running about all the time, but endlessly fidgeting, wriggling, and restless. These children constantly drum their fingers on a table, swing their feet, or tap their pencils; continually hum or sniff; or get out of their seats ten times in ten minutes.

You read more about this earlier in the descriptions of the child who is rocking his chair relentlessly, whose lunchbox is swinging into the nearest leg, and whose mouth is going nonstop. The amount of motor activity does not fit the situation and reminds us of a developmentally younger child. A two-year-old can run you off your feet in half an hour. A hyperactive ten-year-old can do the same thing (*hyper* means "excessive"). Such purposeless, scattered, mindless, disordered activity is exhausting to cope with, but it is important to remember that *the child is not bad.* Instead remember that the child's development is lopsided and irregular. Nobody calls a normal, energetic two-year-old hyperactive, yet by age seven or eight, the same behavior is problematic. The degree of activity and its inappropriateness in a school situation may disrupt other children from learning; if so, it poses a big management problem for teachers.

Children with ADHD have particular difficulty following rules. "She's not paying attention," the teacher says, but the teacher frequently means that the child does not listen and follow directions within the given time limit. One teacher said, "Marie is okay when no demands are made of her. She's suffering from a disability in rule following." Teachers and parents frequently see hyperactivity as oppositional behavior that can be controlled. They do not recognize that it is organic and neurologically based. They punish the ADHD child by restricting free time—often taking away the very activities in which the child excels and releases excess energy. The child, who often cannot control excessive movement, is made to feel bad about herself and develops a negative self-image.

It is important to remember:

> Not all hyperactive children have learning disabilities; in fact, many don't.
> Not all learning disabled children are hyperactive, impulsive, perseverative, emotionally labile, or visibly distractible.

Dr. Russell Barkley, a specialist on ADHD, has reported that 20 to 30 percent of children with attention deficit disorder are not hyperactive. Dr. Barkley suggested that ADD without hyperactivity be renamed focused attention disorder (FAD). Even though DSM IV did not include this category we, at The Lab School, see these children all the time. They are characterized by hypoactivity—excessive daydreaming, poor memory, vagueness, social reticence and very little involvement with playmates. Hypoactive youngsters seem to have a lower-than-average activity level and react slowly to everything. Well behaved and well controlled, they pose little trouble for parents and teachers. They may daydream quietly in a corner for hours. But hypoactive youngsters who have learning disabilities withdraw because they cannot process what is going on. With their attention scattered elsewhere, they may not even be aware of what is going on, including in the classroom.

Whereas the hyperactive child cannot tolerate any frustration and impulsively throws a book, swears, stomps away from the game, or slams the door the moment he can't do something, the daydreamer can either tolerate far more frustration without falling apart or further detaches himself from the scene.

"Earth to robot" Luigi taunts Mark, whose mind always seems to be on another planet. "Mark is in another world, and I can't pull him out," exclaims his teacher, who is frequently more frustrated with students like Mark than with the hyperactive ones, whom she can reach when they are paying attention.

WHO MAKES THE DIAGNOSIS?

The diagnosis of ADHD can only be made by a medical doctor or psychologist who sees the child and uses the official classification system. The DSM IV is a revision of the system in the third edition of the *Diagnostic and Statistical Manual of Mental Disorders*, published by the American Psychiatric Association. It says: "The essential feature of Attention-Deficit/Hyperactivity Disorder is a persistent pattern of inattention and/or hyperactivity-impulsivity that is more frequent and severe than is typically observed in individuals at a comparable level of development." There are some researchers who see ADHD as the basis for learning problems and do not believe that the field of learning disabilities even exists. One administrator of a learning disabilities program said, "The doctors want to quantify everything. Learning disabilities are too subtle and variant to be totally quantified, but don't tell me they don't exist. With or without ADHD, I've been working with learning disabled students for eighteen years! They're different from the regular population and different from the retarded and disturbed."

A combination of clinical judgment and objective assessment goes into the identification of ADHD. Doctors who make the diagnosis must study an individual's medical, educational, psychological, and behavioral functioning, and must also listen carefully to the child's parents, the school, and other professionals who have worked with the child. Many doctors ask parents and teachers to fill out forms that have rating scales, to provide more information on which to base the diagnosis and treatment. These scales themselves will not diagnose ADHD.

PARENT RATING SCALES

The Conners series of parent rating scales have been the most widely used. There are three forms: the original ninety-three-item version, the revised forty-eight-item version, and the ten-item Abbreviated Symptom Questionnaire. These scales focus primarily on hyperactivity, reflecting the state of knowledge at the time the scales were developed. They do not adequately assess impulsivity and attention.

The Child Behavior Checklist, developed in 1983 by Achenbach and Edelbrok, is also widely used. It concentrates on hyperactivity, leaving out distractibility, and contains a list of behavioral problems and competencies that fall into the two broad categories of Internal behavior (e.g., withdrawal, somatic complaints, anxious/depressed behavior) and External behavior (e.g., aggression and delinquency). It is a good measure of other social, emotional, and behavioral problems that frequently accompany ADHD. Scores are obtained on nine scales: anxious, depressed, uncommunicative, obsessive-compulsive, socially withdrawn, hyperactive, aggressive, delinquent, and having somatic complaints.

New instruments such as the Child Attention Problems Scale (Barkley), the ADHD Rating Scale (DuPaul), and the Attention Deficit Disorders Evaluation Scale (McCarney) address problems of inattention and impulsivity as well as hyperactivity.

The Yale Children's Inventory assesses multiple factors related to ADHD, learning problems, and emotional difficulties. There are eleven scales: attention, impulsivity, activity, tractability, habituation, conduct disorder–socialization, conduct disorder–aggression, negative affect, language, fine motor, and academics.

TEACHER RATING SCALES

Many schools employ the Iowa Conners Teachers Rating Scales (1982) of which there are several versions. The primary focus is on hyperactivity and inattention in the classroom. The Conners Abbreviated Syndrome Questionnaire, developed by Conners and Barkley, is frequently used in school systems and is a ten-item list that seeks to isolate behavioral problems and hyperactivity. The Conners Teacher Rating Scale from 1969, containing thirty-nine behavior problems (including distractibility and hyperactivity) is still used in some classrooms today. The Teacher's Report Form (Achenbach and Edelbrok, 1986) obtains teacher ratings on the same problem areas covered by the Child Behavior Checklist, providing a multidimensional profile of behavior problems as well as adaptive behavior and school performance.

DIRECT OBSERVATION

A number of schools have trained observers who sit in a classroom and note specific targeted behaviors. They will count the number of times a child gets out of her seat, how often she interrupts the teacher, how frequently she talks to the person next to her, or how much noise she makes opening a book or getting out a piece of paper.

Written reports by teachers frequently provide just the information the doctor is looking for, such as, "She could learn if she could just pay attention," or "He rarely completes any task," or "She says whatever comes to mind, never screening any thought."

After the doctor sees the child and reviews the data, he then consults the following official guidelines to see if the child meets the following criteria:

DIAGNOSTIC CRITERIA FOR ATTENTION-DEFICIT/HYPERACTIVITY DISORDER

A. Either (1) or (2):

   (1) six (or more) of the following symptoms of **inattention** have persisted for at least six months to a degree that is maladaptive and inconsistent with developmental level:

   Inattention
   (a) often fails to give close attention to details or makes careless mistakes in schoolwork, work, or other activities
   (b) often has difficulty sustaining attention in tasks or play activities
   (c) often does not seem to listen when spoken to directly
   (d) often does not follow through on instructions and fails to finish schoolwork, chores, or duties in the workplace (not due to oppositional behavior or failure to understand instructions)
   (e) often has difficulty organizing tasks and activities
   (f) often avoids, dislikes, or is reluctant to engage in tasks that require sustained mental effort (such as schoolwork or homework)
   (g) often loses things necessary for tasks or activities (e.g., toys, school assignments, pencils, books, or tools)
   (h) is often easily distracted by extraneous stimuli
   (i) is often forgetful in daily activities

   (2) six (or more) of the following symptoms of **hyperactivity-impulsivity** have persisted for at least six months to a degree that is maladaptive and inconsistent with developmental level:

   Hyperactivity
   (a) often fidgets with hands or feet or squirms in seat
   (b) often leaves seat in classroom or in other situations in which remaining seated is expected

(c) often runs about or climbs excessively in situations in which it is inappropriate (in adolescents or adults, may be limited to subjective feelings of restlessness)

(d) often has difficulty playing or engaging in leisure activities quietly

(e) is often "on the go" or often acts as if "driven by a motor"

(f) often talks excessively

Impulsivity

(g) often blurts out answers before questions have been completed

(h) often has difficulty awaiting turn

(i) often interrupts or intrudes on others (e.g., butts into conversations or games)

B. Some hyperactive-impulsive or inattentive symptoms that caused impairment were present before age seven years.

C. Some impairment from the symptoms is present in two or more settings (e.g., at school [or work] and at home).

D. There must be clear evidence of clinically significant impairment in social, academic, or occupational functioning.

E. The symptoms do not occur exclusively during the course of a Pervasive Development Disorder, Schizophrenia, or other Psychotic Disorder and are not better accounted for by another mental disorder (e.g., Mood Disorder, Anxiety Disorder, Dissociative Disorder, or a Personality Disorder).

Code based on type:

314.01 Attention-Deficit/Hyperactivity Disorder, Combined Type: if both Criteria A1 and A2 are met for the past six months

314.00 Attention-Deficit/Hyperactivity Disorder, Predominantly Inattentive Type: if Criterion A1 is met but Criterion A2 is not met for the past six months

314.01 Attention-Deficit/Hyperactivity Disorder, Predominantly Hyperactive-Impulsive Type: if Criterion A2 is met but Criterion A1 is not met for the past six months

> **Coding note:** For individuals (especially adolescents and adults) who currently have symptoms that no longer meet full criteria, "In Partial Remission" should be specified.

These criteria are not foolproof. When a teacher who has heard about ADHD sees that a child cannot concentrate, is very restless, talks excessively, interrupts, and cannot control his impulses, often she or he is sure the child must have ADHD. However, these behaviors cannot be attributed only to ADHD. They may also indicate family trauma, acute anxiety, a clinical depression, or some other form of emotional illness. Childhood depression is more rampant than mental health professionals ever believed. When depressed, a child has difficulty concentrating and following through, and may also be distractible, restless, easily irritated, and moody. Acute anxiety, the stress of living through a death in the family, a terrible divorce, or some other overwhelming occurrence can also produce these symptoms. This is why a mental health specialist has to make the final diagnosis. However, most of the time the symptoms *do* point to ADHD and then the next question is, "What do we do about it?"

TREATING ADHD THROUGH MEDICATION

Throughout this book you will find practical ways for parents and teachers to handle children with ADHD and LD. There is no easy answer. There is no one way. Parents at home, teachers in school, and other adults who spend time with the child need to experiment to discover what works best with each individual youngster.

Parents and teachers need to know the nature of the condition and provide whatever structure they can in order to help this child walk the path of success. Sometimes structuring is not enough, particularly if the child is so hyperactive and so distractible that he can't focus on one thing for more than a few minutes at a time. In these cases, the condition may require chemical treatment. A physician—a pediatrician, neurologist, or psychiatrist—treats the child with medication to help the youngster focus and be receptive to teaching.

It is typical for parents to be afraid of giving drugs to their child. Parents often say:

> *My child has to be drugged? No way!*
> *He'll become a druggie.*
> *She'll show all kinds of weird side effects.*
> *His height will be affected.*
> *Her appetite will diminish.*
> *She won't sleep.*
> *He'll look like a zombie.*

According to the latest research, these concerns (although very real) appear unfounded. Physicians have been treating ADHD with medication since the 1930s, and follow-up studies of adults who took these medications as children found no apparent long-term side effects. Stimulant drugs such as Ritalin, Dexedrine, Cylert, and other medications calm hyperactive children, make them less active, and consequently enable them to concentrate. Teachers at The Lab School, where approximately 43 out of our 250 students are on medication, see dramatic results. Students become more alert and focused and develop better motor control, apparent from their improved handwriting. Overall, medication seems to help this small group organize their activities and thought processes. On medication, they tend to demonstrate planning skills that were never evident before and can blot out many of the unfiltered messages from their senses and bodies that habitually overstimulate them. In so doing, the medication calms them down. Research postulates that medication increases the amount of the neurotransmitter that is lacking in the brain of the hyperactive child. This neurotransmitter allows the brain to function effectively and the child calms down and thinks before he acts. No longer bombarded by excess sensory information, the child is free to pay attention. The drugs do not sedate the child or tranquilize him.

Medications used to treat ADHD are no longer limited to psycho-stimulants such as Ritalin (Methylphenidate), Dexedrine (Dextroamphetamine), and Cylert (Permoline), which seem to have dramatic effects with 75 percent of the population that requires this treatment. Some children need antidepressant medications such as Tofranil (Imipramine) and Desipramine (Norpramine). Much less frequently prescribed are the antidepressants Fluxetine, Chlorimipramine, and Buproprion. For some children an anticonvulsant, Carbamazepine (Tegretol), and an antihypertensive drug, Clonidine (Catapress), have been effective.

The physician determines the appropriate medication, the dosage, and how often it is given. It is adjusted according to the child's response and feedback from parents and teachers. If a teacher tells the physician, "John's attention, impulse control, and activity level are well controlled until about eleven-forty-five A.M., and then it goes from bad to worse," a second dosage may be added. Some children demonstrate no difference in behavior, so the physician will adjust dosages and, if necessary, medications; sometimes the physician determines that no medication is to be given, due to the child's lack of response. It is very important for the physician to obtain information about any changes in the child's classroom behavior in response to the medication so that he or she can assess treatment and prescribe the optimum dosage. This teacher input is usually obtained through the behavior checklists discussed previously. If the physician does *not* pay attention to teacher reports, parents need to ask why.

Research has shown no long-term side effects from medication. For the first week or so on a medication, a child may show a loss of appetite or have trouble getting to sleep. This should disappear, but if it doesn't, parents should alert the physician by the end of the week. The same holds true with headaches and stomachaches. If the child develops tics, alert the physician immediately and the medication will be changed or eliminated.

At The Lab School, we suggest that parents introduce medication to their child by showing him a ruler and saying, "You have to do eleven inches of the work—" (have them feel how long eleven inches is). "The medication does one inch of the work—" (have them feel the one inch). This exercise shows children that they are still in control and that they must do most of the work, but that the medication gives a helpful boost. Eventually, the child should aim to do all twelve inches himself. A child is usually on medication for a couple of years. There are, however, a few children who need to take medication until or through adulthood.

It is common practice for parents and doctors to tell the principal of a child's school, but not necessarily his classroom teacher, that an experiment with medication is taking place. Usually within a day or two the teacher will mention the child's improvement to the principal. The teacher is not told ahead of time because her unbiased reaction is helpful in telling the drug's effectiveness.

Medication is not the right treatment for every child. Some children respond well to a tight structure, novel learning environments, a small student-teacher ratio (as much one-on-one as possible), and certain behavior management techniques and counseling. Others have tried all these routes with no success and reluctantly turn to physicians for medication.

Medication has to be carefully controlled and monitored. Drugs have been badly abused, especially in the 1970s, when schools, not just doctors, prescribed medication for hyperactive youngsters. In many cases, however, medication has enabled previously impossible children to listen and concentrate, making them receptive to learning. But medication alone is rarely enough.

OTHER MEANS OF TREATING ADHD

Psychologists, clinical social workers, and psychiatrists can counsel the parents, the child, or whole families. They can check on medication and assist in developing strategies that will help a child achieve, focus, and control impulses both at home and at school. Parents can benefit from going to CHADD and LDA meetings (see appendix 5) to learn what other parents have found useful. Some parents go to parent training programs. Whatever action they decide to take, the more parents know about ADHD, the more they can help their child.

For some children, behavior modification programs work best to change behavior. A child receives a token, food, toys, or extra privileges when he performs appropriately. At The Lab School, behavior modification has been extremely helpful in getting a child past obstacles over a limited period of time. When it continues for a long time, however, the child tends to expect *ex*trinsic rewards for behaving correctly instead of enjoying the *in*trinsic reward of feeling good about himself. Also, some adults lose track of the whole child because they become so involved with rewards and scorekeeping. Martin's family used tokens to attempt to stop Martin's unconscious humming. He received a blue token every time he hummed so that he became aware of what he was doing. He received a white token for every half hour he was able to control the humming. When he had fifteen white tokens, he could choose a toy he wanted. It worked with Martin, but it didn't work for Sandy, who didn't care if she had more toys, extra food, or special privileges. For Alice, it worked only for the first two weeks. Effective behavior management programs require frequent monitoring to change and revise conditions and to maintain their effectiveness.

Teachers too need as much knowledge as possible about ADHD because they need to know what constitutes distraction and when more structure is most needed. Lunch, recess, physical education, and field trips are traditionally difficult times for a child with ADHD. Teachers who understand the nature of ADHD can anticipate problems and set up procedures that work.

IMPORTANT POINTS TO REMEMBER:

Children with ADHD and often LD produce many behaviors
> *that irritate*
>> *exhaust*
>> *defeat*
>>> *their parents*
>>> *their teachers*
>>> *and others*
> *that irritate*
>> *exhaust*
>> *defeat*
>>> *themselves,*
> *that emanate from "the condition,"*
> *not*
> *from devious minds that have*
> *stayed up nights plotting*
> *to annoy and defeat adults.*

These children feel bad about themselves.
These children are the recipients of constant criticism.

> *NEGATIVISM*

Parents and teachers need to look at what's working and praise them
> *to help them feel competent*
>> *to help them feel O.K.*
>>> *TO FEEL GOOD ABOUT THEMSELVES.*
>>> *POSITIVISM*

FIVE

THE NEED TO LEARN
HOW TO LEARN

Teaching the learning disabled child the approach to a task is as important as, if not more so than, teaching the task itself. To begin a task, the child has to focus on it, look at it, listen to directions, integrate several processes at once, and establish priorities or at least an order of procedure. All of these constitute areas of difficulty for a learning disabled child, which is why he has so much trouble starting tasks. Teachers often remark that there is no logic to how these children begin something, and they refer to a child's approach as "scattered," "totally disorganized," or "inappropriate." Teachers describe the learning disabled child who begins telling a story in the middle or who starts writing on the bottom of a page or who circles a smudge on a worksheet, obviously missing the point of each exercise. One teacher said, "They don't know what to do with their bodies, much less their eyes, their ears, and their mouths. We have to teach them all that before they can get to work."

Very immature children may randomly attack every task in a desultory manner. They may pay no attention to what they are doing, but just do something and do it fast. Jane was so impulsive that she would begin every worksheet before listening to or reading the instructions. She required an adult at her side to monitor what she was doing and to say to her what eventually she had to learn to say to herself: "Stop, Jane. Think. What are you to do? Now begin." Slowing her down, focusing Jane was enough, for she had enough organization skills to draw on after that.

Clive did not. When he finally learned to help set the table and put spoons on the right side of each place, he would ritualistically put out spoons for every meal thereafter, even if the spoons were not necessary. Clive had not yet developed the maturity to distinguish what belonged and what didn't. He lacked the basic skills of discrimination, the organization to select the appropriate way to handle the task. A learning disabled child may find one way to do a particular task and, due to his internal disorder, stick to that way of doing it forevermore, down to the last detail. His procedure may not be right the second or third time he does it, because the situation itself may have changed, but that makes no difference. You could almost give him a new name: the One-Way Kid.

When do we tend to become rigid and inflexible?
. . . when we don't know what to do.
. . . when we are most uncertain.
When do we tend to look for one answer?
. . . when we are confused.
. . . when we are most unsure of ourselves and everything seems out of hand.
When do we want to cling to the familiar?
. . . when we are overwhelmed.

The learning disabled child is overwhelmed by unscreened stimuli bombarding his brain; he is confused, uncertain, unsure. It is not surprising that he grabs onto one way and doesn't let go, particularly when we think of this child as lagging in development, like a very young child who feels secure only with routine. Swamped by an overload of sensations in a world that often appears to him as an undifferentiated mass, he opts for one way to do things and rebels if there is a change. This child dreads the unknown and the unfamiliar. There is so little that makes sense to him. Sameness makes sense.

THE ONE-WAY KID

The learning disabled youngster is reminiscent of a very young child who cannot deal with alternatives at the immature level of his age. She becomes anxious when she is taken to the park by an unfamiliar route. She is upset on a Sunday morning when her parents have breakfast in their pajamas, breaking the known routine of dress first, breakfast afterward. She won't accept a broken cookie because a cookie is round; if the broken piece is jagged, it can't be a cookie. She doesn't recognize a teacher outside of school. She may appear paralyzed when faced with two equal choices, unable to select either one.

Sometimes the learning disabled child can unintentionally be very destructive. "He breaks all his toys!" says Tommy's sister. He pushes and pulls too hard. He continues to press one lever when he is supposed to press and pull; he can't switch easily from one movement to another. He's often the One-Way Kid. He pulls the wheels off his toy cars, he winds too far on the windup robot, he presses too hard on the pencil and breaks it, and he nearly squeezes the life out of the pet turtle. He's called careless, irresponsible, hostile, when, in fact, in his immature fashion, he is continuing an action too long, almost mindlessly. The technical term for this is *perseveration*.

Not allowing any deviation from his one way, the learning disabled child often cannot bear to see another child using a different method to attain the same goal. He will correct the child, insist that his way is the right way, pick on the child, and stand over him to be sure that he does not err. Sometimes the One-Way Kid is so busy minding everybody else's business to make sure they do things his way that he neglects his own work completely.

The order he has created around himself is so fragile that he may rush to an adult to announce that Johnny has broken a rule or Suzie has taken the wrong book. Other children see him as a tattletale and shun him. His inability to tolerate differences may make him suspicious of black or white people (whichever he is not), or of people with foreign accents, thereby causing embarrassment to his parents, who wonder where he picked up such prejudices.

THE NOW CHILD

Anything sudden or unexpected throws the inflexible child off his track. On the other hand, he expects his wants to be met instantly: "I want it right now! Do it now!" The concepts of "later," "in time," "wait" are meaningless to him. The inflexible child who wants what he wants when he wants it, no matter what is going on around him— a storm, a riot, an accident, a crisis—is the same child who doesn't see wholeness. He gets caught up in the details and misses the big picture. Occasionally he sees the big picture but has no understanding of the parts and their relationship to one another.

Any kind of postponement, delay, or change of plans immediately upsets the learning disabled youngster. Bobby said, "People are tricking me. It's not fair," whenever a sudden change of routine, such as a substitute teacher's coming, took place at school. Susan simply cried at these times. Jamie exhibited more excess energy than ever and would ask a series of compulsive, nonstop questions to find out about the change but would not wait to hear the answers. Many a scream in a restaurant, a tantrum on the floor of a department store, a grab at someone else's ball in the playground can be tracked down to the Now

Child. In the first years of life, this behavior is understood by the passerby, who comments: "Poor little thing; he's overtired." But the older child is dismissed as a spoiled brat, and his parents are criticized for having done an inadequate job, or the teacher is reprimanded for having poor control of her students.

No matter how conscientious the parents have been (most parents of learning disabled children do a superb, superhuman job), if the child is in a very early stage of emotional growth due to delayed development, he is not ready to delay or postpone. No matter how excellent or outstanding the teacher, a Now Child cannot wait and take turns like others in his age group. He is completely egocentric. The world is composed of his wants, his urges, his impulses. He has separated himself out as an individual, but he has not yet integrated himself into the reality around him. He doesn't think of others and their needs. He's a bit like the child who keeps looking at himself in the mirror to reassure himself that he exists.

THE CONCRETE CHILD

The very young child has to see what is in front of him in order to make sense of it. We call that child very concrete. A neurologically immature child is also very concrete. In the development of all children concreteness must precede the ability to deal with abstractions, according to the Swiss psychologist Jean Piaget. This child needs to see the material he is taught, hear it, touch it, smell it, feel it, "be" it. He needs to have enough experience with it to know it well. For a word to have meaning, he must associate it with an object, a picture, or an experience. For example, when asked to copy the word *hill*, severely learning disabled Patrick, age twelve, drew a picture of a hill next to the letters in order to give meaning to the word before copying it.

Quentin, age eight, was asked if his grandfather was coming to the Grandparents' Day festivities on Friday. Quentin said, "I don't have a grandfather." The teacher said, "But I met your grandmother and she was with a man." Quentin replied, "Oh! That was *Grandpa!*"

Jean, age nine, heard on the radio that a man who had been shot might become a vegetable. "How could he turn into a carrot or a string bean?" she asked her mother.

The very concrete child is a literal child. Subtleties, nuances, and inferences escape him. Sarcasm goes over his head. "That's just great!" says the neighborhood bully derisively. "Oh, thank you! I didn't think I did that well," answers Bruce gratefully. "Get him!" says the bully, laughing, and all the other children join in ridiculing poor Bruce.

Bruce didn't pay attention to the bully's tone of voice. He didn't separate the tone from the words in order to understand that the meaning was not friendly. Abstractions and oblique references pass him by. That's why it is rare for a learning disabled child to have a sparkling sense of humor. Double meanings, exaggeration to an absurd point, distortion, innuendo—key ingredients of humor— escape the learning disabled child. Unfortunately, her literalism often provides humor for others. Eight-year-old Rosie asked what the nose looked like when told that somebody "had a nose for business." Nine-year-old Thomas, having just heard the story of John Henry, was serious when he worried out loud, "It must have hurt John Henry's mother when he was born with a hammer in his hand." Ten-year-old Christine wondered where the stack was when a friend said the gym teacher was "blowing her stack." Eleven-year-old Jason looked anxiously at his feet when an adult remarked, "My, you've grown another foot!"

Eleven-year-old Eugene is also very concrete in his thinking. He was listening to a record that told a story about covered wagons when he heard the narrator call them "ships of the prairie." Eugene thereupon insisted he was listening to the wrong record because this one was about ships, not covered wagons. He was unable to grasp the metaphor and understand that "ships of the prairie" could mean "covered wagons."

Sidney insisted that a mountain lion could not live in a zoo, only on a mountain. Warren was equally vehement about Mount Vernon being the mountain where George Washington lived.

These children are intelligent but very literal because of their delayed development. The immature, concrete child is often stuck in the rut of one interpretation. Yet this problem is understandable when we realize how overwhelmed this child is with the indiscriminate mass of information assaulting him.

Clyde, a sophomore in high school, announced, "The Republicans win everything. They even got our country named for them—calling it a republic."

THE PERFECTIONIST

Often the inflexibility that results from extreme immaturity makes the learning disabled child a perfectionist. Of all people, this child does not need that self-imposed burden on top of the others. She can't bear to make a mistake and may react to her error as if it were a catastrophe, dooming the whole of her project. Twelve-year-old Mitchell slowly, carefully wrote a letter to his grandmother. He proudly showed it to his mother who commended him on his very good effort but suggested, in a matter-of-fact way, that he should correct a spelling mistake before he sent it. Mitchell snatched the letter from her hand, crumpled it up, and stomped on it. "And I could have found him an eraser in two minutes!" bemoaned his mother later, as upset by the incident as Mitchell had been by his spelling error.

Or the child may not blow up. She may simply drop her work and walk away, never to return to it. Blow up or quit—either tendency makes the learning disabled child extremely reluctant to undertake something new, where a mistake-proof routine has not yet been established and errors are almost a certainty.

The learning disabled child also often equates mistakes with failure. She cannot see that one mistake in a project is not a disaster but can easily be rectified. She may be hypercritical of a teacher who makes a mistake, and make a big issue of it. The teacher's error disturbs the learning disabled child's very precarious sense of order, or it may reflect her deep conviction that mistakes equal failure, and she doesn't want her teacher to be imperfect. The adults working with learning disabled children need to give themselves permission to make mistakes and thus allow the children to do the same without collapsing.

Fear of making mistakes is unfortunately reinforced almost every time a child watches an ad on television, where intelligent, athletic, stunning, clean, clearly competent people serve as an example of perfection, achieved with no effort beyond buying the right floor wax or the right car. In our world of "instant products," success and perfection occur within minutes, and there's no time for error. "A perfect solution for every householder," "the answer to your prayers," "the way to meet a perfect mate" describe a simple soap or deodorant. Learning disabled children feel very particularly imperfect surrounded by all this perfection. The child often projects this feeling of inadequacy by picking on the faults of others. He looks for defects. He tells Aunt Lily that she has a big mole on her chin. He calls everybody's attention to a run in the principal's stocking. He points out the falling plaster, the uneven shelf, the barely chipped cup. He informs each of his classmates as to their ugliest feature. And yet he yearns to be well liked.

It is a rare learning disabled child who can be sportsmanlike in a game. He sees every loss as yet another confirmation of his worthlessness, and he will do anything—even cheat—to win. Occasionally a child will fear winning. A win this time makes losing next time more likely and more terrible. He has been raised from infancy in our competitive society, which emphasizes achievement and winning above all else, where the second best are downgraded as also-rans, has-beens, and losers. There is no way he can simply enjoy an activity for its own sake when everybody around him presses onward toward success and wins because he loses.

THE PERSEVERATING CHILD

Besides wanting to perform a familiar action in his own rigid way, where he can't go wrong, the learning disabled child may start doing it over and over again like a mindless habit. To persevere is good, and learning disabled children are usually very hard workers. They have to work far harder than other children because they must consciously think through even simple actions like sitting down or taking a book off the shelf. But to *perseverate* is to go beyond perseverance and do the same thing again and again, without thinking, without even being aware that the habit exists. This describes that child mentioned earlier who drew circles over and over again.

Often the perseveration is verbal. When a child comes up with a good thought, he has to interrupt you to say it. He's afraid he'll forget it. Then he says it over and over again to be sure you heard. Sometimes he simply says the first thing that comes to mind and repeats it until he is stopped. He may get hung up on a subject—submarines, ambulances, or a trip he took—which he talks about endlessly until everyone is tired of it. Or having accidentally said something amusing, which was appreciated, he may go on saying it in a stereotyped way long after it has stopped being funny.

She may want to wear the same clothing every day, or she may become attached to one color and want blue blouses, blue shoes, blue sheets on her bed, and blue walls in her room. Harry was always in need of bandages for real or imagined cuts; he perseverated on talk of ailments. Monique persisted in drawing Snoopy. Holly gave the same response, modeled on her first response, to all arithmetic problems. Barry wrote the same letter or sometimes the same word down the entire page. Cary sang the same tune over and over again. Frank cleared his throat every few minutes. Mary asked for a drink of water before class one hot day and kept on wanting her drink of water all through the fall and winter as though she could not get into the classroom without it. Paul ate a cheese sandwich every day for a year. Jack kept on hammering so many nails into the boat he was building that when it was time to sail the boat, it sank from three pounds of extra nails.

THE DISORIENTED CHILD

The One-Way Kid cannot deal with priorities, alternatives, or even choices. Choices can produce anxiety, for they demand organization, isolating the prime characteristic or pleasure in each choice. Once the essential factor is extrapolated, then the two choices must be compared. This requires retaining several things in the mind and switching back and forth to study them. The learning disabled child generally experiences difficulty switching gears. It's as though each time he tries, he becomes settled in a permanent position and is thrust out of it and disoriented with the next move. Choices among many alternatives can drive him frantic. Open classrooms, which offer maximum choice and flexibility, can be agonizing for this child. Unstructured time, such as recess or lunchtime at school, can tax his powers of organization beyond the limit. He doesn't know what to do with himself. He may sit and stare, run around aimlessly, talk incessantly, or go from one thing to another. He has to be taught explicitly how to behave and what to do at lunch and recess in order for him to handle these situations properly. He may have to be taught many times over, in different ways, so he can manage the normal exigencies of these periods. The ability to transfer learning from one situation to another is a prime difficulty of the learning disabled child. It is related to his great immaturity, his concreteness, his being the One-Way Kid. You can transfer something, if the situation is not exactly the same, only if you have the maturity and organization to recognize the prime factors, to isolate the essentials, in the situation.

At home, the choices of what to do with free time can be upsetting to the learning disabled youngster. Jeremy's mother complained that every day this eight-year-old came home from school, went to his room to play, and burst into tears within a few minutes. She was mystified: "He had a whole roomful of fascinating toys, and there he'd sit in the middle of the floor bawling!" Finally she discovered that he didn't know which toys to play with. When she structured the situation by asking, "Jeremy, would you rather get out your soldiers or the Tinkertoys?" he was able to relax and start playing.

Substitutions and alternative ways of doing or being baffle the learning disabled child. James made great friends with the janitor, Freddy. When a boy named Freddy joined his class, James became quite angry, insisting that it couldn't be his real name because Freddy was a man's name, not a boy's. James also could not find the cups in the kitchen when someone had placed them upside down on the shelf; with their bottoms up, they did not appear as cups to him. Nor could he recognize the letter *a* if it was written in another type or on a different texture of paper. He could not read the word *cat* because it was printed in red. He insisted that the word *haul* meant to carry something and that the corridor outside his classroom could not be called *the hall*. To say that something is the same as another thing is pure nonsense to such a child. It can't be the same. There can be only one way.

THE NAÏVE CHILD

At this stage of development, a child fixes on one superficial aspect of the thing he perceives and fails to isolate the essential characteristic that binds it to others of its kind. She believes exactly what she sees, and she is easily fooled. In a Lab School class, a group of children made fresh lemonade and tasted it. They poured the lemonade into three glasses, then added orange food coloring to one glass and purple food coloring to another. When they tasted it again, they insisted that only the untouched glass contained lemonade; the others contained orange juice and grape juice. Even though they had added the artificial color themselves, they could not be persuaded otherwise. They clung to a single aspect of appearance—color—and could not yet identify the essential fact that they had made the juice in all three glasses from lemons. Franz banged his package of Fritos against his desk each lunchtime. Why? "I'll have MORE to eat," he said.

Betsy had two balls of clay of equal size. She rolled one of them into a long sausage and then claimed that there was more clay in the sausage than in the remaining ball, even though she herself had rolled it out from the ball. She was beguiled by the new shape and could not remember the two equal balls. The same child understood that $2 + 2 = 4$ but found it totally unreasonable that $3 + 1$ should also equal four.

Garrett gave some dimes to a neighbor's child but clutched on to his nickels. He insisted that a nickel had to be worth more than a dime because it was much bigger. Once Garrett got into a fight with his older brother over a similar error. The two boys had agreed to share the job of making brownies. They had the same sized pans and equal quantities of brownie mix. When the brownies had cooled in the pans, Garrett cut his batch into four rows of four big brownies, sixteen in all. Garrett's brother cut his batch into six rows of six little brownies, thirty-six in all. When Garrett compared the two batches, he flew into a rage and accused his brother of cheating by making so many. He fixed on the finished number of brownies and could not understand that the total volume was the same. Such errors frequently lead to misunderstandings, fights, and punishments for learning disabled children because their thinking is at a more primitive level than is expected for their age.

THE DEVELOPING MIND

The Swiss psychologist Jean Piaget (1896–1980) proposed that intellectual development progresses in stages and thinking is qualitatively different at each stage. He developed a theory of human development that has become well respected and that is particularly pertinent to the child with learning disabilities. Teachers of the learning disabled need to be well acquainted with Piaget's theories so they can best meet the needs of the student who is delayed in development.

Piaget argued that all children's minds develop in four distinct stages in a specific sequence that is the same for all, but that the rate at which individual children progress can differ widely. He points out that it normally takes the first six or seven years of life before a child is no longer fooled by the external physical appearance of objects and finally acquires the logical structure and mental understanding to recognize the *underlying constancy of matter*, i.e., a cup is a cup even if it's upside down or looks bigger or smaller according to where it's placed.

Piaget postulated that the four stages are characterized by different types of thinking, and that a child cannot move into the next stage without the foundation of the previous stage.

STAGE 1: THE SENSORY MOTOR STAGE (AGES 0–2)
   The child learns about the world through all his senses; handling and testing things is an essential preamble to the formulation of concepts.

STAGE 2: THE PREOPERATIONAL OR PRELITERAL STAGE
(AGES 2–7)

Dominated by what something appears to be, rather than what logically must be; there is magical thinking. Symbolism appears in play and language develops rapidly. The child is no longer completely dependent on his senses.

STAGE 3: THE CONCRETE OPERATIONAL STAGE (AGES 7–11)

The mind has to see it to believe it. Thought is still limited to concrete experiences and very literal.

STAGE 4: THE FORMAL OPERATIONAL PHASE (AGES 11 AND ON)

The child becomes logical and can form abstract ideas about objects that are out of sight. The child can understand nonliteral uses of language.

When the central nervous system is delayed in development or is dysfunctional, the child often remains in the concrete stage. A twelve-year-old can be in the preoperational stage and thus needs to be taught with those characteristics in mind. A teenager may be in the concrete operational stage and must be taught abstract principles through concrete activities.

The mistakes a child makes are vital clues to his intellectual development. When Garrett accused his brother of cheating him on the brownies, as mentioned above, he was demonstrating that he was fooled by appearances. He thought his brother's brownie pan cut into thirty-six pieces offered far more food than his four rows of four big brownies. What stage was Garrett in? His thinking or developmental level was in the preoperational or preliteral stage (closer to six years of age) when his chronological age was eleven.

Many learning disabled children are very developmentally delayed, perhaps by four to eight years. They may not have obtained the skills of the early sensory-motor stage that a two-year-old usually masters. Teachers must therefore incorporate more direct sensory-motor experience into the learning process regardless of the children's chronological age. Learning disabled children need much more teaching with objects and manipulative materials than the average child before they can start dealing with abstractions. Experience is the key to intellectual development. A child who has had physical experience with a concrete object, such as a ball, can then form a mental picture of the ball and think about it in the same ways that he experienced it.

This is why at The Lab School we teach much of the material through visual and concrete means. Influenced substantially by the theorists Jean Piaget, Jerome Bruner, and John Dewey, curriculum is designed to suit each child's developmental level. It also appeals to the child's interest levels, which correspond to his chronological age. Students need to learn basic concepts through the use of their senses. Every activity has to have a clear sequence of steps to be mastered one by one. A hands-on, multisensory approach involves the whole child and gives him or her a chance fully to assimilate information and master learning techniques.

For example, Lab School students start out with miniature figures in a sand tray that they play with to develop a story. They arrange human figures, animals, trees, buildings, furniture, landscapes into a story that clearly has a beginning, a middle, and an end. Their story has to have some action to appeal to a reader. Once they think the story through, they present it to their peers, who critique the story. Then they put the story on a Macintosh computer and develop it into a 16- to 20-page book with illustrations that has an artistic cover, a title page and a page at the end with a photograph, entitled "About the Author." In June 1991, The Lab School won the Computer World/ Smithsonian State of the Art in Technology Award in Education for these kinds of innovations.

In a drama class, Brian was asked to play the parts of a strong king and then a weak king. From his portrayal, the characters appeared to be identical, although he knew they should be different. He could not isolate the main characteristic of each king and therefore could not exaggerate that quality in order to communicate the difference by his acting. He was unable to integrate gesture, movement, and speech. The actress who was teaching him first demonstrated a strong walk and then a weak walk so the children could see the difference. They practiced strong walks, accenting their struts, and added strong gestures and strong facial expressions. In time, they also gave strong oral commands. Following the same step-by-step method, they learned to act the part of the feeble king. Subsequently, they played guessing games that involved the concepts of strong and weak, first verbalizing what they had to remember: What will the walk be like? The gestures? The facial expression? The voice? Their increased capacity to organize and integrate effectively in drama carried over into the classroom.

Until children are seven or eight years old, they ordinarily have trouble looking back in time and then forward in order to make a sensible judgment. They are inflexible, and only one way makes sense to them. The learning disabled child may continue to exhibit this characteristic long after others grow out of it.

Frequently this child develops one way to act in a social situation and applies it to all other situations. He dances into a classroom, waving his arms, going "beep bop-big boy is here—ya dee da!" The first time—he amused his classmates, but then he adopted this behavior as his stereotyped entry. "Heil Hitler!" says Albert every time he is given an instruction. "Yes, Your Majesty," says George perseveratively to each teacher's or his mother's requests. The parents wonder why the child doesn't understand that these remarks or this behavior don't belong in the present situation. The teacher wonders if this is an attention getter, a misfired attempt at humor, or simply rude behavior. The outsider finds it bizarre. Other children label him "weirdo kid."

Just as Sandy has trouble visualizing pictures, letters, and words, he has difficulty visualizing his impact on others. Seeing the consequences of his behavior is not in his repertoire, and he is being truthful when he says, "I never thought about that." Mary, who can't read, also has trouble reading faces; she can't see when somebody is happy, angry, sad, or bewildered. She doesn't look carefully to begin with, or she overlooks the clues that are important. Many learning disabled children are extraordinarily perceptive about people's feelings and relationships, but still they rarely can anticipate their impact on others or even recognize it afterward.

Teachers of learning disabled youngsters often live in dread of transitions, for trouble erupts at those times. Those are times of shifting gears, accommodating to change. Putting away what he has been doing starts the storm. The hyperactive child frequently explodes; he shouts, swears, and throws down his work. The hypoactive youngster or the one who doesn't overreact tunes out or daydreams at this time and needs constant reminders to get ready. Many learning disabled children seem not to hear the directions. Lining up to go to the next class brings problems of who has which place in the line, who touches whom, and what's to be taken to the next class. Down the stairs, not watching where he's going, overhearing a remark that he thinks, rightly or wrongly, to be about him, a casual touch on the shoulder misinterpreted to be a hostile gesture—all these may lead to blows. This is followed by entering the next class, where his chair may not be in the right place, the materials have been moved, and he is now so furious with the remark and the touch on the shoulder that he can't settle down to work.

Each transition seems to wear out the learning disabled child so that he can't function effectively until well into the next activity. But we know that his neural development is delayed and that he is very slow to integrate more than one thing at a time, if at all. And his difficulties are easier to understand when we realize that planning and preparing oneself for change take organization, the ability to project ahead and to look backward. These are the disabled areas of this child, areas that have to be taken over for him by the teacher until the child can learn to handle them himself. The teacher must be superbly organized herself, be able to see far enough ahead, and be well prepared in advance to help the child plan for the approaching transition. Each child reacts to change in his own pattern and can be helped to discover his own best strategies for coping with it.

Too much going on in the child's mind at once leads to difficulty with discrimination, separating out one thing from another, and then integrating them to make sense. Impulsivity leads to scattered approaches, random action, random thought, or perseveration. A fragile sense of order begets the inflexibility or rigidity of ONE WAY and contributes to a fear of making any mistakes. Egocentricity of the Now Child combined with concreteness, literalness, and relying on appearances as truth are evidences of extreme immaturity. All of these factors contribute to the learning disabled child's inability to deal with alternatives, to choose, to substitute one thing for another, to transfer learning from one situation to another, to switch gears, or even to start a task.

THE TEACHER'S JOB

When we are aware of all these factors, what can we do? We cannot change them willy-nilly in order to make the child easier to educate. They will change as the neural development takes place. What we can do is keep these factors firmly in mind while programming for a learning disabled child. If we know a learning disabled youngster cannot begin any task, then we invent ways to help him establish a routine that will work to help him program himself to do it. This is why teaching the learning disabled child how to learn may be more important than the task itself. Part of the teacher's job is to teach him how to sit in a classroom, how to organize his materials, and how to get to work. We would not expect a three- or four-year-old to know how to begin work in a formal classroom setting, yet we do expect a six- or seven-year-old at this developmental level to do so. At first, how to deal with regular school routines becomes more important than learning content, for otherwise the learning disabled youngster cannot survive, much less progress, at school. But also, the child's good-to-superior intellect must be challenged, stretched, and excited at the same time that simple routines are learned.

A good percentage of children with learning disabilities are also gifted and talented. The concept of being both learning disabled and gifted and talented is rarely accepted by teachers in the 1990s. For the most part, if a child appears to be very smart, teachers tend to think the child is just not trying. "He's clearly lazy," said Miss Vator, "because I know if he just tried, he could read!" Because the child is so verbally astute, sometimes teachers decide that the child takes pleasure in mocking his teachers, that his problem is oppositional behavior or that he's disturbed. Mr. Robinson told fellow teachers that "Judy just needs discipline to stop flouting authority. She's spoiled."

The worst problem with gifted children who are learning disabled is that they are quick to see that other children their age have acquired the skills they haven't, and then they feel rotten about themselves. Self-esteem problems are even worse with this population than with children of average intelligence who are not as quick to pick up on what they do not know. All kinds of defense mechanisms build up. The gifted child uses her swift brain to manipulate the school situation so she won't meet failure, or the talented boy uses his "smarts" to make a comedy out of the situation. Too often, the "giftedness" is directed toward avoiding work and certainly toward avoiding failure.

Teachers must challenge the "giftedness" in children by following their interests and talents, enticing them into inquiry, and stretching their intellects wherever possible while recognizing their need to learn how to learn.

SIX

MANAGING SPACE AND TIME

What's the difference between 1 2 3 and 123?
What's the difference between b and d?
What's the difference between act and cat?
What's the difference between + and ×?
What's the difference between OIL and 710?

What's reading? It involves a series of graphic symbols placed in a certain order in space.

What's math? It involves groupings in space, location of angles in space, order, and placement of numbers in space.

What's geography? It involves land space, water space, relationships in space.

What's history? It involves spaces in time—relationships of one space in time to another.

What's art? It involves the creative use of space.

What's learning? It involves exploring new space: discriminating, integrating, organizing spaces in the mind, in time.

The learning disabled child has difficulty with learning in general, usually with reading and spelling and often with math, geography, and history. The child experiences confusion in regard to spatial relationships and time concepts.

Space and time are organizing systems. We organize the way we view a room. We organize the way we enter it and choose a seat in relation to what's going on and who is there. We organize our bedrooms for maximum comfort and convenience. We place the furniture where it can be easily reached and arrange our clothes in drawers and closets so that we can find what we want easily. We organize what we will do within a given time period. We organize where we are going in relation to our starting point. We *have* a starting point. The severely learning disabled child does not.

Children copy the way in which adults use space. They recognize the different atmospheres that exist in classrooms where the chairs are lined up facing the teacher and classrooms where the chairs are placed in a circle. They recognize the feelings and attitudes that underlie the work spaces, play spaces, and eating spaces. They take note (often unconsciously) of a family's way of using space and a community's handling of outdoor spaces. Being able to enter a room and immediately organize it visually so that we place ourself in it comfortably is a skill we take for granted. Knowing instinctively how we'll use space gives us a sense of safety, confidence, and freedom to relate to people or ideas. When we are lost in space, we are groping, stumbling, shaking; with no borders, beginnings and endings, no directions, we feel unsafe, alien.

The learning disabled child is most often lost in space: lost in up-down, left-right, above-below, top-bottom, in-out, under-over, apart-together. He does not know automatically how to operate in space; he cannot visualize or organize spaces nor can he find his way easily in space. He does not know where the top shelf is since he is not sure that his feet are below his head. He can't make reliable judgments about space since his body is not a reliable instrument of measure.

The learning disabled child is lost in space, so he very often covets one space, one corner, one chair. What if someone takes your chair? Or places himself in a space that you consider yours? What if someone crowds you? What if someone leans on what you feel is your territory? How do you react to this infringement on your space? Multiply that reaction by ten and you can feel what the learning disabled child experiences. His reactions appear to the observer to be way out of proportion to the situation. They are, in fact, that way because his sense of space is so very precarious that the least bit of trespassing threatens his entire being, and too much space is equally threatening.

With a faulty perception of space, this youngster either clings with desperation to an adult or gets lost in a big department store, the supermarket, or at a ball game. A class of learning disabled children from The Lab School was invited to visit the White House with three of their teachers. When they entered the great ballroom with its huge space and vast, shiny floor, the children began running, sliding, rolling in different directions, whooping, and yelling. Such an enormous, unstructured space was more than their senses could manage. "It was as if each of those children had blown a fuse," reported one of the teachers later. "And it was the worst half hour of my life!"

Without our being aware of it, most of us follow unwritten rules in the way we organize our work space, our recreational space, our conversational space. Space is important in our conversations with others—not just with the words but in our conversational distances. How close do we talk to someone we like (or don't like), to an older person, to a child, or to a sick person? We instinctively know what we want to do. However, frequently the learning disabled person does not. Too often he comes up so close that we back off, or he stands so far away while he talks to us that we can't hear him. Relationships in space cause trouble between people from different parts of the world, even from different cultures within one country. In the Middle East and in Latin America, people usually come very close, often making body contact, to talk to someone. Americans back off, finding these people aggressive, pushy, and fresh. The others feel Americans are cold, distant, hostile. Similar judgments are made regarding the learning disabled child. His indiscriminate sense of space affects how others perceive him. It affects his relationships, as does his poor timing.

LEARNING ABOUT SPACE

How do we develop a sense of space and spatial relationships? A newborn baby learns about his body little by little, starting with his mouth, which sucks, and by sucking obtains food. Awareness spreads to his face; his eyes follow movements, and he gives a smile of recognition. Then comes awareness of hands and arms, which grope for what the eyes see. Next come the feet, pushing against his mother's lap, defining his length and his place in space, building a body image. A baby who does not yet know the limits of his own body responds to the world with the whole of it, using great energy at random, with no order or pattern. When he smiles, even his feet are part of the action.

His own body is the baby's reference point by which he gauges the whole world—size and shape—far and near. All his judgments about space are related to himself. If his body image is accurate, he is getting good sensory feedback and is integrating it properly. All along, in the normal developmental pattern, he has been gaining a sense of himself by being held, hugged, rubbed, stroked, and patted. He is moving and being moved. If he does not receive this stimulation or if his nervous system does not properly interpret these tactile messages, the baby does not come to feel the dimensions of himself. When he learns to crawl, he tries to squeeze through spaces that are too small. The feelings in his shoulders and sides help him to determine how big he is in relation to the space. He learns by trial and error. As he remembers, he organizes his experiences and builds up a body memory with which he can compare his movements and sensations. His whole body will tell him when he is about to lose his balance, and he will isolate out parts of his body to do different jobs. His mother takes her child's hand and says, "Look at your hand. See Mommy's hand?" She touches it, she shows it to him, waves it, kisses it. Words too then become a part of his body image. The information is stored in his brain, pulled together to make a more and more detailed image, organized so as to make sense of his body. Starting with himself, using all his senses, he is beginning to perceive the world.

But if a child's senses are not conveying accurate information, if the body image is fragmented, if the parts remain scattered and do not relate to a whole, then the body cannot be used as a reliable instrument of measure. The body is not functioning as a prime information-gathering tool; it is not processing, storing, and applying the needed information. If the body is out of kilter, the whole world is out of kilter. If a child does not have complete body awareness, she can't isolate the different parts of her body and make them work together. She must be taught specifically how to do this step-by-step.

Muscular control and coordination develop from head to foot. A baby can raise her head after two or three weeks but does not walk until she is ten to eighteen months. She throws a ball before she can kick it. As she gains control of her muscles, learns which parts of her body do what, and improves her eye focus, she finds she can do things faster and more efficiently; later on, she can tie her shoelace standing on one foot, talking all the time, and without dropping the tennis racquet under her arm. With good organization, she can do many tasks at once and automatically. She reacts fast. But when a child wastes energy and motion in superfluous movement, then she does everything more slowly, more inefficiently, and more clumsily.

If our body's messages are coming through to the brain clearly, we get quick feedback. If we lean too far forward or backward, we are acutely uncomfortable knowing that we are about to lose our balance, so we straighten up and resume a balanced posture. Children with poor body feedback can fall off their chairs easily. Balance and equilibrium develop in stages also. A child of three can usually stand on one foot, at four he can hop, at five skip, but a child with motor learning disability may not have the balance to do some of these things at nine or fourteen. An eight-year-old may swing from one part of the car to another each time it swerves, and a ten-year-old may struggle to ride a bike. They do not have sufficient body control.

Normal development proceeds from bilateral (the use of both sides of the body at once) to unilateral (the use of one side at a time). At first, both hands hold the mug and both feet stand on each stair; but as they grow, children learn to reach with one hand and to walk downstairs with alternating feet. By age five or six, they show a definite preference for one hand over the other; they become clearly right- or left-handed. As part of average growth, children develop an understanding of the two sides of their bodies and learn to use them separately.

The right side of the brain controls the left side of the body, and the left side of the brain controls the right side of the body, with an imaginary midline. Both sides of a baby's body move together toward the imaginary midline but do not cross over. Normally by the time a child is five or six and his separate sides are working together in a coordinated way, with one side preferred over the other, he easily crosses the midline. The immature child, in contrast, has no separate feeling of right and left; he does things on the left side of his body with his left hand, things on the right side with his right hand, and avoids crossing over the midline. Dana is sawing a plank of wood in half. She starts sawing and saws through to the middle of the board, then stops. She now goes to the other side and again proceeds to saw toward the center. Horace tries to conduct music without his arm's ever crossing the midline; the music teacher finally takes his right arm and tries to push it way over to the left, but at the middle of his body she meets rigid resistance. Anne Marie starts writing on the left of her page and then way over to the right; the middle of the sheet is empty. Richard's drawing of a clock is equally strange. All the numbers on the round face—out of sequence, reversed, and rotated—are crowded on the left side, leaving the right side blank.

A true inner awareness of left and right is called *laterality*. If a child does not have laterality, his movements become helter-skelter from both sides. When he writes on a piece of paper, both his hands and arms move. When he kicks with one foot, the other one moves too, and the child falls down. This child frequently mirror-writes. Without laterality, he cannot follow directions to find an object or a point in space. Poor body image leads to delayed development of laterality, which leads to poor directionality, so that he is lost in space. He can't put his name in the upper left-hand corner of his page. If he cannot differentiate the left from the right side, how can he memorize a symbol that has a right or left side? He does not even know if he is right-handed or left-handed.

Until recently, and even now, both-handedness (ambidextrousness) has been mentioned as a cause of reading difficulties rather than seen as an indicator of immaturity. It doesn't matter which hand a child uses as long as the maturation has taken place for him to feel two distinct sides of the body, differentiate them, and integrate them. Most of the world is right-handed. Archaeologists have dug up ancient tools that show that humans seem to have preferred their right hands as far back as the Bronze Age. Taboos and superstitions have centered on left-handedness. Even the term *left-handed* is called *sinistrality*—a word with the same root as *sinister*—yet there is nothing wrong with a child's being left-handed.

The child who "sights" with his left eye and uses his right hand (or who sights with his right eye and uses his left hand) is said to have *mixed dominance*. For years, doctors and reading experts tended to believe that this was the cause of reading difficulties; then studies showed that half the people who read well have mixed dominance but do not reverse letters and numbers. Thus what had been a convenient answer to the cause of learning disabilities until the 1960s was proven incorrect. Mixed dominance does not matter, but body awareness and the way a body is organized do.

LEARNING BODY AWARENESS

A child who does not have awareness of his body also lacks mastery over the directions in which his body goes. He would have trouble following directions such as "turn to the right" or "move forward and then come back." He might not know what the teacher means when she says, "Put that aside. Find the paper above the desk and on the shelf to the right." Franklin would say, "Put it *faceup*," when he meant "put it *right side up*," and "put it *out* to the center" instead of "put it *into* the center," but even these efforts were a great improvement over his previous inability to give any spatial directions at all.

Frequently the learning disabled child cannot create pictures in her mind. She cannot visualize "up and down" any more than she can visualize *b* or *d* when she tries to write them. She has to do much more looking, touching, and talking to try to remember what she has seen. The difficulty that the learning disabled child faces in visualizing space often causes her to act like a much younger child. She is like the nursery-schooler who loses her jacket and runs around to every place she can think of where she has been, looking for it. At a later stage of development, the child can sit still and picture in her mind where she has been until she can logically decide where she probably left it. Until she is able to visualize space, a child cannot plan how to use it.

By school age most children can dress themselves quickly in the morning—if they want to. A few will even lay out their clothes neatly the night before. But not Bobby. Even before he started school and began writing his letters backward and upside down, Bobby had trouble getting his shirt on the right way around. He would habitually put both legs through one leg hole of his shorts and put his shoes on the wrong feet. He couldn't coordinate his muscles. He knew the result he wanted, but he didn't know how to organize to get it.

For a child to plan his movements well, he must know where his body is in space, and he must be able to coordinate several parts of his body at the same time into one action. A learning disabled child with poor laterality may find this extremely difficult. If you have ever tried to mount the obstacles in a difficult obstacle course, you know what kind of planning he needs simply to move around without knocking things over, bumping into the furniture, or falling down. This is called *motor planning*. Motor planning is the ability of the brain to conceive of, organize, and carry out a sequence of unfamiliar or nonhabitual actions. If you try to write your name backward, you will experience the kind of difficulty in motor planning that a learning disabled youngster may experience in writing his name forward.

Occupational therapy is a health profession concerned with improving a person's occupational performance (a child's occupation is to be a preschooler or a student) and his ability to adapt successfully to the tasks he must perform in his environment. Working with the physically handicapped (i.e., the victims of strokes, brain damage, and cerebral palsy), occupational therapists work with clients on relearning how to dress, feed themselves, hold a pencil, and other functional tasks. Sometimes a child with learning disabilities who is physically able to put on his clothes cannot figure out how to do so. This is a problem with motor planning (or praxis). Occupational therapists have found that a child with a faulty sense of his own body usually does not efficiently organize or integrate information he receives through touch, movement, muscles, joints, and ligaments (proprioceptors). Thus, it is not surprising that the child finds it difficult to plan his activities or coordinate several things at once.

Occupational therapists developed treatment programs for motor-planning difficulties and began applying the principles of this treatment to learning disabled children who are disorganized and have difficulty with sensory-motor skill development. This treatment approach, known as sensory integration, assesses a child's ability to take in information through the visual, motor, tactile, kinesthetic, and balance (movement) systems, organize it in his brain, and use it to adapt successfully to his world. Treatment involves activities that provide certain specific sensory stimuli and require goal-directed motor responses. An occupational therapist working with a child on body image and consequent motor-planning problems would work to improve a child's processing of information regarding his body and what it can do. In a step-by-step sequence, the therapist would encourage the development of movement, balance, kinesthetic body awareness, and sense of touch. The activities gradually increase the demands on the child to make an organized, more mature response. Activities could include rolling, jumping, pushing, pulling, use of specialized swings and ramps—anything that gives a child a more accurate awareness of his body. The OT helps the child develop his reflexes and equilibrium, the natural mechanisms necessary to cope with gravity and movement through space. Occupational therapy also helps a child modulate an overresponsive or oversensitive sensory system. (See *tactile defensiveness* in appendix 1.)

It may be necessary for the therapist to teach the child the most basic concepts of space and direction. For instance, one exercise involves repeating together the word *up*, integrating language with sensory-motor learning to identify the upward movement of the body as the child is moving. An occupational therapist working in a school will also work on specific skills that a child needs to function in the educational environment, such as handwriting.

What the occupational therapist frequently does with the body is exactly what parents and teachers have to do with all aspects of learning; she breaks each task into its smallest units and then puts them into their proper sequence for teaching. This is called *task analysis*. It requires identifying the steps a task involves and which ones the child has already mastered. We cannot take for granted what a child can and cannot do. Keen observation of a child with motor difficulties is crucial.

A clumsy child takes longer to learn to remember what he has seen, heard, felt, or done ... longer to make sense of information from two or more senses ... longer to get meaning from looking, listening, touching, moving ... longer to answer a question or repeat what he has been told. Her timing and spacing are off. She does not have enough internal organization to put everything together rapidly. This is not surprising when we realize how much excess, random energy the child employs uselessly. Her efforts exhaust her, making her slow and inefficient.

Ivan was standing under a cliff when rocks began to fall. His father had to race over and grab him up to save him, scolding him furiously for not obeying. Ivan was not being disobedient or stubborn. He simply could not get himself organized fast enough to meet the emergency. Over and over again we yell accusingly, "What's the matter with you?" when a learning disabled child does not react quickly. How he wishes he could answer that question! And by asking it, we make him even slower, for under the stress of being pushed and being yelled at, he becomes almost paralyzed.

Distractibility and disorganization can cause clumsiness. Combine this with being lost in space, with poor coordination and poor timing, and what do you have? You have a child who can't look, listen, and move at the same time. Often he can't learn by watching others demonstrate. He can't eat and talk at the same time. When he reads, he can't translate words into sounds and think about their meaning at the same time. He stops all learning in a classroom while he picks a pimple. He cannot integrate several processes at once.

Ruthie always dropped her boots—or her books or her homework or her hat—when she carried them to school. She couldn't organize herself to carry all these things at once. She was clumsy in brushing her hair, brushing her teeth, and putting on a kerchief, and she couldn't organize herself to cut meat with a fork and a knife. Hilda literally tripped over her own feet as though they were some alien objects attached to her, having nothing to do with the rest of her. Elizabeth's zeal to be helpful in the kitchen often led to too many, or too few, ingredients in the bowl and rude remarks from her brothers at the table later. Robin wanted more than anything else to be considered grown up and responsible. She begged her mother to let her help dress her three-year-old sister, but somehow the clothes were never put on right, and dressing took so long that her little sister usually ended up bawling.

Friendly and clumsy, an older learning disabled child may long to join the neighborhood children in their games but finds himself rejected, run away from, or the last one to be picked for a team. His awkwardness makes him a liability because he is sure to miss the ball, or drop it, or be too slow getting to first base, or lose track of which direction he is going.

Chuck's family had just returned to America from overseas. They were still living in a hotel, but Chuck, age nine and a half, was already enrolled in a special school for learning disabled children. One Friday, his mother arrived by taxi to pick him up after school. As Chuck ran happily out the front door, he didn't look where he was going; he tripped on the sidewalk and went sprawling, while the contents of his lunch box rolled into the gutter and under the taxi. Chuck, lunch box, thermos, half-eaten apple, and uneaten sandwich were all picked up and put into the taxi. The following conversation then took place:

"Mom, guess what! I've got a new friend!"

"That's great, Chuck! What's his name?"

"I don't remember, but we're going to meet each other tomorrow."

"Where are you going to meet?"

"At school."

"Tomorrow's Saturday, Chuck—remember? No school."

"Oh . . . Well, that's okay. I asked him to come swimming in the hotel pool. He's gonna come."

"When did you ask him for?"

"Um . . . Oh! . . . Maybe that was yesterday!"

"Well, we'll just have to wait and see if he shows up. Did you tell him the name of our hotel?"

"Sure, the Hilton."

"Chuck! We're staying at the Sheraton!"

At this point the taxi driver turned around and said, confidentially: "Lady, you've got a PROBLEM with that kid!"

The taxi driver may have been right, but the real problem was Chuck's, not his mother's. Who . . . what . . . where . . . which . . . when . . . had all escaped him. With no firm ground under his feet, no fixed points in time to grip onto, he could only stumble and grope, and the result was a well-meaning but inept and clumsy performance. This lack of orientation brings with it a lack of grace. The child is awkward in the disconnected way he moves his arms and legs; he blunders into the furniture and trips over the rugs. He is frequently graceless in his social interchanges with other people—talking too much or too loudly, making an inappropriate spontaneous response, or not reacting when he should. But all learning disabled children cannot be categorized as awkward physically and socially; some appear to be well coordinated, gracious, thoughtful in social situations.

Henry was awkward. He misjudged space and had little sense of time. He was delighted when his mother and father had company because he loved people. He helped his mother set the table, and in spite of his mistakes, he and his mother enjoyed these times together. Henry would greet the company, and one time he insisted on taking their drink orders. How he wanted to do it well! "Good for his memory as well as his spirit," said his father. But the task turned out not to be too good for his spirit. He forgot the orders and had to ask all four guests to repeat them, several times. Then, when he finally came in, triumphantly carrying the drinks on a tray, he did not judge the space correctly, tripped, and sent the whole lot crashing to the floor.

Typically the learning disabled child can't remember where to go;

he frequently gets lost, loses not only himself but also his possessions, and doesn't see things that are in front of him. When he's asked to stand in front of his desk, often he stands behind it. When he's asked to put the paper into the box, he frequently puts it beneath the box. He is disoriented in space. When asked to write something on the bottom of the page, many times the learning disabled youngster turns over the page. It is extremely common that a learning disabled child cannot write his name in the upper left-hand corner of a page; instead he scrambles the letters together in some indiscriminately chosen space or makes the letters so big that they go off the page. When asked to place a dot in the middle of the page, he puts it on the edge—or anywhere else. When asked to touch his left knee with his right arm, he'll frequently mask his confusion with a sneeze or a joke.

Nine-year-old Melissa stopped a teacher in the hall and asked, "Where is 'around the corner'?"

"Which corner?" she replied mystified.

"Around the corner!" Melissa insisted.

"There are many corners, Melissa. Which one do you mean?"

"I don't know. The sports teacher told me to get the ball from 'around the corner.' "

"Where was the sports teacher standing?"

"I don't remember!"

"When did he tell you this?"

"A long time ago."

CONFUSED BY TIME

Melissa was very intelligent, but she had severe problems with time and space; she had no reference points. Both time and space demand selecting out, remembering, integrating, and sequencing. They demand order, just what a learning disabled child does not have. This is why parents and teachers must immediately provide the structure in space and time for such a child.

Some children need help only in specific areas. Some are good athletes who deal well with their bodies in large spaces yet can't organize space on paper. Others require a clearly defined place and time and space for everything in their lives. Well-marked spaces, or small spaces, spell safety to such a child. He does not know how far his body extends or how much space it takes up. This is why security often depends on the same seat at the dining-room table, the same place in the school bus, the same chair in the classroom.

Space is something that the learning disabled child can see; he may see it distorted, out of proportion, and askew, but he can see it. It is tangible. Time eludes him totally, for it is more abstract; it is something that happens between two points he can't see. He cannot feel a minute.

An infant's time is body feeling related to his needs—time for milk, time to change his diaper. It is personal or egocentric time. His needs are time. What begins in egocentric, concrete terms moves steadily outward toward an abstract, universal scheme. The child can see a day and a night; he can see a season and know if it is winter or summer. A two-year-old's sense of time centers on the present, but he is beginning to understand *wait* and *soon*. At three, he usually knows *yesterday,* but he is much more able to talk about the future. By then he can tell how old he is; he knows he goes to bed "after supper and after a story"; and he can talk about what he will do tomorrow. At four, he knows what happened throughout a day, what to expect in the morning, what happens before, during, and after lunch, how the afternoon is spent, and he knows the sequence of supper, bath, story, and bedtime. After five, he knows the days of the week; he can tell what day follows Sunday and project how old he will be on his next birthday. He uses the words *yesterday, today,* and *tomorrow* with ease. By seven or eight, he knows the months and the seasons, and he can usually tell the time. The learning disabled child, occasionally as late as age fourteen, still does not know the days of the week. His perception of time is that of a preschooler.

Just as the two-year-old, the Now Child, understands no time but the present, so the learning disabled child becomes sullen or cries, screams, and stomps around when he does not get what he wants now. Long time, short time, more time, less time, do not mean anything to him. Before, after, not yet, soon, later, wait—all this is mumbo jumbo. Scolding by adults only shows him once more that he is out of phase with everybody else, that he is doing things wrong, and that he is bad. He needs an adult to place him in a time slot, to provide a system for him whereby he can structure his activity to fit into the adult time scheme. Structure of space and time can be lifesaving for the learning disabled child.

Time is order. It is made up of sequences. Because a learning disabled child has no order, he is lost when he tries to tell the days of the week (or the seasons or months), to remember the alphabet, to count or to tell time. Counting is the basis of measuring time. Counting what you don't see is what time is all about, and if you are a concrete child, you need to see it.

A little child who says that Grandma will be coming "one sleep away," is charming, but a ten-year-old who says that is considered peculiar. Primitive people and preschoolers cannot deal with the abstractness of time either. They see it as a time to get up, a time to eat, a time to work or play, a time to sleep. Intervals of time, periods, and durations have no meaning for them unless related to their own life experiences. An abstract time system based on counting does not exist for them. If asked when a story took place, eleven-year-old Norman always answered "in the day" rather than giving a historical perspective or even stating "a long time ago." Ten-year-old Isador wondered if Christmas might come sooner by his coming to school earlier each day. This made no sense, but Isador could not make any sense of time.

On his first day at The Lab School, twelve-year-old Basil was told,

"It's two o'clock, time to go, Basil. Your father will be here to pick you up."

"That can't be," protested Basil. "My father works in Virginia, and it takes him an hour to get here."

His teacher explained to him that by starting an hour earlier, at one o'clock, his father could indeed arrive in Washington at two. But Basil, unable to visualize the interval of an hour and connect that to the distance from Virginia, continued to repeat, "Dad *can't* get here at two—it takes him a *whole hour!*" until his father astonished him by walking in.

Basil had no concept of time, even the meaning of the terms *before* and *after;* Basil was also poorly coordinated and lost in space. It was not enough for a teacher simply to work on Basil's nonexistent time concepts. He needed a whole remedial program of locating his body in space, learning left from right, working on visual, auditory, motor, and tactile discrimination, as well as memory. He needed to understand the terms *before* and *after* with his body in space before those words conveyed meaning in relation to time.

Intervals of time regulate our lives. Time is precious, hurried, closely watched. Time is money.

> *We invest time,*
> *save time,*
> *borrow time,*
> *budget time,*
> *charge time,*
> *spend time,*
> *steal time,*
> *waste time,*
> *lose time,*
> *check time,*
> *share time,*
> *squander time,*
> *take time.*

We hurry our children to grow up and tell older people to stay young. We hurry to learn. We crave shortcuts, quick solutions, easy answers.

Speed is a way of life: sports cars, jet planes, instant cake mix, electronic communications. If you don't get where you're going today, tomorrow may be too late. Yet with all the emphasis on speed and saving time, boredom and the use of leisure time are big national problems today. So it is with the learning disabled child who cannot tolerate the pressure of time and yet cannot make constructive use of leisure time. Sleep is regulated by time. Meals are regulated by time. We time everything.

LEARNING TO JUDGE TIME AND SPACE

"HURRY UP!" How many times a day do we say this? But the learning disabled child can't organize himself to hurry; he falls apart instead. With his random, excessive movement and his immature lack of planning, he expends more time and effort getting anything done and is therefore slower than normal. His distractibility and inefficiency keep him from accomplishing anything on a time schedule. His perceptions are slow and frequently inaccurate.

A child's failure to grasp concepts of time can cause a wide variety of problems at school. Most obviously, the child may be continually late. He cannot pace himself if he does not have a reliable time sense. He cannot pace himself to finish a job, a paper, or a test on time. The study of history is dealing with time past and sequences in the past. The past is more difficult to deal with than the present or even the future. A five-year-old knows the age she will be on her next birthday but not what it was on her last birthday. Walking backward is harder than walking forward; you can't see where you are going, and you have to visualize what is behind you.

Dealing with anything backward is much harder than doing it forward. It takes more organization. The past tense is difficult for many children: "I've got it" and "I'm gonna get it" are much easier than "I had it." Subtraction is harder than addition. Repeating numbers backward requires additional concentration. Double negatives such as "it is not unusual that" are often baffling, for they demand reversing to translate them. It takes years before a learning disabled child can cope with any of these things. He cannot figure out what letter comes before *E* without going back to *A* and reciting forward again. To find out what number comes before 9, he must go back to the beginning and count up from 1.

To apply reason to time, to understand cause and effect, you have to reconstruct time that is past. A child cannot normally do this until the age of eight, usually the third grade. Switching back and forth from past to present to future time demands organization and a great deal of memory. Impeded by impulsivity, distractibility, poor memory, and disorganization, the learning disabled child becomes lost in this process. With no concept of time except what has just happened, she may answer "How was your day at school today?" with "Good" or "Terrible," depending only on what happened during her last activity of the day.

Her timing is off in her speech; she doesn't know when to begin and when to stop. She has difficulty perceiving pauses in people's speech and in understanding the implications of those inflections. She has trouble with raising and lowering her own voice. Her rhythm may be off. Frequently she can't sing in established tempos. Often she can't rhyme. She's a poor judge of time and lingers after class and then is late to the next one. Her timing is off in planning schoolwork. She can't complete projects, can't estimate the time needed for homework, can't judge how much time to allow for each question on a test, can't pace herself to produce a term paper, can't do work on three different subjects in one evening, even when the assignments are very short.

The concept of self is essential in order to locate oneself in space and time. Until a person can see himself as quite separate from his environment, different, unique, yet related intimately to it, he has no real sense of self. Under those conditions, space and time happen to him, and he is helpless. The immature being starts there and slowly achieves a mastery over the present and the past, planning for the future as a defined, independent, fully functioning self.

A very young child believes that somebody big must be older than somebody small because he cannot see time or comprehend age. He does not know whether his mother or his grandmother was born first and cannot imagine them ever having been children. He senses only that he himself is growing; he expects to catch up and overtake his older brother, his parents, and his grandparents.

By seven or eight years old, children with normal development are accurate judges of both time and space, and it is this ability above all others that gives them the solid foundation on which to base formal school learning. Some school systems, such as Switzerland's, devote the first two years of school to intensive readiness activities—the arts and handicrafts—postponing formal learning of reading, writing, and arithmetic until the children are at least seven years old. Since school-age learning disabled children are delayed in their development, they remain at the stage of preschoolers who are not clear about the location and use of their own bodies, not yet ready to undertake the tasks of formal schooling. They tend to grope in time and space. They are lost without two of the major support systems of daily life. Lost in the space and out of pace with life around them, learning disabled youngsters fall many times along the path of progress, and yet most often get there . . . in time.

Teaching learning disabled children how to manage time and space means giving them much more experience with motor development—more dance, more sports, and more perceptual motor activities in the classroom to make them aware of their bodies and teach them to use their bodies in a more organized fashion.

Their bodies then become more reliable instruments of measure through which to gain accurate feedback about the space they move in. Organization of the body helps children ready themselves to begin mastering the organizing systems of our society: space and time. The foundations necessary for this mastery are the same foundations necessary for mastering the three Rs at school.

SEVEN

LEARNING THE THREE Rs

Henry was so smart that he could guess a word from all sorts of clues—pictures, the name of the book, his teacher's expression. It was only when he was faced with plain words on a page that he developed a mysterious bladder complaint that obliged him to flee, tripping and stumbling, to the bathroom as soon as the reading lesson began.

Katie said: "I don't want to read. You can't make me!"

Andy was a good boy. He was quiet and well mannered in class. Much of the time he was off in a daydream. He was a whiz at sports, and the other children admired him. But he could not speak well. It was so embarrassing for him to talk that his teacher let him read silently rather than aloud in front of the class, and she missed the fact that he couldn't read at all.

Teddy lost everything. He lost his pencil. He lost his homework. He lost himself going from one classroom to another. He lost interest in the middle of a project. And he lost his memory for the words that he could read perfectly well yesterday.

Here are some of the comments their teachers sent home about these four children:

"Henry does not take the time to be careful or neat. His large vocabulary indicates a high degree of intelligence. He will not sit still long enough to master his reading thoroughly, although he could easily do the work if he tried harder. He needs to be more motivated."

"Perhaps the source of Katie's uncooperative attitude toward language arts may be found in her home environment."

"Andy has adjusted well to the group. He is academically a 'slow bloomer,' but his shyness in class is more than compensated for by his outstanding abilities in the gym and on the playground, where he assumes responsibility and leadership. It is a pleasure to have him in class."

"Teddy is all over the place. He seems to make things deliberately harder for himself. Teddy is a careless student. His handwriting is messy and illegible. Unless he is threatened with punishment, he will not do his work. We have found no other way to gain Teddy's cooperation."

Henry's teacher knew he was intelligent; his large vocabulary and lively interests convinced her of it. She recognized that he was clumsy and restless, but she was sure that if he could just be made to concentrate, he would read as well as any other child in her class. He needed only to try harder. She did not see the need for any special testing or tutoring.

Katie infuriated her teacher by her attitude. The teacher was at her wit's end and felt the parents must have fostered this degree of stubbornness in Katie. The teacher did not recognize that a learning disabled child will most often say, "I won't" or "I don't want to" rather than admit the truth: "I can't."

Andy's teacher thought there was nothing to worry about. The fact that Andy could assume responsibility and even leadership in his area of competence led her to believe that he was basically doing all right and that time alone would do the trick for his reading. It did not occur to her to have him specially tested or that he might need tutoring or other forms of special help.

Teddy's teacher could not believe that Teddy wasn't being so disorganized or having some of his accidents on purpose. More discipline was her answer. She found that he would sometimes go through the motions of working when he was under threat of punishment, and she fell back on this method more and more.

As a preschooler, Henry knocked over the blocks and spilled the juice while he talked in an adult manner about unidentified flying objects. And Katie had a tantrum every time she was asked to perform for her nursery-school class. Andy sat quietly in kindergarten but was inattentive to the stories that were read aloud. Words were as unmanageable to him as zippers, buttons, and coloring books were to Teddy. None of these four children was identified as learning disabled because many preschoolers have these same problems and soon grow out of them. It was only when they started to fail in school that people panicked.

A child with an outstanding talent, like Andy, can manage to slide by for a while, with goodwill around him. A child who can sit still, who can follow directions, talk appropriately, and who has a good memory can also get by. But sooner or later,

 failure to learn to read
  usually spells
   failure at school,
    which usually spells
     a feeling of failure in life.

What are some of the common school characteristics of a learning disabled child?

1. Erratic, inconsistent, unpredictable. Appears to be lazy. Good days, off days. Forgets what was learned yesterday. But without reteaching, he may remember it two days hence.
2. Poor attention span. No sustained focus.
3. Works very slowly. Never finishes work in allotted time or works carelessly, finishing in half the expected time. Feels need to hurry, without thinking.
4. Poorly organized. Desk a mess. Always losing his coat or lunch.
5. Late to class. Lingers after class.
6. Loses homework, or hands it in late and sloppily done. Doesn't understand or forgets assignments.
7. No study skills. Doesn't know how to organize work, how to plan in regard to deadlines, how to organize time.
8. Low frustration tolerance. Gives up easily or explodes.
9. Freezes when required to perform on demand. When he volunteers information, he can tell what he knows; in responding to questions, he appears dull and ignorant.
10. Can't plan free time. Daydreams, acts silly, or repeats same activity over and over when given free choices.

The school difficulties of the learning disabled child revolve around organization, sorting out, differentiating, remembering, and integrating. Learning means doing more than one thing at a time. It means making many connections and plugging them all in at once. It's connecting sounds and symbols. Sounds and symbols linked together in the proper order have to be perceived correctly in the first place.

Perception is the ability to read the environment. It is making sense of the environment through the stream of messages coming into the brain from the eyes, ears, nose, mouth, hands, skin, and the whole body. It is the brain's picture of the world and the organized relationship of one sensation to another. *Perception is the foundation on which all learning is based.*

SCHOOL READINESS

A baby under a year old with a cookie holds the cookie in front of him, beams, and looks at the whole satisfying treat. It looks round, feels round, is round. He experiences totally the cookie with his whole body. He proceeds to suck it, smell it, smear it around, drop it, and perhaps sit on it. He has seen the whole cookie, and now only part of it is left, a morsel. Does he still know it's a cookie? If he is handed a square cookie, he may not know it is a cookie until he tastes it, smells it, and remembers, recognizing its prime characteristic—its good taste.

When he grows older and yells "Cookie!" he has a picture in his mind of how it tastes, feels, and looks. He creates a mental picture, a visual image, of the object. This is his visual memory, stored in his mind and ready to be recalled for future use. He learns by experience with other objects to recognize what makes them identical, similar, or different. This discrimination later is transferred into seeing the difference between *want, went,* and *won't* (visual discrimination). And the same discrimination must be applied to the sounds he hears— hearing the difference between *berry* and *very,* between *think* and *drink* (auditory discrimination).

His memory is trained during his preschool years as he remembers what he's seen, what he's done, and the names for everything; he memorizes labels of all kinds. This, though he doesn't know it, is visual and auditory memory training, the underpinning of reading readiness. He will need to remember not only individual letters with their names and sounds but total configurations of letters:

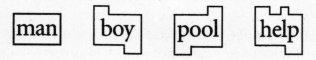

In the early years of a person's life, listening is the first way of connecting meanings to words. A baby can stop when he is told "no" as early as ten months. He can respond to "Give me that" by fifteen months. Soon after that, he can point to his own nose, eyes, and hair. But his brain is not ready for him to start speaking until he is close to two years old.

After the age of three, language is the most important tool a child has. If he does not have adequate use of language, then he continues to communicate through pointing, gesturing, and other body language. If language develops normally, he uses it to discover more and more about the world he lives in, to develop concepts and ideas about the world. He uses it to express his feelings and opinions, to transcend the now world of things he can see and touch in order to talk about things that are out of sight in another place or another time. Eventually he uses language to reason and to discuss ideas.

But in order to use this amazing tool of language properly, a child must have an intact nervous system. He must be able to receive language: listen and hear, understand what he hears, and store it away in his memory, ready to be recalled and used later (the same system of sorting out, differentiating, integrating, and remembering that applies to every other mode of perception). He must also be able to express language by finding the right word in his memory and speaking it correctly—but this skill depends partly on having heard the word correctly in the first place. Speech reflects hearing. A toddler says *aminal* for *animal* or *pisghetti* for *spaghetti* because he hears it that way. Amusing in a three-year-old, it's a sign of poor auditory perception and sequencing difficulties in a seven-year-old.

Good listening is demanded of a child when he enters school. He has spent six years listening to dos and don'ts, to television, records, and songs, to toys with bells, beepers, and squeaks, to stories and counting games, to people talking all around him (happy talk, loud talk, angry talk, gentle talk), and in the normal way of development he is now ready to sit still, listen carefully, and follow directions.

In kindergarten he is taught many skills that are designed to make him ready. He learns to listen and look. He learns to count, although he probably won't be able to remember his own telephone number until he is seven, and he may not yet comprehend that four is bigger than two even though he sees that two here, and two there, make four when they are all put together in one pile. If his teacher taps her drum three times, he learns to answer with three taps on his own drum. He learns to speak clearly. If he is still saying *aminal,* he now learns *animal* as if it were a new word, and he puts it in a new place in his memory. Most important of all, he learns to follow directions. This ability requires the child:

1. To be able to stay still and pay attention.
2. To hear all of the directions so as to get the main point and know what he is supposed to do. This also means understanding the sequence, getting the details in the right order.
3. To remember what he's heard—the main point of it and the parts of it in their right order.
4. To translate it all into terms of himself, organize himself accordingly, and turn those instructions into action as he carries them out.

The child whose nervous system is developing at an uneven rate may meet his first troubles in the area of sounds. He finds himself bombarded with noises, and he pays equal attention to them all, slow to sort out the meaningful ones from the background. He may not talk until after he is two and a half or three, and then he may use only a limited number of words with no connecting links. When he gets to nursery school and kindergarten, he may not be able to repeat a sequence of three claps after the teacher. He may not understand what his teacher says to him because he was distracted when a fly flew by his face, or he may have heard the first part fine but started thinking about that instead of listening to the rest, or he may have heard it all but forgotten it right away, or he may have confused some sounds or not known the words, or he may not be able to get himself organized to do what he's been told. He may be called willful, stubborn, or uncooperative because he doesn't follow directions.

LANGUAGE DIFFICULTIES

He may also be unable to organize his speech so that it has a clear beginning, middle, and end. A learning disabled child's mind often leaps through many ideas before the words can come out. The struggle is similar to that of a child who can't get his body organized and moving in time to react properly. He may speak slowly, groping for words, making him the butt of many jokes and imitations. His immature speech may make him sound ignorant. Ten-year-old Sidney, from an educated family, claimed, "He got dead," when he was trying to say, "He was killed." He would say, "I buyed it," "My footses are wet," and "My notebook is gooder than his."

Often a learning disabled child cannot make his wants clear because his phrasing of words is clumsy. Anne tugged at her teacher, saying, "Come quick! He wants you because it hurts him!" while her teacher tried frantically to find out who was hurt, where he was, and what had happened. People often do not understand what the learning disabled child is saying, for he begins in the middle of a story, at the end of an idea, or at some point that is unclear. He can't seem to recount the events that happened in order for them to make sense to a listener.

The immature child, beset by distractions and muddled in his language, has a limited ability to control his environment through words. He cannot make reasoned requests or explain his problems, so he uses actions, the way two-year-olds do. Maybe the nonverbal learning disabled child's hyperactive or impulsive behavior is a substitute for his limited language, by which he tries to gain a measure of control over what happens to him. Or conversely, perhaps his immaturity forces him to remain in the concrete world of the two-year-old, and his immature behavior inevitably follows. Does immaturity prevent him from acquiring language skills or does the lack of language skills keep him immature? It's like the question "Which came first, the chicken or the egg?" Whatever the cause, the nonverbal child encounters escalating difficulties at school as he grows older, and often increasing social problems as well.

Hunched in their caves three million years ago, our ancestors could make do with pointing, gesturing, and grunting until they needed to call attention to something out of sight, something that happened yesterday, something about tomorrow. Then a symbol—a word—was needed. People of the Stone Age didn't choose pebbles or scratches on the ground to be the symbols that represented objects to them. They chose sounds because hearing was highly developed. It was their survival sense, their scanning system. They relied on ears for the first warning of danger, picking up sounds from all directions, around corners, in the dark, through walls. An ear placed against the ground could detect sounds from far away. Ears were always alert, even during sleep. They would wake up at any hint of danger, just as parents today wake up at the first cry of the baby or the tiptoed steps of a teenager coming in late.

The cavemen and women developed language when they wanted to leave messages or make plans. Presumably they began with naming concrete objects and moved to abstractions. Languages evolved with different grammars and vocabularies, and language became the channel for culture. Words transmitted knowledge, intelligence, education. For more than two million years, listening has been the chief way of learning, and language has been the primary means of communication. For large numbers of youngsters with learning disabilities, communication through language is their prime problem. They cannot use language effectively to leave messages or make plans.

Language arts are taught to children from the moment they start first grade, yet there is now ample evidence that in any school population there will be some children who are not ready for the standard language arts curriculum. These are some of the typical language problems that impede the academic progress of learning disabled children:

1. Cannot state something in an organized, cogent way. Tends to muddle; starts in middle of an idea. Cannot organize words properly into a question.
2. Has immature word use and ungrammatical phrasing.
3. Has trouble following directions, particularly long sequences of them.
4. Doesn't enjoy being read to, but does like looking at pictures in book.
5. Becomes distracted in class when instruction is presented orally. Learns from watching, not listening.
6. Is very literal. Misses inferences, subtleties, nuances, innuendos.
7. Has poor sense of humor; doesn't understand jokes, puns, sarcasm.
8. Has trouble with abstract words. Defines words by their concrete attributes or function.
9. Can't deal with multiple meanings of words; very rigid.
10. Can't tell a story in sequence or summarize; can only recount isolated and highly detailed facts about an experience.
11. Forgets names of things that he knows and has to describe them (word-finding problem). Later, when not under pressure, will recall the word he wanted to say.

The confusion in what the learning disabled child hears is reflected in his speech and use of words. He often is Mr. Malaprop. He may reverse words without knowing it or use words with similar sounds to the ones he means. Twelve-year-old Morton said that his dog ate *god food*. Eleven-year-old Clyde was explaining that every time he went to the drugstore, he sneaked over to read *Boy Play*. Thirteen-year-old Brian said he played with a pair of twins who were not identical; they were "eternal." Molly's Sunday-school class finished the first part of the Bible, and she was excited that they had just started reading the "New Intestine."

When he begins school, a child is expected to be able to listen well, to speak clearly, to pay attention, and to take the second great step in the process of civilization: writing. For more than two million years, spoken language was the overriding skill of humankind and made all other developments possible. Only in the last five thousand years did a further need arise: the need to say things to people too far away to hear. A symbol was needed for the sound of words, and writing was invented. And so reading and writing became the primary goals of a child's education.

In a society where productivity is prized and a child no longer plays an economic role as he did up through the early 1900s, there is only one area where a child is required to produce, and that is at school. "How's school?" is the question all adults ask.

READING AND WRITING

Going to school is equated with learning how to read and write, and reading and writing, in the minds of many people, is equated with intelligence. If children can't learn how to read and write, they must be "dumb." This is very far from the truth; learning disabilities can occur in children who test out in ranges from normal intelligence to unusual brilliance. Yet parents feel that there is a stigma on their child if he does not learn to read quickly. No matter how much they love him, parents take the child's failure as their own, so they try by every means possible to make him do better. They tell him, as his teacher has told him before, that he is not trying, or that he is not trying enough, that he's too used to getting his own way, that it's time for him to stop being a baby and grow up and to take responsibility by learning to read. They talk to him at length. They bribe and punish, spend hours going over his schoolwork with him. And they can't understand why all that extra effort doesn't bring him more success with the written word.

What is involved in learning to read? Organization of thought, all the perceptual skills, spatial relations, and timing. (See chart on pages 106 to 107.)

WHAT IS A WRITTEN WORD (*WROD, SOJB, DROW*)?

A WORD IS A MESSAGE.	It carries an idea, an object, a person, a place, an action, which links up with an experience you can remember.
A WORD IS A SYMBOL.	Those black marks on a white page mean something; they stand for something specific.
A WORD IS A PATTERN.	Like a code, each symbol in the pattern can be translated into a sound, and the series of sounds in their proper order make sense.
A WORD IS A SEQUENCE.	The shapes that make up the word have an organization of their own —a beginning, a middle, and an end; they cannot be switched about and keep their same meaning.
A WORD IS A TOTAL SHAPE.	It is a total configuration. It may have more than one internal pattern, but the sequence is fixed, and when the symbols are translated into sound, the meaning is fixed and does not change.

TO READ . .

SPACIAL RELATIONSHIPS AND SPACING

- left to right progression knowing left from right

- eye-hand-foot coordination

- directions in space directionality

- judgment in space (motor planning, sequencing)

ORGANIZATION OF

- ability to sort information (classify, categorize, label)

- appropriateness (what belongs, what's missing)

- ability to recognize parts that make up a whole

EYE TRACKING

EYE-HAND-FOOT COORDINATION

VISUAL PERCEPTION

- observation skills
- discrimination
- memory
- sequential memory
- understanding to give meaning

TACTILE PERCEPTION
- discrimination
- memory understanding

SELF-CONTROL TO SUSTAIN ATTENTION

form constancy

figure ground

size

shape

color

INTEGRATING SOUND AND SIGHT TO HAVE MEANING

A CHILD NEEDS:

THOUGHT ORDER

- ability to break down the whole into parts

- recognize sequences

small	first	beginning
big	next	middle
bigger	last	end

SYMBOLISM—VERBAL SKILLS

- vocabulary
- comprehension—understanding of concepts expressed in words
- verbal reasoning
- recognizing the oneness of objects, symbols, words—separate identities
- understanding that a mark, a sound, a pattern, represent an object or idea

AUDITORY PERCEPTION

- listening skills
- discrimination
- memory
- sequential memory
- understanding

RHYTHM TIMING SENSE OF TIME

INTEGRATING SEVERAL PROCESSES AT ONCE

A word consists of a series of graphic symbols in space that have meaning when a series of sounds are linked to them in the proper order.

The process of decoding the symbols can be taught in many ways—by sight, by sound, and by touch. Most important is to match the method to the child. Identify his strengths. If he seems to learn more from what he sees than from what he hears, begin with a visual method of teaching reading. Perhaps his ears are his best channel. In this case, begin with an auditory method. Maybe seeing or hearing have to be combined with touching letters of different materials and textures, or with writing and tracing the shapes of letters to reinforce the learning. One builds on a child's strengths while remediating his weaknesses.

For the new reader, there are two basic methods: visual and auditory.

VISUAL METHOD.	Instant recognition of the total configuration of a word: "look and see" or "look and say." Visual analysis of spelling patterns, leading to pronunciation of the whole word.
AUDITORY METHODS.	Hearing the sounds in a word. Sounding out unknown words. Learning the beginning, middle, and end sounds of words.

Some children cannot use the visual method because they don't have the visual perception—visual focus, visual discrimination, and visual memory—for immediate recognition of words. They have not yet learned to look carefully, find the visual similarities and differences, and remember them. They are most incapable of this when they have laterality problems—rotations, reversals, and problems with their eyes tracking left to right. Reading involves moving the eyes smoothly across a line of print, then back again, a bit lower down the page. This is a hard task for children with space difficulty, and it is why some youngsters need to guide their eyes with a marker—a finger or a moving pencil—to avoid losing their place.

Some children can't use the phonic method because they don't have the auditory perception, the focus, the discrimination, and the memory to attach new sounds to new words. Because they have not learned to listen carefully, they don't hear the differences between two sounds, or, if they do, they forget them right away.

But no matter which strategy works best for a child, reading is still a visual-auditory association. Therefore even though a child is taught through his area of strength, progress may still be slow until the weaker area does its tasks automatically and ensures the association. Some children are fairly well developed in their ability to see and hear differences, but they cannot link the two. In many ways, the ability to make the proper connections is the most crucial of all. It is the only way that experience can become usable. The process of combining and digesting the messages from two or more senses into one coherent meaning is like the process of cooking. You can mix butter, flour, eggs, milk, and spices together in a bowl, but they do not become a cake until you bake the batter. Understanding comes through making connections between things that did not appear connected before.

Once a child has begun to read, structural analysis is introduced. He analyzes syllables, breaking a word into its elements and then pulling them together; he learns prefixes and suffixes. He also uses his reasoning powers to guess the meaning of a new word from the rest of the sentence; he learns to figure from contextual clues what's missing, what belongs, what's appropriate.

These are some of the most typical reading problems encountered by learning disabled children:

1. Confuses *b* and *d*, reads *bog* for *dog*, and often confuses *b, d, p, q*.
2. Confuses the order of letters in words (reads *was* for *saw*).
3. Doesn't look carefully at the details in a word and guesses from the first letter (reads *farm* for *front*).
4. Loses his place on a page when reading, sometimes in the middle of a line or at the end of the line.
5. Can't remember common words taught from one day to the next; knows them one day, not the next. Most frequently forgets abstract words (*us, were, says*).
6. Has no systematic way to figure out a word he doesn't know. Guesses or says, "I don't know."
7. Reads without expression and ignores punctuation. The mechanics of reading are so hard for him that he has no awareness of the ideas expressed by the written symbols.
8. Reads very slowly, and reading tires him greatly.
9. Omits, substitutes, or adds words to a sentence.
10. Reads word by word, struggling with almost each one of them.

Listening decodes sound into meaning. Reading decodes symbols of sound into meaning. But writing puts it into code in the first place. This is called *encoding*. To write something down means going into the mind, plucking out a series of visual symbols with sounds attached to them, putting them in the right order (going from left to right) to produce the word you want, then putting several words in the proper order (also going from left to right) to convey the message you want. It takes more organization, more differentiation, more remembering, more sequencing, and more integration than reading or many other skills. It is one of the most sophisticated activities devised by the human brain, and it clearly demands maturity. Whereas a child may be able to read on an adult level as early as third or fourth grade, only very rarely can a child write well, with precision, clarity, and expression, before the seventh grade. And spelling is often his nemesis.

Lucie was clearly saying something to Mark in a Lab School physical education class that irritated him. Finally, the teacher took both eleven-year-olds aside and asked what was going on between them. Mark replied, "Lucie's calling me 'the G word' and I don't like it. Tell her to stop." Lucie replied that she had every right to call him by "the G word." When she continued to do it, she was sent out of the room. But the physical education teacher was curious as to what the mysterious "G word" meant. He held Mark back when he dismissed the class and asked him to explain it. Mark's answer was, "You know, the G word stands for Jerk."

The learning disabled child, with her disorder, her visual and auditory problems, her connecting problems, is indeed defeated when she must produce the written language. It has been the experience of many teachers in special classes and special schools that even though a child may read and even surpass his grade level in reading, arithmetic, and language skills, spelling will still tend to stay below grade level. Spelling seems to be the area that needs remedial help for the longest period of time.

Some of the learning disabled child's typical spelling problems follow:

1. Writes *b* for *d* and vice versa.
2. Transposes the order of letters (spells *was* as *saw* or *the* as *hte*).
3. Doesn't hear the sequence of sounds in a word and writes isolated parts of it (writes *amil* for *animal*).
4. Has no memory for common words that are not regularly spelled. May try to spell them phonetically (writes *sez* for *says*).
5. Does not hear fine differences in words (writes *pin* for *pen*).
6. Has trouble with consonants (writes *wif* for *with*).
7. Often disguises poor spelling ability with consciously messy handwriting.
8. Uses no capitals and no punctuation in sentence writing.

9. Leaves words out of sentences; can't express himself in complete written sentences.

10. Avoids writing whenever possible because it is so difficult and so demanding.

HANDWRITING

To compound their other problems with writing, children with learning disabilities frequently have poor handwriting too. Their immaturity causes them to confuse the left and right sides, and they frequently have trouble crossing the midline, tracing letters, and staying inside the lines. They tend to leave no space between letters and words and can't visualize which way the letters go and what the letter looks like, much less what a series of letters looks like. They don't capitalize the beginning of a sentence and rarely use punctuation. Punctuations are visual symbols that have to be remembered, that mark endings, or that represent pauses (that a child with poor timing doesn't have). He presses too hard, or not hard enough, on his pencil. His thumb does not help to maneuver the pencil; he has to use his whole arm to write. (This is known as visual-motor difficulty, small-motor difficulty, or eye-hand coordination difficulty.) The child who has severe difficulty with handwriting is often the child about whom the teacher says, "It's as though his brain shuts down when his hand has a pencil in it." All his energy goes into the writing, and there is none left over for thinking.

Here are some typical handwriting problems of the learning disabled child:

1. Holds pencil awkwardly, too tightly, inefficiently. Tires easily by writing.

2. Can't write without lined paper. Spacing is poor. Leaves no space between words. Leaves no margins.

3. Writes letters backward, upside down. Has incomplete formation.
4. Mixes lower-case letters with capitals. Memory for the forms of letters is poor, so he uses whichever form he can remember.
5. Writes letters above and below the line. No size consistency.
6. Writes in very large hand; can't control pencil enough to write small.
7. Holds pencil too tightly and writes very small. Can't relax hand and pencil. Also hides poor spelling.
8. Writes incredibly slowly. Takes five minutes to write a sentence; each letter must be perfectly formed.
9. Can't remember how to form letters, so uses his own way. Forms letters inefficiently.
10. Erases often and writes the same letter several times.

It is not infrequent that one finds a learning disabled child whose handwriting is extremely legible, well formed, and neat. She does not have visual-motor or fine-motor difficulties, but she still may not be able to spell or read. Her good handwriting ability can be used to help her learn to read.

The child who puzzles many teachers is the one who can't remember which way the letters go (she reverses them and rotates them), yet she may be able to draw very well indeed. Her problems are much more related to her visual-spatial perception than to eye-hand coordination.

MATHEMATICS

The writing down of math problems causes many learning disabled children the same trouble as the writing down of letters and words. The number *14* becomes *41*; *6* and *9* get mixed up, and so do *2* and *5*, *3* and *E*. Then *7* comes out looking like *r*, and *4* looks like a swastika.

Somehow the child cannot picture in his mind what the number looks like and thus can't write it.

A child may be very talented at mental math but defeated every time he has to write down his answer or work out his processes on paper. In long division and long multiplication problems, he puts his figures in the wrong columns. Signs like + and × are hard to differentiate and even harder to reproduce, and a page with too many problems on it is too confusing. The child's wrong answers result from visual perception problems plus eye and hand not working together rather than a failure to understand the math.

Sometimes a learning disabled child does superbly in math (though not in reading and spelling) if the math problems are read to her. Perhaps her superior reasoning and memory make this possible. Or perhaps it is because numerical symbols, once learned, mean a fixed set of things. Number 4 means a certain quantity, and there are no inferences, subtleties, or multiple meanings as there are with words.

If a child cannot differentiate sizes, quantities, or measurements and cannot categorize them or put them into sequence by size, we cannot expect her to understand abstract number concepts. Organization to the extent of understanding sequences (first, next, and last) is essential to the awareness and recall of a succession of numbers.

To begin with, a child must understand that one object = 1, that one person = 1, that one symbol = 1. If a child cannot separate herself from the environment to become a single self, we cannot expect her to gain an understanding of this one-to-one correspondence or one-to-one association. Yet we cannot proceed in math without it.

Counting is at the root of all computation. Adding is a shortcut to counting forward; subtracting is a fast way to count backward. Since addition and subtraction are counting forward and backward from a given point, then multiplication is counting forward in groups and division is counting backward in groups. Counting is sequencing. Counting is order. But the learning disabled child cannot remember sequences. She has disorder, a lack of order.

The concepts of *more than* and *less than* are dependent upon our perceptions of larger, longer, big quantities, as distinct from smaller, shorter, little quantities. To know that three is more than two, you have to understand one in relation to the other. Math consists of seeing relationships, and that's what many learning disabled youngsters can't cope with; they can't group one set together as distinct from another set. Math requires focus on the main principles, the binding force, and a disregard of unessential information.

For the One-Way Kid, math may be very upsetting. Four plus six is the same as five plus five is the same as nine plus one, but in his pure sense, there can be no equivalencies and alternatives until he has matured somewhat. The inflexibility of the learning disabled child makes it difficult for him to shift gears, and yet much of math is switching from addition to subtraction and multiplication. What if Maria is asked this word problem: "Ms. Brown had five apples in the cellar. She had twice that number in her kitchen. She bought a dozen more at the store and gave six to the neighbor to make an apple pie. Her little boy ate three of the apples in the cellar. How many apples did Ms. Brown have left altogether?" Even if Maria had no language problems, even if she had no problems clearing away extraneous information, still she might have considerable difficulty translating "a dozen," figuring out which computation process to use, and then switching from multiplication to addition to subtraction. If she had memory difficulties, as most learning disabled youngsters do, you can comprehend the magnitude of the problem.

Holding in the mind several things at once, remembering and integrating them are part of math. Sheer rote memory, such as memorizing the multiplication tables, is part of math, and many learning disabled children have no rote memory; some do have rote memory but can't understand the principles. Very concrete children can reason only on the basis of what they see and in regard to objects they can move around. They cannot deal with abstractions, and numbers are very abstract.

These are some typical math problems of the learning disabled child.

1. Counts on fingers.
2. Cannot commit multiplication facts to memory.
3. Reverses two-place numbers (13 becomes 31, for example). Also reverses numbers (5 to ꙅ) or rotates 6 to 9.
4. Doesn't understand place value.
5. May solve addition and even multiplication problems by counting on fingers, but cannot subtract, the reverse operation.
6. Subtracts smaller number in a column from larger number. In the problem 25 − 7, he subtracts the 5 from the 7 simply because the 5 is smaller, not seeing the 5 as representing 15; thus he arrives at the answer 25 − 7 = 22.
7. Often understands concepts but can't work the problem in written symbolic form with paper and pencil.
8. Occasionally can do rote arithmetic on paper, but it has no meaning; math problems in daily life, such as making change, escape this child.
9. Can't remember sequence of steps required to multiply or divide. Has trouble switching from one process to another, such as dividing and subtracting in long division.
10. Solves problems left to right instead of right to left.

THINKING PATTERNS

If he has trouble grouping like objects or like numbers, if he tends to get caught up in details and miss the main point, or if he has trouble understanding relationships, then he may reason that 4 + 3 + 2 cannot be the same as 5 + 5 − 1 because one problem has subtraction in it. Jessica has difficulty seeing the relationships between number

facts. She knows that $7 + 5 = 12$, but she can't solve $12 - 7$. This may
be the same youngster who at a later age does not understand that
cats, alligators, and hippopotamuses are all alike in that they are
animals, four-legged, and vertebrates: she can focus only on alligators
being in water or hippopotamuses being fat. When Gus was given a
list of animals—dog, cat, tiger, bear, horse—and asked what they
were, he answered "pets" instead of "animals," focusing on only one
or two clues. The child deals with one part of a situation without
relating it to the whole. "You're missing the point," or "You failed to
pay attention" are criticisms he hears over and over again.

The sorting out of the essential from the unessential characteristics causes him a great deal of difficulty. In order to compare two
items, he must define the main characteristics and find similarities
and differences. He must rely on his ability to classify and categorize,
which in turn demands that he sort the information properly. If he is
to compare a red pencil and a green pencil, he must understand first
of all that they are both pencils, that they both have the same function, and both are approximately the same size and shape. The difference is their color. He has to avoid being sidetracked by the fact that
one may have a broken point and the other may have words printed
on it. Organization of information makes possible the drawing of
conclusions and the building up of generalizations. But the learning
disabled child can't do either if he hasn't organized the information
correctly in the first place. His assumptions make little sense and can
cause him ridicule or failure at school. Many learning disabled youngsters cannot even come up with a simple assumption because they do
not yet have the equipment to tie all the information together, let
alone attempt a summary or a generalization. This child is often
labeled as "preoccupied" or "refuses to try."

A child may have trouble with analogies because she can't remember a word or because she can't focus on the prime characteristic
under study. Ten-year-old Letha said, "*Swim* is to *fish* as *hop* is to . . .
jump." She offered her first association to the word *hop* rather than
focusing on the basic structure of the analogy. "*Grass* is to *green* as

snow is to . . ." produces an answer of *ice* or *sleds* from twelve-year-old Mary, who says whatever is uppermost in her mind or what relates to her life. Mary is egocentric. Her world does not yet include many things other than herself. She is very concrete, and she reasons about what she sees in front of her, not abstractions. If she can't remember facts and she can't organize either, Mary cannot participate effectively in a discussion on how the French Revolution differed from the American Revolution. And we cannot expect Mary to be able to predict or foresee the consequences of being a revolutionary.

"The cause was oppression. The effect was revolution." Understanding this kind of statement demands organization. It relates one thing to another—a condition to a consequence, motivation to incidents. It takes a certain maturity to state, "This happened because . . ." The learning disabled child is not a frequent user of connecting links like *because* and *therefore*. In general, he has trouble with linking one thing to another and, specifically, relating cause to effect or vice versa. He doesn't see the effect of his own behavior on others or anticipate its impact. Often he does not understand why he is being castigated or punished, for he does not understand the connection between what he did and what happened. His problems in making connections bring him further defeat at school.

The ability to make decisions, to select choices, and to make judgments rests on being able to weigh several alternatives at the same time, compare them, and choose the one most appropriate to the situation. One alternative has to be seen as more valuable than the others. But the learning disabled child, bombarded by too many impressions at once, cannot tell what values to apply; he is overwhelmed and thrown into a greater state of disorder.

> *Delayed and uneven maturation*
>   *causes*
>   *delayed and uneven perception, which*
>   *causes*
>   *delayed and uneven conceptual growth.*

Often the learning disabled youngster has average or above-average reasoning abilities, but he cannot put them to use when his perceptions of situations are off. He fails at school not only on the evidence of his worksheets but by failing to demonstrate good reasoning and intelligence.

These are some of the typical thinking problems of the learning disabled child.

1. Has difficulty sticking to the main point. Brings up irrelevant, extraneous points.

2. Doesn't grasp cause-effect relationships. Rarely uses the word *because*. Doesn't anticipate and evaluate.

3. Is rigid. A word can have only one meaning. Or knows $5 + 7 = 12$ but can't answer $12 = 5 + ?$. Or knows $8 \times 7 = 56$ but can't solve $56 \div 8 = ?$.

4. Has trouble seeing similarities and differences and understanding relationships.

5. Doesn't see patterns. Must memorize all words because he can't see spelling patterns. All multiplication facts have to be memorized one by one (that's why the child gives up) instead of seeing patterns that simplify the task. Doesn't group ideas together to form patterns of thought.

6. Has a poor memory. Can't remember names of people or places and has trouble also with faces. Reasoning often gets sidetracked because of poor memory.

7. Doesn't organize the facts and concepts the child does have and thus can't mobilize them to solve problems, to predict or foresee consequences.

8. Can't categorize or classify. Each experience is an isolated event. Doesn't summarize. Can't generalize from the concrete to the abstract.

9. Doesn't transfer learning from one lesson to another. Has to relearn each concept anew.

10. Understands concepts too narrowly or too broadly. All four-

legged animals are dogs. Only black and white cats (like his own cat) are cats. Or he may call all cats Puff, the name of his own cat.

PROGRAMMING FOR SUCCESS

The learning disabled child is often very immature in his thinking, as he is in his movement and language. His disorganization betrays his fine intelligence. Frequently this child has not reached the stage yet where others of his age are ready to take off academically. This child does not automatically develop a filing system in the brain that allows the information to be quickly slotted in logical compartments of the mind and retrieved at will. He lacks the internal organization to classify and categorize information or put it into proper sequence, to understand time, or to perceive and use the space around him accurately. Therefore he cannot acquire the skills for academic learning by school age as most other children do and consequently cannot meet the expectations and requirements of his grade. Without the organizational foundations, he cannot approach the norms of knowledge and achievement against which children are measured annually, and he lags further and further behind.

Defeat means losing. The learning disabled child is much too frequently a loser at school because the people around her don't understand what's preventing her from learning. Often she's trying as hard as she can while the world tells her, "You're not trying hard enough." She's doing the best she can, yet we tell her she's not.

Academic success is dependent upon the acquisition of the foundations, the readiness, and the maturation necessary for mastery. Obviously motivation is an important component and motivation is nurtured through successful experience. Success breeds success. In every tangible way, we need to program learning disabled children for success and pleasure in learning. Nothing is more effective than the experiences that produce that unique and exhilarating excitement within a child of "I CAN DO IT!" To provide students with the tools for mastery, a sense of competence, and confidence is what teaching is all about.

EIGHT

TEACHERS: THEIR CONCERNS AND FEELINGS

There are definite principles of teaching and techniques for structuring the learning materials, the space, and the time of a learning disabled child who can't sit still or remain in focus long enough to concentrate. Some specific methods have been tried over many years with thousands of severely learning disabled children at The Lab School. (They will be discussed in the next chapter.) Before a teacher can apply the techniques effectively, he or she must be able to reach the child. They need to provide an environment where learning can take place, and need to understand the feelings of anger, frustration, and defeat that both the teacher and the learning disabled child will inevitably face. This is true whether a teacher is a specialist with a whole group of severely learning disabled children or a regular classroom teacher with one or two such children who disrupt the class.

It is difficult to set limits on a child when the training and inclinations of a teacher make her want to expand, rather than narrow, his world. A high degree of organization and persistence is required to put boundaries on a child's behavior as well as on his work. This includes the way in which children enter and leave the classroom, their seating, and their ways of approaching their work. The teacher must decide whether the group is sufficiently threatened by one child that he must be sent out, even though she wants to bolster and support the child. She must know how to set the tone in class so that the children feel good about themselves and about each other. She must learn how to avoid confrontations where nobody comes out the winner and how to find ways that allow the child and herself to save face. In the end, she must try to teach the child to monitor himself so that, in time, it is no longer the teacher who must tell him, once again, that he has acted inappropriately or has been careless, but rather he who can think, "Is that what I meant to do? Is that what I meant to say?"

The needs of learning disabled children are so great that the demands on their teachers are very great, and they need solid support from their supervisor, principal, and the school administration in general. Learning disabled youngsters, without meaning to, consume their teachers, exhaust them, and bring out all their fears of inadequacy and incompetency.

The teacher of a learning disabled child must be willing to give and give and give, in turn receiving criticism and facing defeat and failure. He has to absorb the child's frustration, anger, guilt, and defensiveness, all of which seem to be directed against him. A learning disabled child can give a teacher the constant feeling that he is doing the wrong thing, which only adds to his frustration in trying to find the right thing. It is painful after hours of effort to give success to a particular child to hear that same child say, "You always work with the others; you never work with me." A learning disabled child can make an adult feel that nothing the teacher ever says or does is good enough, and in the end he finds himself with no more to give. The child with learning disabilities is like an insatiable sponge, draining off all his effort and energy. In fact, that is the effect the child often has on adults in general. They find themselves worn out by the child's constant demands. The teacher is exhausted by the amount of anticipating he must do, the planning, the extra preparation, and the perpetual tension that never lets the atmosphere in class become relaxed. In a classroom of thirty-two children, one or two who can't sit still, who keep interrupting, who demand help incessantly, who constantly drop, lose, mess up papers, can easily extend this exhausting quality into all its activities and drive the teacher almost to distraction.

Not all learning disabled children are hyperactive, disruptive, and vocally demanding, however. Yet in some ways the quiet daydreamer is equally draining because he is very hard for a teacher to reach and very easy to forget. When a hyperactive, scattered child can be made to focus, he usually responds quite fully. The quiet one may be simply "not there," unavailable for response. He may be a reliable, well-behaved child who has no friends but never bothers anybody; he can fill a teacher with guilt because the teacher has never had time to give him her extra attention. Or the teacher may become overprotective of him, finishing his sentences for him, shielding him from the gibes of other children, inadvertently bringing him the label of "teacher's pet" and further rejection. The daydreamer may avoid focusing or trying to put in a word for fear of being wrong, making a mistake, and risking failure again. It can be exhausting for a teacher to attempt continually to get any reaction from this child.

Although at first a teacher may feel very positive about what he can do for all the students, the normal response of a classroom teacher faced with one or more severely learning disabled children in the class is:

Either this kid goes or I go. The principal has to do something! This child can't learn.

He won't listen to me.

I can't teach him.

I can't control him.

I can't reach him.

He takes all my time from the other children.

He destroys my class.

He distracts the others.

He keeps me from doing my best.

He doesn't belong in my class.

CATCHING THE CHILD'S FEELINGS

It is common for a teacher to feel completely helpless to deal effectively with the learning disabled child. It is common for her to feel woefully inadequate as his teacher. It is normal for her to feel resentful at being placed in that position and then be ashamed of her resentment and anger. Her attitudes are understandable, for none of us likes to feel incompetent. Beyond the deep wounding of her feelings of competency, the teacher is also prone to catching the intense feelings of the learning disabled child. They are very contagious.

When the teacher says, "This child will never learn!" she has caught the child's own feelings of defeat.

When she says, "No matter what I try, it doesn't work," she has caught his frustration and mixed it with her own.

When she says angrily, "There's no point in trying to teach him!" she is probably reflecting his angry feeling that there's no point in trying to learn.

When she says, "If only I could do better by him, make more materials, give him more time!" she is probably mirroring his guilt at not learning.

At one moment she feels she can help him; at others she knows she can't. These feelings correspond to his own ups and downs.

When she says, "He's impossible. There's no way this child will ever learn," she reveals her feelings of total inadequacy, the same feelings the child has.

Parents and teachers of learning disabled children know all too well the experience of coming into a room feeling cheerful and competent and, after five minutes of work with the child, feeling angry, guilty, helpless, and exhausted. They have absorbed precisely the feelings of the child. But they cannot help him effectively if they are caught up in his cycle.

> *Usually a teacher's feelings about a student*
> *tell*
> *how the student is feeling.*
> *Therefore a teacher's feelings about a student*
> *are important diagnostic tools.*

This is why it is important for teachers of learning disabled children to be in touch with their feelings, to recognize them, and to acknowledge them.

When the teacher can say, "I'm not feeling angry. But the moment I'm with Agatha I feel anger, so Agatha must feel angry," then she is in a position to help Agatha. If she does not recognize that it is Agatha's anger she is feeling, the chances are good that she will become really angry herself and make Agatha angrier, until the two become locked in a battle for supremacy.

For many years, when The Lab School was one-fourth to one-third of its current size of 250 youngsters, a psychologist spent most of each Wednesday at the school. Rather than work with the youngsters who had severe learning disabilities, she met with their teachers, individually and in groups, and talked with them about their feelings. She helped them to identify their feelings, trust the feelings, and relate those feelings to their students. She preferred to employ this process rather than work directly with the children because the teachers were on the front lines daily and could do the most for the students if they knew how. The director sat in on those sessions so that she could reinforce this work throughout the rest of the week. In general, the more the teacher understands of herself, the more she can understand her students. The more support a teacher receives, the more she can support her students.

Learning disabled children produce anxiety in teachers. And when teachers are anxious, they become more tense, more demanding, more punitive, more scattered, more clumsy, less patient, less humorous, less sensitive, less organized, less confident. Anxiety can wear out the best of teachers and reduce effectiveness.

Parents often do not understand how infuriating these children can be for a teacher. Conversely teachers usually do not realize how utterly exhausting and consuming the children are at home. Parents tend to blame teachers for not providing their child with the proper educational experience and for letting the child bring home his feelings of failure. Teachers frequently blame parents for the child's inattentiveness, his rudeness, and his messiness, feeling that these qualities would surely improve if the child were properly cared for and disciplined at home. Teachers and parents alike are exceedingly vulnerable when they try to deal with a learning disabled child because much of their pride and their feelings of self-worth depend on the child's performance.

THE TEACHER'S SELF-ESTEEM

A teacher's ego is closely tied to the responsiveness of her students. It is unfortunate, but too often true, that some teachers measure their success by their popularity, by the degree to which their students show their appreciation of them. Others measure it by the degree of control they achieve over the students. Occasionally teachers feel uncomfortable with other adults and at ease with children; such a teacher may tend to depend excessively on children for ego support. However, if her ego depends on a learning disabled child, a teacher is in trouble. She will be up one minute, way down the next—and she will feel defeated.

If there ever was a field that needed teachers with intact egos, whose gratifications are gained elsewhere, it is the field of learning disabilities. The learning disabled child has so many desperate needs of his own that he cannot be burdened with an adult's needs as well. He cannot tolerate the pressure, and he can only make a needy adult needier. There is already more than enough frustration, fear, anger, guilt, and anxiety that the child is passing on to his teacher. She is asking him to learn, knowing full well that his equipment for learning is faulty. This is a difficult situation at best, but it is impossible if the teacher's feelings of worthiness as a person depend on that child's succeeding immediately or the child's showing appreciation or affection for the teacher.

Miss Bayard, in charge of a special education class, wanted to be loved by her students. She would let them do whatever they wanted and did not help them to control themselves for fear of losing her image as a lovable person. As a result, children were hurt more than once in her classroom during the one semester that she taught in the resource room.

Mr. Toby tried to impose discipline by behaving like a military commander with his learning disabled class of ten. He nagged the students for every small infraction of his rules and was always looking for any possibility that they might be contemplating trouble. He spent very little time teaching. Like his students, he was indiscriminate; he did not set priorities; he did not identify the most important issues that deserved reactions or consequences.

Mrs. Martin would whine in front of other teachers, "But Jerry won't listen to me!" Her feelings of helplessness made the other teachers uncomfortable and alerted Jerry to the fact that his teacher couldn't cope with him. To make matters worse, Mrs. Martin would seek Jerry out at the end of the school day, saying, "Let's talk about our relationship." She put an unfair responsibility on the child, who was carrying more than his share of problems anyway. Mrs. Martin's needs were too great for her to be working with learning disabled youngsters.

Young Andy Cole, straight out of college, had an idealized view of learning disabled children. He claimed, "They see life in its purest form. They've got the right idea. They can teach the rest of us." He romanticized the lack of control to represent a positive expression of spontaneity and vibrancy. He saw the child's inability to follow instruction as an admirable way of flouting authority, and he encouraged it. Andy was too much an adolescent himself to assume an adult role. He felt that the children could enrich him and help him to "find himself." He lasted in a learning disabilities classroom for one month.

A superior science teacher in a public school system was given the title of master teacher. He taught and supervised other teachers in the system and demonstrated new methods and curricula. At age thirty-five, he was clearly one of the best in his field. Yet when he went into a special school for learning disabled children, he could not cope. In addition to his supervisory work, he taught six severely learning disabled, hyperactive youngsters three times a week. He talked with the principal about how difficult the work was, and they developed some new approaches together. The third week came, and he did not show up for his appointment with the principal. He did not show up at his next scheduled class, and he did not telephone. He could not be reached. Unable to face the fact that he, a master teacher, had been defeated by a handful of children who didn't learn, he ran away from the job. The principal, to whom this reaction was no novelty, tenaciously pursued him, called him back, and helped him to see that he had caught all his feelings of frustration and despair from the children themselves. She helped him to separate out his own feelings from theirs and aided him in programming for his success as a teacher in this special situation.

Deep concern and love for children (particularly for those who provoke rejection) is necessary, but it is not enough by itself. Many caring teachers have failed with learning disabled children because they have not been able to provide the borders for the children's scattered attention so they can focus, provide the control that will help them behave appropriately, and provide the tight organization and structure that will allow them to approach a task successfully. For solid learning to take place, a teacher needs to limit the amount of material she gives to a learning disabled child, being sure that the child thoroughly learns each part before moving on to more and using as many creative ways as possible to repeat and reinforce each step. It is common for a new teacher to introduce too much, to cover too much material in her eagerness to see a child move ahead quickly. The faster the student learns, the better the new teacher feels about her teaching abilities. She is pleased with the child and pleased with herself as he seems to move along at her pace, but too frequently she is serving her own shaky ego rather than his needs. A child knows when he has not learned a lesson, and his failure makes him feel bad, but he may hide the fact to please his teacher and maintain her enthusiastic approval of him.

Howard slid along like this for a whole term with a new teacher. When the same material was reintroduced the next term, he resisted it vigorously. He refused to go over it and reveal his inability to grasp it, insisting instead that he had done all this before and it was boring. The new teacher had ended her term feeling that she had succeeded where others had not, but she had done a real disservice to Howard.

Since many learning disabled youngsters are very concrete, sometimes teachers need to explain difficult situations to them in concrete terms. Leroy was ridden by so much anxiety that he could not learn. He seemed to carry the whole weight of his many problems—his inability to master reading, writing, and arithmetic. His teacher longed to ease the burden of responsibility he felt. She wrote two columns on a page:

Your Strengths	*Your Problems*
You work very hard.	Reading
You are determined.	Writing
You care.	Spelling
You are a good artist.	Arithmetic

Then she tore the paper down the middle. She handed Leroy the list of his strengths. "You keep these," she said, "and it's my job to take care of the others." Leroy could see and understand the division of responsibility, and it went a long way toward relieving his anxiety. As he was more able to deal with his problems, his teacher was able to engage him more in the process of learning, and pass more of the list to him, but her first job was to relieve his anxiety.

Because of their disorder, learning disabled children need the certainty and safety of a confident adult in charge. But this is quite a different matter from the dogmas of the self-proclaimed experts. These are more like the great black and white truths that we discovered in college and that our exasperating parents insisted on seeing in shades of gray. Growing maturity allows a teacher to define what she doesn't know, to rely confidently on what she does know, and to make occasional mistakes.

SETTING A MODEL

It is crucial for adults to give themselves permission, frankly and out loud, to make mistakes so they can give learning disabled children permission to make mistakes too. Miss Rockford, who gave one of her students the wrong workbook, said, "Whoops, I made a mistake here. I'm sorry about that. But there's something I can do about it right away." Mr. Hart, who sawed off the wrong end of a board needed for a puppet theater, said, "Well, look at what I did! I wasn't thinking

properly. But now I am thinking well and I see there's a way to fix this."
Neither mistake was the end of the world. When a teacher is dealing
with the One-Way Kid, she must remember that he cannot visualize
alternatives and that each mistake, to him, means total defeat. A
teacher needs to demonstrate through her behavior and her reactions,
as well as her words, that mistakes can be useful and that they can lead
to new solutions.

Similarly a teacher must be willing not to know all the answers. By
being able to say, "I really don't know but I can look it up and find
out," he sets a model for the child who fears that every admission of
ignorance is a confirmation of her worthlessness. Often the learning
disabled child will not admit that she doesn't know something and
will not dare to say or do anything unless she is sure she is right.

Frequently the learning disabled child is so defensive that it is easy
for his teacher to become defensive too. Defensiveness in students
shows through comments like these: "I don't care," "It's boring," "I
don't want to do this anyway," "I've done it before," "It's too easy." The
child is always making excuses for why she can't do something, and
often we hear her teachers making excuses for why the teaching
materials aren't easier, more interesting, or more relevant. The defensiveness of the learning disabled child appears at the hint of criticism.
If a teacher says, "It's windy in here," a learning disabled child may say,
"Well, I didn't leave a window open." The teacher may respond with,
"I didn't either," catching the child's overreaction to a simple statement about a cold day when nobody, in fact, left a window open.
Some teachers become so caught up in self-defense of this sort that
they are continually apologizing, a device that does not help the very
unsure child to learn. Others show defensiveness through an exaggerated response to a simple question, comment, or criticism. The ultimate defeat occurs when a very caring teacher says, "I don't care."

A lot of the child's intelligence and good reasoning are devoted to
manipulation: how to get out of work, how to get somebody else to do
it, how to hide his fear that he can't do it, and how to irritate the
teacher or cause a disturbance that will change the focus from his

accomplishing a specific task. Every teacher likes to keep control of her classroom and to engage the cooperation and respect of the children. The people who go into the teaching profession usually are interested in minds; they like sharing; they enjoy ideas. The word *educate* from its Latin derivation means "to draw forth" (not "to fill up a container" as, alas, it has sometimes been interpreted). In drawing forth a child's ability to use his mind, a teacher counts heavily on the child's response, a child's demonstration of understanding for her professional satisfaction. In the learning disabled child, too often she meets a blank wall.

Traditional educators—many of them excellent, caring, fine teachers—have a body of information that they want to impart to their students. They like their subject, and they like to see it become part of each student's intellectual formation. These teachers meet nothing but frustration with a learning disabled child. Progressive educators—many of them excellent, caring, fine teachers—hope to spark the student's imagination so that he can take off on his own and chart his own course. This teacher too meets only frustration with the disordered child who can't organize himself or his work.

What keeps the average teacher working with such difficult children above and beyond his regular, overloaded classroom schedule? For one thing, the learning disabled child needs help badly; in some cases the teacher believes that his efforts can make a difference and improve the quality of the child's life. Sometimes he can succeed, and that makes all the other efforts worthwhile. There is a great reward in the pleasure the child may feel when she finally succeeds in making a step forward. Her guileless enthusiasm and her sweetness emerge visibly, and for a little while her teacher can forget the exasperating, slogging hard work that led up to this moment.

A teacher can sometimes become militant on behalf of a learning disabled child. Mrs. Higgins took on her whole school administration in battle, demanding a language therapist, extra tutoring, and special books for a child whom her supervisors would prefer to have forgotten about. In this case, the extra help was sufficient. The child was able to catch up; Mrs. Higgins had indeed rescued him in time. That knowledge bolstered her and gave her the courage to take on many more learning disabled youngsters.

BECOMING AN ADVOCATE

Learning disabled children need a committed advocate to explain the special situations arising from their handicap. For instance, the behavior of a child who talks aloud to himself, reminding himself not to forget his homework or repeating key words to keep his mind focused, may irritate those around him. When it is interpreted for other teachers by the advocate, the behavior can be seen as helpful to the child and tolerable rather than bizarre.

The advocate, like Mrs. Higgins, needs to muster the necessary services available to the child, coordinate them, and act as a clearinghouse for parents, school, and outside professional services. The learning disabled child's advocate needs more than normal courage in the face of inadequate resources and often insensitive institutions. She must be willing to step boldly forward and, if necessary, take leadership.

Miss Pendle, a regular classroom teacher with many years of experience, had rarely seen a child as disorganized as Jake. She found him annoying, infuriating, and worrisome yet challenging. She was puzzled by him because often his remarks were brilliant, yet he couldn't add 4 + 2 or read beyond the preprimer level in second grade. She tried every approach she knew, read some new books, turned to colleagues for help (unusual for her), and finally consulted a specialist in learning disabilities.

Mrs. Higgins had become an advocate for a mildly learning disabled child who needed extra services from specialists. Miss Pendle, who was faced with a much more severely learning disabled child, needed help in how to manage and structure this child to learn within her classroom. She met regularly with the specialist in learning disabilities who knew how to manage, reach, and teach these children effectively. Miss Pendle became Jake's best ally by providing the very structure and limits that he needed.

SETTING UP A STRUCTURE

"Jake has the attention span of a flea!" said one of his former teachers. Miss Pendle found she had to stand right in front of him, use a louder or softer voice, a bigger or smaller gesture, a touch on the shoulder to catch his attention even for a minute. Besides Jake's inability to focus on any task for more than a few seconds, he was in a moment, if given half a chance, at the pencil sharpener or putting gum into his mouth. He would then have to be told to sit down or be reminded, once more, that chewing gum in class was against the rules. By the time Jake arrived in class for the first period on a typical morning, he was already frantic. He had thrown one tantrum while he was getting dressed and couldn't find one shoe. By the time the shoe was found, it was time for the school bus, and he had missed his breakfast. An older child taunted him on the bus and brought him close to another tantrum. In his anxiety to get off the bus, he tripped and fell on the sidewalk. As he entered the classroom, he was chattering a mile a minute and not looking where he was going.

First, Miss Pendle would catch Jake's eye and stop him talking; then she would point him in the direction he must go to find his seat. She had placed Jake's seat closest to her desk, and she had marked out an area around his chair with masking tape on the floor. The outline of his own space helped to curb his restless wandering, and he was close enough for her to put her hand on him for reassurance or restraint. When the children moved their desks around, Miss Pendle made sure that Jake's place faced a wall, where distractions would be minimized. As his ally, she helped hold him together until he could learn to hold himself together, and she helped to supply the emotional brakes. Yet Miss Pendle knew better than anybody else that what worked yesterday might not work today.

All children need the security of predictable rules and limits. They need to know precisely what to do and when to do it and in which order. Structure provides a framework that can be changed to allow the child to succeed. Teachers often confuse structure with rigidity. The latter inhibits growth, for it doesn't allow for any flexibility. Every child needs supportive structuring of her time, and for a learning disabled child it is essential. She needs a time and a space for everything. Routines are the backbone of her structure: how she enters the room, where she sits, what she puts on her desk. These must all be structured for her. She must be taught routines, step-by-step, until she's mastered them and can do them almost automatically. The things she uses must be kept in the same place. The place for puzzles is on the shelf by the window—big puzzles on the right, small puzzles on the left. When the child takes a puzzle to use, she must always put it back just where she found it. Miss Pendle's masking tape on the floor around Jake's own space served the same purpose. Jake knew exactly where he belonged and where he would always find himself. Three squares of masking tape on Jake's desk visually organized his work space. The upper left-hand square held the papers he was going to work on; the lower center square was for his current work; the upper right-hand square was where he put his finished papers. Later Miss Pendle removed his squares, one by one, as he internalized the organization.

Classroom materials, such as puzzles, worksheets, counting blocks, and a book, were introduced to Jake one at a time whenever possible because he could not integrate several things at once. Miss Pendle made a card with a picture on it to represent each material. When Jake was given a card with a picture of a puzzle on it, it was his cue to fetch the puzzle, put it in front of him, work it, and put it away. Then he would turn over his card and wait for another. When the other children in the class were given their assignments for a period,

Jake would receive three or four cards from Miss Pendle, which she put into a special holder on his desk. It had a pocket for each card, clearly marked to show the order—first, second, last—in which the assignments should be done. This was his schedule, his checklist, his review of accomplishments.

Whenever a child in her class did something she had never done before, Miss Pendle made a point that not only she, but the children as well, showed recognition of progress. She set the tone and gave the word so that each child's accomplishment, whatever it might be, was acclaimed. Besides progress in the three Rs, she pointed out that Russell now came into the room smiling instead of scowling, that Betty had remembered to water the plants every day, that Jake had sat still and listened to her instructions all the way through. "What do we say to Russell, Betty, and Jake?" she would ask. The answer from the class was a resounding "Well done!"

Due to his distractibility, Jake was always knocking things off his desk. Pencils and crayons would always find their way onto the floor. Depending on the total class situation, Miss Pendle would point to them, thereby giving Jake a nonverbal clue, or she might ask him directly to pick them up. Or she might gain his cooperation by using a light touch and pretending to talk to the pencils, "Hey, you pencil under Jake's chair—can't you get back on his desk? Don't you think he'll help you?"

DISPELLING THE TENSION

Humor is an important teaching tool. If a child can begin to see the funny side of a bad situation, he can often find his way out of it. A teacher who can laugh at herself in an easy, accepting way is an important model for the children who see themselves only as a source of worry to others and despair to themselves. The use of humor and the absurd, with a light touch, can be effective tools for discipline, teaching, and testing. A school where laughter abounds among staff members and permeates classes is usually a place where children are given many opportunities to enjoy learning and living. The problems of learning disabled children are serious and need to be treated with utmost concern, yet nothing dispels an atmosphere of tension faster than laughter.

Some of the dilemmas that a teacher faces are not funny, however, and seem to have no easy answers. The child who craves attention, for example, makes noise, says inappropriate things, and throws erasers, forcing the teacher to interrupt the lesson and reprimand her. If the teacher does so, she gives the student the attention she is demanding, thereby rewarding her negative behavior. If she doesn't, the student disrupts the class to a point where it is impossible to teach the others. She frequently ends up sending her to the principal's office. What to do about a defenseless child who is being teased? If the teacher steps in to rescue him, he will not learn for himself how to handle one of life's recurring situations. If she doesn't, she risks allowing his weak ego to be eroded even further, making him still more defenseless next time. Both solutions can seem wrong. How to handle the child who can't bear to be touched? There are many such dilemmas with no one solution.

All teachers know that a transition causes difficulties. When the children are changing classrooms, moving to the library, or going to the cafeteria, the most trouble occurs—pinching or hitting, teasing, or cruel remarks. A buddy system often works best at these times for a learning disabled child. A well-controlled child can be asked to be his buddy, to help him find the way, help him to remember his books or his lunch box, be his friend during the transition. The learning disabled child can hold up his end of the bargain by saving a seat for his buddy or by rendering some other little service. Even when the children make their transitions in an orderly manner, the change and the relative lack of structure and focus can cause considerable anxiety to the disordered child.

Physical education or gym can be extremely upsetting to the learning disabled child because these times may have less structure. Routines are likely to be looser and the level of noise much higher than in the classroom. If he is consistently upset and behaving badly after such a period, it is sometimes preferable to excuse a learning disabled child from physical education and use the time for special tutoring. The daily trip on the school bus can be more stimulating than some learning disabled children can handle. If teachers are on the lookout for trouble in this area, they can sometimes help parents to arrange car pools and avoid an unnecessary upset in the day. Walking to school in a group can also be overstimulating. Walking alone can lead to many adventures for the distractible, impulsive youngster who might follow a stray cat or walk along a new trail. Parents and teachers need to analyze the strengths and the hazards involved in how a child comes to school and then build in ways to make the trip a calmer, more focused, pleasurable experience. Arrival and dismissal times, unless they are very orderly, can also be periods of great stress. Learning disabled children may be helped to cope if they are assigned a particular place to wait until the hubbub dies down.

Unexpected changes of any kind can devastate learning disabled children. Over one Christmas vacation, Mrs. Henry decided to paint and redecorate her classroom as a New Year's surprise for her class. Although some of the children were delighted, the ones with learning disabilities met her efforts with tears or tantrums. Halloween, Christmas, Valentine's Day, and other holidays need a long lead-in period so that when the change in routine occurs, the learning disabled children are well prepared and expecting it. They tend to perseverate on holidays, becoming obsessed with one aspect or symbol of it. The day on which such a child is going to a birthday party after school can end up being a wasted one for him because he can think and talk of nothing but the party. This is one reason why special schools or classes, with totally integrated school days and a minimum of overstimulation, are necessary for seriously learning disabled children.

GIVING INSTRUCTIONS

Most learning disabled children experience great difficulty in listening to, remembering, and following a series of oral instructions. Most teachers are unaware of how wordy they are and how fast they tend to speak. It's important that teachers listen to themselves. One school requires each teacher to be taped so she will hear herself. If a child has language problems, the child cannot deal with many words. If the child is learning disabled, remembering a sequence of directions that exceeds two or three steps is usually impossible.

Count the steps that are involved in the following set of instructions given to a fourth-grade class last year: "Please sit down, take out pencil and paper, write your name on the upper left-hand corner of the page, put the date on the upper right-hand corner, draw a picture of a man in the center of the page, fold the paper in half vertically, place it on the left side of my desk, and return to your seat." A learning disabled youngster could not carry out this exercise effectively.

In giving oral directions, it helps to have the children look at the teacher, to catch the eyes, to reinforce the sound. For some, it is necessary to give the reinforcement of being touched or held in a position facing the teacher. It's important to be clear, precise, and succinct with directions. It is vital to speak slowly enough and yet loudly enough to be heard. Often it helps to limit directions to one or two steps until a teacher is sure of a child's capability in understanding directions. Sometimes it helps to break down directions, giving one small part at a time. This practice follows a basic tenet of remedial education that one goes down as low as is necessary to discover what a child can do and then it's possible to move up from there.

It may be helpful to have the children repeat the instructions before carrying them out. "First we'll put away lunches, then we'll line up at the door, next walk quietly down the stairs and out to the playground. Now what will we do first? Second of all, we'll line up. You tell us what's next. Last of all, we'll walk to the playground." And the next set of explanations takes place at the playground. When the child follows oral directions properly, he deserves much praise and encouragement.

Sometimes teachers have to say the same things over and over again, in different ways, to help focus the children, to interpret to them what they are doing, to deal directly with their fears and their learning disabilities. Here are some stock phrases that might be helpful to teachers of learning disabled children.

FOCUSING

> *Look at me. Eyes on me. Now think through what things you need to bring with you.*
> *Stop. Think. What are we going to do first?*
> *Are you ready now? Ready to sit down? Ready to concentrate? Good!*
> *Calm down. Pull yourself together.*
> *Slow down now. Organize your thoughts. We have time.*
> *Keep your eyes on what you're doing.*
> *We'll do it step by step, systematically.*
> *It's hard for you to stop what you are doing, so I'm going to give you a warning and then ask you to stop.*
> *Let's review what we did. First we went outside. Then what did we do? I remember what we did next. . . .*

DEALING WITH FRUSTRATION

> *It's okay to be angry. Everybody gets angry at times. It's how we handle it that counts.*
> *I know it's hard for you, but you can master it. I'll help you. You try first. I'm here.*
> *When you're frustrated, it helps to tell us about it, and then we can help you deal with it.*

You may have learning problems, but that's no excuse for poor manners!

When you say something is too easy, it really isn't. It's hard. I know it is, and I can help you do it. (Also a response for "It's boring" and "It's babyish.")

You and I know now that when you say you are too tired to do this you are afraid that you can't do it well. Let's try it together.

Encouraging Appropriate Behavior

Yes, I am bossy and I'm going to continue to be bossy until you can boss yourself a little better.

That's not appropriate behavior. (It does not fit the situation.) This is the appropriate behavior. Let's try it.

I'm helping you to help control yourself. It's hard for you to control yourself. Sometimes it's best for you to be away from the group for a while until you can pull yourself together.

When we see you tease others that way, we know that someone has hurt you very badly with teasing. Let's talk about that hurt. When people tease you it's because something really bothers them. They have a hurt.

Dealing with Disabilities

Some babies walk at nine months, some at a year and a half, and others don't walk until they are two years old. They walk when they are ready. The ones that walked earlier don't walk better than the others. Some children read earlier than others. You will read! You need more time, but you will read!

It's good thinking that counts in this world. You have a good mind, and I like the way you use it. That's what's important!

The most important thing about mistakes is that we can learn from them. Don't worry about making mistakes, for you can learn so much from them. Many great inventions have come as a result of mistakes.

You don't have to be perfect. Nobody is perfect. How dull the world would be if people were perfect.

How great that you can laugh at yourself.

First, let's look at what you are good at, what you can do. Then we are better able to tackle what you can't do.

It's hard to lose a game, but I'm sure you'll win one soon. This is a game of chance anybody can win or lose. It has nothing to do with how smart you are!

Nobody likes to lose a game (of skill). That's hard for you! Let's work on it together for a while. You'll see that you'll improve. (Or: "Let's change positions. You take the one that is ahead and I'll take the one that's behind.")

Sometimes it's hard to win too, because you worry about whether you can win the next one as well.

You don't have to cheat to win. You're winning as a person, and you'll get better at the game!

Try to accept my knowledge that you're making progress. You will see it for yourself soon.

Remember how hard this was for you in September. Look at your work now!

TEACHER SUPPORT SYSTEMS

Just as the teacher must build on a child's strengths, interests, and unique talents, so must principals and supervisors. The tone of a school is set by its top administrators, by how willing they are to look at themselves and listen to their reactions, by how they deal with problems and uncertainty. The teacher of the learning disabled child is dealing with an uncertainty—an erratic, inconsistent, misleading, puzzling youngster. She may need help in sorting out what she knows from what she does not know. One of the significant signs of a mature person is the ability to recognize the areas where her knowledge is insufficient, be able to state it, and ask for help. This skill is crucial for teachers of learning disabled children because at times there is a need for help, since the job is so difficult and demanding.

A teacher is thrown on her own resources when schools do not recognize the special problems of a child with faulty perception who cannot learn normally despite normal intelligence. Where schools adopt *mainstreaming* (regular schooling) as a philosophy, the responsibility of meeting the special needs of a learning disabled child falls upon the regular classroom teacher. She has rarely had special training, and often she does not know how to proceed. She cannot be expected to perform this job proficiently without proper support and guidance.

Schools need to build in more supervisory services that are less judgmental and more supportive. Teachers need supervisors who will listen to the details of their worries about a child. Often the process of talking clarifies problems for them. Sometimes a fresh view helps. Teachers frequently need the help of a supervisor or master staff in designing new materials for the child, creating a model lesson, making a learning game, or constructing learning aids together with the teacher, instead of just hearing advice on how to do it. At times they need inspiration. The nourishing of teachers needs to become a top priority of school administrators because then the children are assured of being well nourished educationally.

School support systems that encourage the sharing of ideas and feelings are essential for teachers. Staffs need to be trained and treated in the same way they are expected to train and treat children—by drawing on their experience, building on their strengths and interests, by helping them to overcome areas of weakness, by establishing trust. Tapping their hidden resources, giving them experiences that tickle their intellect, excite their imaginations, stimulate hearty laughter, and give satisfaction need to be a conscious part of staff training.

If administrators don't want the staff to stand in front of their classes and lecture all the time, then they must not do this with their faculty. If the goal is to provide more experiential learning, then administrators need to set up situations for the faculty to explore new situations that use as many senses as possible. When teachers are asked to develop programs that totally involve their students, they will be helped if they see models provided on an adult level where they have been totally involved themselves. Too often school faculty meetings deal with immediate logistical concerns and announcements, not with the true issues of education, with great ideas, with a myriad of ways to solve a certain problem. They don't bring out the best of the human resources that fill the meeting room. They don't bring out a commitment to inquiry, a seeking of new knowledge.

Staffs need to be helped to prize each other's uniqueness, recognize each other's special talents, and rely on one another for help in those areas. Brainstorming in small groups within an established time frame to work out new systems for the operation of the school, or forming teams that present alternate ways of solving a particular intellectual or behavior problem, are ways in which a faculty can learn to work together.

The more ways a faculty is helped to grow . . .

the more a faculty can do for its students . . .

the more students grow.

TEACHING TEACHERS

Teachers serve as models to most students. The ways teachers carry themselves, react, speak, and handle their own feelings are emulated by many of their students. All students, learning disabled students even more so, pick up the emotional atmosphere of a school, feelings about the institution, the relationships between and among teachers, attitudes toward authority. Too little of our teacher training attends to these human factors. In fact, not enough attention is devoted to the quality of those applying to be a teacher or for teacher training. Too much attention has been paid to grades and prerequisite courses. In ancient times, the purpose of education was for children to be near the finest adults possible to absorb their wisdom, their values, and the way they dealt with feelings and relationships. Should it not be so today?

We want all of our children, and particularly those who are disabled in learning, to be near adults who are constantly learning and growing and are excited by the very process of living. Universities need to select human beings to become teachers who care deeply about children, who desire to probe ideas in depth, who want to build up a storehouse of knowledge, systematically, layer upon layer. Teacher training programs must prize the ingenuity, creativity, and problem-solving attitudes of adults so they can draw on those reserves when there are no set paths, no predestined routes. Liking children is not enough. To develop fully the intellects and imaginations of their students, the adults need to be mature, growing people who will tap every resource within themselves.

As the job market for teachers shrinks, and as the mainstreaming of children with disabilities becomes common practice in schools, universities must become much more selective in their admissions to schools of education, seeking out more candidates who are multidimensional people. Teachers need solid training in theory, a vast exposure to methods and techniques, and then highly supervised practicums under master teachers to put the theories to practice and to develop their own unique styles and teaching approaches. They need experience in creating their own teaching materials, worksheets, and games to be able to meet the specific learning needs of each child. They need to be encouraged to develop nontraditional approaches. At the same time they need exposure to all the commercial materials available so they can select appropriately.

HELPING TEACHERS

School is more than an institution for the acquisition of information and knowledge. It needs to be thought of as a place for students to experience mastery in all areas of learning and human relationships. For learning disabled students, school needs to be a source of comfort as well as a challenge. It can be this if teachers are resourceful and imaginative, well trained in the needs of children and in a vast array of teaching methods, and thoroughly supported by the school system.

Evaluations by supervisors need to explain the positive aspects of the teacher's performance and provide constructive advice to improve teachers' weaker areas. Very specific suggestions, brainstorming sessions, fueling her up to get on with the job, giving her more resources are ways to develop a better teacher. In some schools, supervisors merely rate the condition of the room, the bulletin boards' appearance, the children's behavior, and the orderliness of the lesson plans. One classroom teacher with five learning disabled children in her class of thirty-two first-graders said, "All my supervisor told me was that she rated me highly on how nice my room looked and how green the plants were, but she thought my behavioral control was only fair. She never had the time to listen to my plight with these five kids who aren't learning anything. Mrs. Jones reminds me of my mother—too busy to take the time to really help." Fortunately most supervisors aren't like Mrs. Jones. Nevertheless the roles of supervisors need to be examined in depth. Perhaps the nomenclature is too judgmental. Maybe school systems need advisers, backup support provided by master teachers who welcome the challenges of helping teachers deal with their most difficult students and produce learners. Those who advise or supervise teachers need to present examples and to pose questions. They need to help make lesson plans for these youngsters and, with the teacher, seek out the most effective methods. The advisers need to be part of the process to support the teacher.

It may be helpful for a teacher with learning disabled children in his class to make a checklist of questions to ask himself. The following examples might be typical:

What did I do that worked today?

What did I do that should be avoided?

Am I looking at the strengths each child brings with him?

What are his interests?

What are the areas of my strengths, my weaknesses?

Am I too tough on myself?

Do I have enough change of pace in my program?

Do I always have enough alternatives to fall back on when the program is dragging?

How flexible am I?

How important is it to me to be right all the time?

Instead of merely disapproving of negative energies, am I finding ways to divert these negative energies into more constructive channels?

Am I devoting so much attention to negative behavior that I am reinforcing it?

Can I remember to praise positive behavior, the things we tend to take for granted?

Am I talking too much?

Am I unintentionally encouraging their "answer-grabbing syndrome," their feeling that they must have an answer for all situations?

What kinds of questions am I asking the children?

Am I a good listener?

Am I encouraging the children to ask questions?

Since the basis of all relationships lies in the feeling of trust, what can I do to establish it? Can I rush it?

What are the cues that the children are not being reached? Can children be listening even when they seem to be focused on something else?

Do I bring humor, laughter, and smiles into my classroom? How can I make more use of the absurd mistake, the absurd example, both as a learning tool and a source of humor?

What do I do with the child who stands on the perimeter?

What do I do with the hyperactive child or the child who may leave the room?

What do I do with the very aggressive child?

At what point do I send a child to the "crisis teacher"?

Is it helpful for the children to be told at the beginning the goal or goals for that period and to know if they reached them?

How important is it at the end of each period to repeat, rephrase, refresh, and restate the concepts, vocabulary, and information that have been taught?

How do I know when a child is really tired or using fatigue as an excuse to escape work? Why does he need to use an excuse?

What special plans must I make for a rainy day?

How can I stimulate the children to recognize not only their own progress but each other's and to praise their peers?

What can I do in my classroom to foster respect, to promote a positive look at what each child can do?

Am I setting a model of inquiry?

How do I approach the unknown?

How can I help the children to see that mistakes are useful, not to be laughed at, but to be learned from?

Do I fear failure?

BASIC QUESTIONS

What will I teach? (What do the children need to know?)

Why should I teach it?

How will I teach it?

How will I know I taught it?

NINE

TEACHING APPROACHES

Every child can learn. It is up to us, the adults, to seek out and discover the routes by which he learns. Detective work is required. Vital clues can be found through precise observation of the child, keen listening to the child, and careful study of his work. Patterns of learning can be discerned through close scrutiny of all formal and informal test results, teachers' records, and the history and information given by parents. Experimentation is needed to decipher what works and what doesn't. Astute analysis of all the evidence demands strong reasoning, alertness, attention to detail, and precise record keeping in order to uncover a child's unique learning style. All this detective work does not imply that it is a crime to have learning disabilities, of course. The crime is allowing a child to go through years of schooling without learning the basic skills.

To program a child for success, the necessary starting point is to ask very basic questions:

In general, what are the child's strengths?
What are his interests, his hobbies, his pleasures?

What does he have going for him?
Does he seem to learn best through his eyes, his ears, his hands,
*   his body, through associating one thing with another, or*
*   through a specific combination of these?*
What can this child do?

We have to know in detail what a child can't do, but some teachers concentrate only on what a child can't do. It is too easy to say that since we taught him and he didn't learn, the child is dumb, lazy, willful, manipulative, or badly brought up. Sometimes the child does have limitations on his intelligence, or he is disturbed, or he has learned to manipulate adults to avoid working. Usually, though, the child desperately wants to learn and doesn't know how to do it. *It is our job to find out how he learns and then teach him how he learns.*

School needs to be a place for a child to experience mastery. Our teaching approaches must *program for each child's success and pleasure in learning.* No matter how far down we have to go to find an activity that a child can do, and can do independently, we must find it to offer the child success. Each success leads to further success. That exultant feeling of "I can do it!" needs to become part of each child's daily school experience.

Knowing the child and defining his *learning profile* is necessary but not enough. It is only the beginning. *Knowing what he needs to know* is next.

The child needs specific educational tasks to learn. Clear, precise objectives are a must. No matter how the child learns best, or which teaching methods are used, a tightly structured treatment program must lead to a well-defined goal. The teacher must analyze first whether the child has the skills to reach the goal or which skills the child has and which ones must be built in first.

A child may need to be taught a whole spectrum of readiness skills before any attempt can be made on the goal itself. She may not have the foundations on which to begin, and so the building up of these foundations becomes the short-term goal. A ten-year-old learning disabled child, for whom the objective is learning to read, may not yet have developed the most primitive, preschool abilities. For instance, she may not be able to distinguish loud from soft sounds, to recognize similar sounds, to know left from right, above from below, to discriminate shapes and forms, to see the background of a picture as separate from the foreground, to be able to classify and categorize on a simple level. She may first need very specific instruction in one or several of such areas, and a learning prescription that pinpoints these precise needs must be produced for her.

TASK ANALYSIS

Any task presented to a learning disabled child must be explored in depth by his teacher. For this, *task analysis* is required. The teacher may find performing the task himself to be a good starting point. After noting what he did and how he did it, he breaks down the task into its components and isolates the steps that were involved, ranking them from the simplest to the most complex and putting them in logical sequence.

Marie wanted to skip, but she lacked the coordination. "Teach me to skip, Mrs. Willis!" she pleaded. Mrs. Willis analyzed what skipping entailed. Before Marie could skip, she must know how to hop. Before she could hop, she must know how to stand on one foot. Before standing on one foot, she must stand on two feet. Marie could hop, so Mrs. Willis began by having Marie stand on one foot, the point where she could succeed with ease. She explained that Marie would have to practice standing on one foot and hopping, first on one foot and then on the other, before she could skip. They started out the same way each time, and then Mrs. Willis varied the routine, creating games to help her hop on alternate feet, and finally to combine forward motion with alternate hopping. Much repetition ensured that Marie could skip automatically. Marie was involved in the learning process with Mrs. Willis; she understood what was going on to help her reach her goal. Each time she was able to hop on one foot and then the other, she would fill in a colored square on her graph paper. She built up colored squares into a bar graph and kept a visual record of her progress. Each step required a more sophisticated set of readiness abilities than the step before. Each step needed to be broken down into its own components and examined in the light of Marie's readiness.

To ensure the child's success and keep his enthusiasm, the place to begin teaching is just below his point of mastery. From there, each step can be structured into a lesson plan and taught systematically, one step at a time, reintroduced and repeated again and again until the goal is reached and the child responds automatically.

The chart entitled "To Read . . . A Child Needs," shown in chapter 7, shows a beginning task analysis of an extremely complex task. Only the largest components appear on it. Each one of those could make the subject of a chart of its own. Each part needs to be magnified until the teacher thoroughly understands what is involved and what, precisely, the child needs to be taught.

In preparing a task analysis, a teacher might ask the following questions:

What am I asking the child to do?

What are the main components of the task?

What are the smaller components within the larger parts?

Which parts come first and which later?

Can I rank them from simple to complex?

What does the child have to know in order to perform each stage?

At what point in the sequence of the hierarchy does the child have mastery?

What steps will I teach, one by one, from there?

Can I set clear, precise goals for each step?

The task analysis combined with the profile of the child serves to prepare the way. The teacher then must have access to and be familiar with a multiplicity of teaching materials and their various levels of difficulty. No one method or set of materials is foolproof. Many of the very best teachers subscribe to no one method but draw on the many that they know, matching a variety of materials to the child's age level and interests, as well as to his developmental level. Methods and approaches must fit the child rather than the child having to adapt to a particular method or approach.

Still another ingredient is necessary. This is the part that challenges all the resources of a human being and makes teaching exciting. It is *problem-solving ingenuity*. Creativity is needed for a teacher to present material so that it entices the child and lures his participation. Inventing materials to present the same lessons in hundreds of different, imaginative ways until it is learned and has become part of the child's very being is surely the spice of teaching. There are many excellent commercial materials available today for teachers to choose from but teacher-made materials are also necessary. "You made this game just for *me!*" said nine-year-old Jane Ellen, who loved games and relished the fact that something had been designed especially for her. Not only can teacher-made materials focus on a specific child's interests and needs but they motivate the child's focus right away.

PREPARATION FOR THE TASK

Before he starts his task, the learning disabled child needs to be *structured to focus*. He needs to be told the purpose of the task and what is expected of him, told what to look for, what to attend to, and what to ignore. He needs to be shown explicitly how and where to begin a task. Things that we take for granted with children who have no learning problems must be spelled out, step-by-step, to the learning disabled youngster. If he is approaching the task of circling all objects that begin with the letter *t* on a page, the preparation may include teaching him how to sit most conveniently for the job, where to look first, how to begin in a systematic fashion, what to say to himself as he does it, and what to do when he comes to the end.

Overloaded with stimulation when faced with complexity, the learning disabled child needs to be given only one thing at a time to do. He does not need widening horizons and enrichment. He needs limiting. *By limiting the amount of materials, the number of words used, the quantity of procedures, the choices, and the amount of work,* we are not limiting the child but, in fact, allowing him to learn. Establishing *regular routines, familiar procedures,* and *prescribed ways of behaving* are ways of giving parameters or borders to the child who is disorganized and distractible.

By *establishing a time, a space, and a place for everything in the classroom,* the teacher is providing the structure that gives the child the safety to learn. Then he does not have to expend all his energies on where to put his body, so often lost in space, where to put his belongings or his work, or how to organize his time; this careful structuring helps him to concentrate on his work. Structuring the day for the learning disabled child in terms of events, instead of hours, helps the concrete child. Preparing him for the end of class and *giving advance notice of changes in routine* helps make the transition for a child who has so much trouble switching gears and who has such a precarious sense of order.

The child who has difficulty processing language hears most of the instructions she receives in the course of a day like the gabbling of a record that is played too fast. *Clear, precise directions* that use a minimum of language and are delivered one direction at a time—and never more than two or three—ensure her success in following them. The learning disabled child needs eye contact, a teacher's gestures, modulation of his voice, and, at times, a certain animation on his part, to help her focus.

The child with a learning disorder, whose energy is as scattered and random as his attention, tires quickly. Many learning disabled adults who have achieved professional success tell us that their hardest job remains to block out the extra stimulation. They have to work very hard to contain the overload of their senses; they talk of the enormous energy this takes and the consummate fatigue that results. In teaching the learning disabled child, professionals must take account of this fatigue that results from so much inefficient functioning. It is therefore helpful to *change the pace of instruction* frequently, to prepare several different activities for a given time period, to give *short-term assignments*, and to *alternate energetic activity with a more restful exercise*. The child's fatigue cycle forces a teacher to *prepare alternate plans and backup material* to draw on when necessary. The teacher needs to know the fatigue cycles in order to reserve the most intense teaching for the time when the child tends to learn best. Many learning disabled children are most alert the first hour of the morning; others need an hour or two to become organized to learn. Most learning disabled youngsters *need extra time* because of their slow processing. Many cannot finish a paper or a quiz in class within the time limits but, if given extra time, can do exceedingly well. Recognizing this fact, the College Entrance Examination Board and Educational Testing Service make provisions for certified learning disabled students to be given extra time for finishing their SATs and other standardized tests. It is acknowledged that the abilities and performance of these youngsters cannot be properly evaluated when held to a time limit.

A MULTISENSORY APPROACH

Learning disabled children need to use every available channel for gaining knowledge and retaining it. By using their whole bodies, by learning and reinforcing what they have learned through experiences of touching, tasting, smelling, seeing, hearing, and doing, they seem better able to organize and integrate information in the brain. The *multisensory approach to teaching* is effective with most, but not all, learning disabled youngsters. For some children, the use of too many senses produces confusion. The total-immersion approach is too much for them, and the use of the senses has to be limited. However, all learning disabled children *need repetition* of lessons until they are fully learned and have become automatic.

To be able to transfer the learning of a task in one situation to a totally different situation causes great difficulty for most learning disabled students. It becomes part of the teacher's responsibility to *attempt to teach transfer,* the recognition of the same task in many different forms. This means encouraging the pupil to discover relationships and structuring the lesson so that the child is led to the place where transfer becomes the logical next step.

Whenever possible, a teacher must *link what is unknown to a learning disabled child to his own experience and knowledge.* The student is helped to learn by referring back to himself and to his familiar world as often as possible. A child who was making a simple musical instrument in the Lab School woodwork shop was taught the word *vibration* and its concept. Her teacher encouraged the child to hold her hand against her own throat as she made a series of sounds in order to feel the vibrations. She then felt vibrations on the teacher's throat and on the musical instrument. The word *vibration* proceeded to have meaning for the child when the function of a musical instrument was explained. A history teacher wanted to get across the idea of *preservation* when her class began to study Egyptian mummies. She demonstrated the concept by using a concrete object that the children knew well. She asked them each to take an apple, slice it in half, and encase one half in plastic wrap. In a couple of days they saw one half of an apple rotted and one "preserved."

CONCRETE EXAMPLES OF
ABSTRACT PROBLEMS

Many learning disabled children have difficulty remembering, and
some have a word retrieval problem. If they can't find the right word
when they need it, the teacher can avoid unnecessary frustrations by
supplying the word immediately. *Memory can be jogged by experience
with concrete objects.* An artist, who was also a very creative teacher,
found that her class of learning disabled children could not remember
basic historical facts. For example, they could never remember what
Columbus was looking for when he discovered America. One day, she
came to class with a heaping bowl of plain, boiled spaghetti, which she
promptly offered to the children. Nobody wanted any.

"Why don't you want it?" she asked.

"There's no sauce!"

"What is sauce made of?"

"Tomatoes and stuff."

"What stuff?"

"Spices and stuff like that."

"Aha! Spices! Now you know what Columbus was looking for!"
And the children never forgot it.

Because learning disabled children are so concrete, they need to
be introduced to *abstract ideas through their bodies and objects and
pictures.* Evolution is a topic that is not only complicated for six-to-
eight-year-olds but contains the added difficulty for learning disabled
children of many sequences that have to be remembered in their right
order. At The Lab School it is taught by games played on an ordinary
flight of stairs, with each step representing a stage of life—fish,
amphibian, reptile—each with its own objects and pictures to identify it. The physical action of going up the steps, following the stages
from fish to man, and touching and seeing the objects at each level
helps to make the ideas and sequences stick.

Very sophisticated material can be presented to these children only when the teacher thoroughly understands it herself and breaks it down into simple parts to teach it step-by-step. Conversely *very elementary skills,* which are ordinarily introduced to much younger children, need to be and *can be presented in a sophisticated way* so as to lure learning disabled children who are older into doing what they must. When a group of eleven-year-olds at The Lab School needed the nursery-school experience of touching and discriminating among textures, we set up the Tactile Museum. The children helped create the museum out of a wide variety of materials for touching—Styrofoam, sponge, velvet, fur, and metal, among others. They guided visitors around it, having them identify different surfaces, and they helped to develop scavenger and treasure hunts and all kinds of other games that seemed adult to them. In short, they provided for themselves the very preschool experiences they needed. The children were very proud of their Tactile Museum since no other school had one, and they felt that they were performing an adult activity.

KEYS TO HIGH-QUALITY TEACHING

The secret to high-quality teaching often lies in the imaginative presentation of what appears to be a grown-up activity. Learning disabled youngsters need every possible opportunity to feel pride in what they are doing, to be able to share some of it with the rest of their family. Six-foot-tall, fourteen-year-old Van was mortified when his eight-year-old brother saw that he was plowing through a second-grade reader for homework. Twelve-year-old Kristina crumpled up the homework of simple addition and subtraction problems that she took from the resource room into the school bus so that none of her peers would see it. A wide variety of teaching materials are available and are pitched at very elementary levels. They appear sophisticated and are tuned in to the times, reflecting interests close to the child's chrono-logical age. A teacher can also make her own, for format (as well as suitability of content) is an important consideration if we wish to secure a child's full cooperation. Children must feel good about what they do. Yet they need to know that there are some very elementary exercises they need to do, but that work is better left to the privacy of a classroom desk.

Often teachers face a dilemma when a child must be taken out of class to meet with a tutor or a resource teacher or to receive other supplemental services. The child needs the extra help, but he is resentful of being separated from the group. Ways must be found to help him save face, such as scheduling his remedial sessions during periods when some of the rest of the students are out of the class-room. It may mean doing battle with specialists who are on tight schedules, but it can be worth it for a sensitive youngster; his lower level of resentment may allow the remediation to become more effective.

Mr. Backral found that Jeff seemed to learn best when he was lying down on his back to read or listen to a story. At home, Jeff always listened to the radio or watched television lying down. Learning while sitting up presented a real problem for Jeff; the occupational therapist who worked with him speculated that Jeff's vestibular system did not allow him to deal easily with gravity, and she felt it was justified to have him lie down in order to be more productive. However, Mr. Backral had a problem when Jeff refused to be the only one in the class lying down. His solution was to place a number of big, comfortable, brightly colored pillows and a rug in the back of his classroom and announce that anybody could make himself comfortable there during silent reading time. Jeff was never alone there.

When a child makes slow progress, it is necessary for him to *have visible proof of his progress.* He has heard too many easy platitudes—"Come on, you're doing fine," "You're doing great; keep trying." He needs to be convinced. If his teacher keeps a folder for each month of

his work, in February he can look back on his September work and
see the progress. He can be encouraged to keep bar graphs, charts,
or stars pasted on a page. With each tiny accomplishment, he can fill
in each step up to the grand prize on top, paste in each slice of pizza
that will lead to that treat, complete each part of the electric system
until the lightbulb goes on. His teacher can help him draw a train,
with a new car to be added for each achievement, a caterpillar that
grows longer with each book he has read, or a simple checklist to
check off if he can read well enough. How many words did I learn
today? How many times did I raise my hand instead of blurting out
a question?

Fernando's teacher decided she wasn't doing her duty unless she
recorded every failure too, and she made him put them in his graph
alongside his less frequent successes. As Fernando started to see his
graph go down, he became disruptive, he made frequent trips to the
bathroom, complained of headaches and tummy aches, and stopped
trying. Marie's teacher neglected to put down most of the failures, and
that chart, as well as Marie, continued upward. Sometimes a child
simply cannot do a task, in which case it is better not to continue it
and certainly not to keep a visible record.

Do we *value a child's intangible achievements* enough? Do we
praise effort, hard work, and perseverance, even when the result may
be less than we hoped for? The willingness to be taught (availability
for teaching), constructive enthusiasm, and sensitivity to others are
qualities that deserve recognition and encouragement. When a child
becomes aware of their existence in herself and has them pointed out
for her with appreciation, in a specific situation, she is more likely to
try to draw on them again. Even when she does not fully succeed, she
needs praise for attempting to make a change, for making progress in
learning from mistakes, for getting started more quickly, being better
organized, and following through a bit more. Recognition of each
little step spurs the child on.

An important approach that helps a child keep track of her own progress is *self-monitoring*—evaluating what she is doing as she goes along. A child may have to learn stock phrases to repeat to herself. "This is what I just said. Is that what I meant to say?" "Before I go outside, have I got on my jacket, my mittens, and my hat?" Mr. Constable trained his students never to say they had finished a piece of work until they had said to themselves, "Look carefully at what I have done. Now look again. Did I do what I was asked to do? Am I satisfied?"

A PROBLEM-SOLVING APPROACH

The teacher acts as a *model* for a child in how to approach situations, how she treats others, what she says. But the learning disabled child often needs more than a model. In certain situations, she must frequently be taught carefully and systematically *how to react appropriately and what to say.* For example, Jenny had to be explicitly taught that when people said "Hello" to her each morning, it was important to look at them and respond. Besides handling such everyday situations as riding on the school bus, eating in the cafeteria, and using the playground equipment, a learning disabled child also needs to *be taught how to deal with unexpected situations.* If she is lost, she must know whom to ask for directions. If she doesn't know what is expected of her, she must know how to get clarification; she must know whom to go to. Coping with this sort of uncertainty before panic strikes requires familiarity with some strategies. It becomes part of a teacher's role to teach alternative options. Taking typical life situations of the children's age group, a teacher can create exercises with one solution, then provide alternatives and try to have the children produce even more. Problem solving—not just in arithmetic or social science but in the children's own lives and concerns—is an approach that needs to be used more in our schools.

TELEVISION: A TEACHING TOOL

When there is *any activity learning disabled children thoroughly enjoy doing, then teachers need to use it to teach the children the skills they need*. Television appeals to all children. They become enthralled by its magic, fun, silliness, excitement, and humor. To the learning disabled child, television can also be a haven, a safe place to escape from a difficult world that makes exhausting demands on him and makes him feel picked on and confused.

While the learning disabled child relaxes in front of the television, it is bombarding several of his learning channels at once. He can see it, hear it, and associate his own experience with it. He knows and learns to predict the sequence of the program formats, the plots, jingles, and ideas. The repetition endears television to this child who loves familiarity, who loves to know what will happen next. He can absorb what is presented with no fear that he will have to perform in response to it. It is safe and sure.

Teachers need to show parents that they can help a learning disabled child best through television by helping him to organize in his mind what he has seen. The parents will occasionally have to watch his programs too so they can get patterns of thought started, an exercise that can be extremely valuable to him.

> *What was the show about?*
> *What happened—first, next, last?*
> *When did it happen? Where? How?*
> *What was the result?*
> *What was the main point, the theme?*
> *What do you predict will happen next?*
> *What do you predict the ending will be?*

By asking these questions in different ways again and again, over a period of time, the parents can help the child to build up the patterns, understand the logic of sequences, and link cause with effect. If the child can't put his thoughts into words that make sense, the adults need to do it for him until he can do it for himself. This may take quite a period of time, even a year.

Police and detective shows are very simplistic, logically organized, and easy to understand. They show a clear relationship between cause and effect. A child who has difficulty with abstractions can see everything in concrete terms. He can be asked why the action occurred and what resulted from it. If parents are worried about the violence in police shows, television can be a good way to explore these values together.

Family and situation comedies also have strong learning possibilities. The relationships between people touch the child's own experience and are a fruitful base for discussion. The plots tend to follow the humorous ramifications of a single event. The child can be helped to recognize and isolate the repeated patterns. The people in the stories are usually predictable stock characters, each of whom has one outstanding attribute: the kind, helpful person with a heart of gold; the insensitive bore; the efficient, impatient boss; the flighty scatterbrain. These oversimplified characters can be used to help a learning disabled child understand cause and effect in social situations, especially his own. Perhaps for this reason comedies about "cool" teenagers hold such a fascination for learning disabled adolescents.

The role of adults concerning cartoons often has to be one of interpretation or a conscious decision to leave this area alone. Although the drawing is usually clear and the animation is simple, the narrative is often far too sophisticated; the dialogues are full of adult nuances and adult humor, which are incomprehensible to a learning disabled child. Yet he seems to enjoy cartoons. Many of the good educational specials, which delight most other children and adults, can be resented by children with learning disabilities. It is as though the television, which has been his friend and fortress, is suddenly seen as a traitor, allying itself with teachers and schools, trying to teach him something! Educational programs, like "Sesame Street," are likely to have some parts that are paced too fast and include too much, although he does enjoy and profit from other parts. Newscasts can interest a learning disabled child if he develops some expertise in an area such as politics, the environment, or the stock market and follows it closely. From one special interest, he can be helped to find similarly engrossing qualities in a second area and then a third.

Medical shows offer parents a chance to talk with their child about illnesses in general. They can discuss the causes, the symptoms, and the cures. This may be a good time to reassure him about his own troubles, which he may identify as an illness or a terrible injury. Quiz shows may help him to add to his fund of knowledge (but are more likely to add to his interest in money or the prizes). Sports programs can be a source of real interest and growing expertise. Once they have been taught the rules very explicitly, the youngsters can frequently understand football games better on television than on the field, where they have trouble locating the ball and following the action.

Some parents look on television as a pure waste of time for children. They may demand, "Why aren't you reading a good book instead of looking at this junk? Why aren't you out in the fresh air instead of cooped up in front of the television? Why aren't you doing your homework?" Professionals can help parents realize that *television is not a waste of time for a learning disabled child if he is helped to use it properly.* It can serve to expand a child's vocabulary and train the child in the skills of focusing, observing, and listening carefully. It can help him sustain and lengthen his attention span. It can reinforce the skills of readiness that the child needs for academic learning—classifying and categorizing, seeing parts in relation to a whole, and improving language skills. Parents can make extensive use of television as a teaching instrument and enlist the willing cooperation of the child as well. Parents can build on their child's interest in order to work on his weak areas, *programming what he needs into what he likes to do.* Sylvester needs to organize, he needs practice expressing a sequence of ideas clearly, and he needs a larger vocabulary. Sylvester's favorite program is "Star Trek," so frequently at dinner, his mother, father, and older brother ask him to describe the latest episode in a straightforward, concise way. Sometimes they try to predict how the show ended, and he has to correct them.

Teachers can use television constructively for homework by creating simple forms that the child has to fill out, requiring him to name the program correctly, write down the day of the week and the time it appeared, categorize it as a mystery, a comedy, a quiz show, or science fiction, name the main characters, and describe the main theme in one or two sentences. Furthermore teachers can play category games by having the children group their favorite programs into medical shows, detective shows, quiz shows, and so on. Comparative thinking games can be built around television programs.

The same activities can be done with movies. Learning disabled children enjoy being movie critics, and those who can write may spend hours writing movie reviews and illustrating them. Class discussions on movies can be organized to teach a myriad of skills.

Radio programs also offer many opportunities for teaching. The child has to listen and has no pictures to help him remember what he has heard. A soap opera, a special broadcast about a famous person, a sports program, or a newscast can be used as assignments.

CHALLENGE THE INTELLECT

It is vital to challenge the intellect and imagination of the learning disabled child, to tempt her curiosity and spur her reasoning. When I founded The Lab School, I was determined to find ways to help youngsters learn to enjoy fine literature even if they could not read. I wanted to get them hooked on books. It was important for them to have access to the information that others of their age group were learning from reading. They needed to hear good story construction, fine use of language, and an expansive vocabulary. I wanted the minds of Lab School children to be stimulated, and The Lab School Media Center emanated from this wish. In 1967, the Library of Congress allowed "medically proven word-blind children" to use Talking Books for the Blind. The director of The Lab School Media Center made tapes of books that had not been recorded previously. She divided all of what she considered to be the best of children's literature into seven comprehension levels. Then, depending upon the child's comprehension level, he could listen to certain stories or books.

Precise teaching objectives and a set of procedures were developed by the director of the Media Center. Children come to the Media Center to develop their listening and expressive language skills. In an interview with the teacher, they have to relate the main point of a story, identify what came first, next, and last, and describe an episode in detail. Those with limited language place figures on a picture board to show sequences that took place in the story or they draw the sequences to demonstrate their comprehension. Understanding of motivation and cause-and-effect relationships is emphasized. When the students finish hearing a book, they have to locate on a map where the story took place and on a pictorial time line when it took place. The books are chosen keeping in mind the children's age, their interest, their ability to listen, and their comprehension. Children with poor listening skills can listen to only forty seconds of a tape. Some can listen for a few minutes and others for half an hour or forty minutes without discussion. The Media Center is not only teaching them in a systematic way the skills they need for academic success but also exposing them to high-quality literature, universal ideas, and the great concepts of history.

An intelligent child does not stop learning because he can't read, write, and spell. The intelligence of the child must be respected. Too often our schools stop offering education to students who cannot read. They work on remedial techniques and give the students manual work while neglecting the educational journey into great ideas. Learning disabled youngsters need quality education. The world of inquiry is wide-open to nonreaders if teachers are given the training, help, and support to grapple with the difficult task of teaching exciting content without the students' reading any of it themselves.

While the slow process of remediation in reading, spelling, handwriting, and math is taking place, the intellect of the child has to be challenged as far and as fast as it can go. Reading is the passport needed for effective entry into our society. Yet too often we equate it with intelligence and stop educating.

T E N

TEACHING THROUGH THE ARTS AND THE ACADEMIC CLUBS

The arts have been a universal language among human beings since the world began. Gesture, movement, dance, rhythm, paintings, music, and masks carry symbolic meanings that often have no verbal equivalents; they are understood without words.

It took the human race a long time to develop an oral language and far longer to evolve a way to write it down and read it. Children in their early years reenact the history of mankind. They understand gesture, rhythm, tone, and movement before they understand words. They sing and croon before they speak. They draw and paint before they form letters. They dance and leap and act out stories before they read. We need to make more use of this developmental sequence in our schools. Our elementary-school children need to be immersed in the arts, which are considered essential to quality education. They foster intellectual, physical, social, and emotional growth.

Almost every child can be reached and taught innumerable skills through the arts. Yet rarely do schools take advantage of the rich and full education that can be derived from them. Schools tend to sideline the arts by relegating them to after-school activities or allowing drawing and music to be taught only once or twice a week. But some schools allow artistic activities to be scheduled in conjunction with a social studies or science project, or they employ the arts as preliminary training for eventual careers. In special education, the arts are sometimes treated as adjuncts to medical treatment, as therapy. The Lab School of Washington are pioneers in using the arts as vehicles to teach academic skills.

When I founded The Lab School, I wanted the arts to be central to education in the school's unique program. I not only believe in the intrinsic value of the arts to better the human condition, but also that children love to participate in most of the arts. They become totally involved. Further, the arts provide activity learning, and immature children need a great deal of this type of learning to gain that total involvement and to ensure their understanding of the material. The arts lend themselves to the imaginative use of concrete materials and experiences to teach abstract ideas. Neural immaturity makes it very hard for learning disabled children to grasp abstractions. They have to be introduced to abstractions through their bodies, through objects and pictures, and then through symbols. The arts offer opportunities to strengthen visual, auditory, tactile, and motor areas. Through the arts, children can order their worlds, make sense of what they know, relate past experience to the present, and turn muscular activity into thought and ideas into action.

AN ARTS CURRICULUM FOR THE ELEMENTARY SCHOOL

I developed a curriculum where half the day is spent in the classroom and half the day in the arts. Woodwork, arts and crafts, music, dance, drama, puppetry, and filmmaking offer pleasure and tangible results to children. Highly structured, clearly determined objectives have to be pursued through each art form. I programmed organizational skills, essential for approaching academic tasks, into the arts curriculum just as they had to be programmed into the classroom curriculum. If a child has not acquired the basic skills, he cannot learn to read even if he is taught reading several times a day. Reading readiness must be taught in the classroom, but it can also be taught successfully through the arts, and the two together form a more solid base.

Artists, art teachers, and art therapists can work on the same basic skills as a classroom teacher but in different and captivating ways. The same training in discrimination that is required for reading in the classroom is provided by discriminating one shape, sound, color, or direction from another in the arts. The skills for academic readiness are inherent in the arts: organizing and remembering sequences; assembling diverse elements into a meaningful whole; gauging relationships of size, shape, color, or volume; using and recognizing a symbol in varying contexts; and many more. With a prescription of precise objectives, the artist concentrates on the learning process while the child, doing what he enjoys, concentrates on the product he is creating.

There is a discipline underlying every artistic endeavor. People think of the arts as being very free; they are, but they become so only after one has mastered a set of basic skills. These skills must be taught in an organized, purposeful way. Learning disabled children need to be introduced to the arts in a step-by-step progression, as with anything else taught to them. They need to sort, to differentiate, and to integrate several things at once. The special genius of artists must be tapped to offer these experiences in systematic ways.

The most resourceful of artists are needed to teach learning disabled youngsters who cannot cope with the freedom that is usually ascribed to the arts. Their attention is often so unfocused and scattered that freedom is chaos for them. The overload of unrestrained

stimuli on their senses calls for just the opposite of free choice and
unrestricted opportunity; *their world must be limited to allow them to
learn and create.* The artist and the art must do the work of the faulty
"filtering mechanism" of the brain to allow focus, discrimination, and
organization to take place.

TOM: A LAB SCHOOL STUDENT

When Tom first came to The Lab School, he was a handsome seven-
year-old with above-average intelligence, and in some areas such as
verbal reasoning, he was in the superior range of his age group. He
used adult vocabulary correctly, although he often reversed the sequence of syllables. "I gather this decision is *umanimous*," or "The
emenies are encroaching upon us!" he would say, with great authority.
He could talk about the galaxies with the knowledge of a ten-year-old
but couldn't recite the days of the week or the seasons or count to ten
accurately.

Tom could make no sense of written symbols. He could not
perceive the difference between a straight and a curved line; dollar
signs and percentage marks were mere decorations to him. His
eyesight had nothing to do with the problem. He could not link
sound and symbol to recognize letters or read a word. He could not
write or spell. He was not able to follow directions, and he interpreted everything in its most literal sense—when he paid attention.
But in fact he could rarely pay attention in class, for every little noise
or movement distracted him. Tom was totally unpredictable; sometimes he was very alert, and at other times he was very slow. He was
inflexible and unwilling to try new things—even to the point of
bringing the same kind of sandwich to school every day for a year.
Tom threw himself indiscriminately into every activity with inefficient and exhausting energy. He would run around the classroom

and climb on his desk while simply getting a book from the shelf, quite unaware of what he was doing. He was clumsy as well— knocking things off his desk, forgetting his homework, tripping over his untied shoelaces—for everything about him was totally disorganized and scattered. Tom looked like a normal, bright child and in no way appeared disabled. Only his age was surprising, for he behaved most of the time like a child much younger than his age, and he looked younger too.

It took Tom five years to begin to read at The Lab School. It took two more years before he was reading ahead of his grade level and before his math skills caught up. At age eighteen, Tom was a senior in a regular high school and went on to college. His SAT scores in English placed him in the ninety-ninth percentile nationwide and in the ninety-third percentile in math. He continued to have trouble with spelling, but tried to organize his work so as to give himself extra time for heavy use of a dictionary. He continued, however, to have difficulty organizing the workload of five to six courses. Tom left college after a year and went to work in an automobile repair shop for a few years. Then he went to a community college for two years and transferred into a regular university to major in information systems management. Graduating magna cum laude, he was elected to the Phi Kappa Phi Honor Society. He was an Eagle Scout, a coed soccer player, and a confident, well-liked young man.

What was he doing at The Lab School during those five long years before he began to read?

TOM'S CURRICULUM

While the slow, laborious process of reading readiness was being systematically taught to him, Tom's lively intellect was fully engaged;

his imagination was being challenged and stimulated. He was learning history, geography, and social studies—covering material from the Old Stone Age through the Renaissance to American history in a special Lab School program. He was encountering the literature of his own age and going way beyond it through Talking Books for the Blind and tapes in The Lab School Media Center. While he learned the difference between *b* and *d,* he was listening to *A Tale of Two Cities* by Charles Dickens. He was building a desk and a chair, a xylophone, a go-cart, and a six-foot boat in the woodwork shop—planning, measuring, and proceeding step-by-step to completion. (In order to bring home each tangible proof of his success, he had to teach another child how to do the same thing.)

He was playing rhythm instruments in music class, distinguishing high sounds from low ones, fast from slow, loud from soft. Tom was playing games that linked sounds to symbols. At the loud bang of a drum, he would pick up a red poker chip, at a soft tap a yellow one. When his music teacher held up a card with two red circles and a yellow one, Tom could "read" it to mean "loud-loud-soft" and play those sounds on the drum himself. Tom's music program was challenging and fun for him. Every bit of it was planned to teach him reading readiness skills.

Always on the move, Tom was constantly crashing into doors or tripping up the stairs—partly because he was impulsive and didn't look where he was going, partly because he did not judge the space around him properly. Like a child of two or three on unfamiliar turf, seven-year-old Tom had no sense of what was in front of him, behind him, or above or below him, nor could he tell left from right.

To help Tom understand his own location in space, his dance teacher at The Lab School (a professional dancer with his own company) always made sure that Tom—like his classmates—began each exercise at an appointed place against the wall so he was clear about his own point of departure. Similarly Tom's classroom teacher marked the space around his desk with wide masking tape on the floor so he could see where "in front of the desk" or "beside the desk" really was.

Tom's well-formed body was a stranger to him. He had no sense of its parts or how they connected. Without being able to identify arms, legs, head, or back, he could not make them work as a unit. In dance class, he had to isolate his hands and feet separately to become a puppet like Pinocchio. He learned to use his arms and legs as though they were pulled by imaginary strings. In front of a silhouette screen, he had great fun stylizing his movements and guessing what the movements of his classmates represented. As he grew older and the dance exercises became more sophisticated, he moved as part of the gang in *West Side Story,* isolating body parts and unifying them within a dramatic and exciting framework. From the beginning, imaginative obstacle courses demanded that Tom look carefully in front of him, judge distances, and plan the movements of his body.

The ancient Greeks knew that educating the body as well as the mind led to an educated citizenry, yet we have eliminated much of the work with the body from our elementary schools. Few schools have dance or drama in their curriculum. We know that the ordering of the body leads to organization in the mind. It is imperative for the progress of learning disabled children that great attention be paid to teaching organization of their movements, which will help organize their minds.

As Tom began to plan better and move more efficiently, his use of paper space in the classroom also improved. The orderly placement of his math problems on a page was a welcome change from the previous scramble, with all the problems usually crowded down one side of the page. He was able to follow directions such as, "Write your name in the upper left-hand corner of the page."

In graphic arts class, Tom printed repetitive designs, always proceeding from left to right and establishing order. Collage helped him to organize visual experiences and to separate foreground from background.

Tom learned the tools of drama with puppets, masks, hats, and other props. A radio station, a spaceship, and a restaurant were among the many settings. Tom could use words like *majestic* and *feeble* correctly, but he couldn't act the parts of a strong king and a weak king and show any difference between them. His drama teacher, an actress, helped him to isolate the main characteristics so he could exaggerate and communicate them by his walk, his gestures, his facial expression, and, in time, his voice. Learning disabled children have great difficulty organizing and integrating several actions at once—skills that, when worked on in drama class, can carry over to the classroom. Tom didn't look at words—and he didn't look at people. He couldn't decipher expressions of anger, sadness, or fear. He had to be taught this skill. It's difficult to size up a situation if you're a poor judge of size, shape, or direction. Through drama, Tom was focused on looking at people's faces, walks, and gestures and matching them to an emotion. The immature, egocentric child doesn't look at the reactions of others. Drama is an effective tool for teaching this skill.

In filmmaking, Tom's class made Super-8 films from their own scripts about slapstick characters who were jinxed or were mummies (wrapped in rolls of toilet paper) and who never knew what was going on, and about battles with a runaway alphabet trying to take over the children.

When Tom and two classmates decided to make a movie melodrama about a hero and a villain, the filmmaking teacher helped them to focus on the main point: the hero wins, and the villain is defeated. When the children started shooting the film in the park with three more classmates playing the hero, the heroine, and the villain, the professional filmmaker frequently reminded Tom to focus and frame, to keep his camera on the main action. The purpose of such constant attention to visual focus in filmmaking was to build more attention to visual detail in the reading program, to see the difference between *stick, stock,* and *stuck.*

The filmmaker had the children edit their own movie, organizing the sequences to make the action interesting, exciting, and under-standable. Their work required that they think out the thread of the story and decide what should be shown first, next, and last. The addition of music and sound effects and the animation of titles called for intense concentration and organization. (All of Tom's film titles were delightfully animated.)

In all the arts activities—in Logic Lab where games of logic and strategy were played, in the Media Center, in the academic clubs, and special classroom projects—Tom's reasoning, language, and general knowledge were developing at a fast clip.

CREATING AND REINFORCING ORDER

In every area and at every level, Tom was immersed in the learning of ORGANIZATION—the organization of his belongings, his time, his work space, his body, and above all, his mind. A system had to be created in his brain where all information could be slotted quickly and retrieved at will. What most children achieve automatically by school age and need never think twice about, Tom had to be taught step-by-step, over and over again.

Throughout the day at The Lab School, every activity had the purpose of creating and reinforcing order. Even while lining up to go from one room to another, the children represented the different days of the week or the months in order and formed the correct sequence in the line. Tom was constantly immersed in patterns and sequences, sorting and classifying information in dozens of different ways through all the arts. He continually was asked: "What comes first? What comes next? What comes last?" "Stop. Think. What are you going to do? Where do you begin?" "Make a picture in your mind to help you remember." "Look—then speak." "Listen—then react."

"Now plan." "Tom, this is what you just said. Is that what you meant to say?" or "Tom, this is what you just did. Is that what you meant to do?" Tom's teachers were providing him with the information that people can normally give to themselves—the monitoring that we do automatically. His teachers were continually asking Tom the questions they hoped he would learn to ask himself.

When Tom started to build his chair in the workshop, his teacher, a sculptor from the Corcoran School of Art, had him look at chairs and then pictures of chairs and then gave him a choice between making a straight chair or a rocking chair. The sculptor helped him to draw the straight chair that he chose. Since Tom could not visualize well, all the dimensions were measured against his own body. The teacher started him on each phase of the work and stopped him, helped him through the change from measuring to sawing, fitting pieces together, to hammering, to sanding, then painting. Together they rehearsed what must be done first, next, and last so that Tom thoroughly understood the parts that contributed to the whole and the order of procedure. The artist imposed the order and the limits that Tom needed until he could do it for himself. Like all the other arts programs in the school, this one was carefully structured for the child's success and pleasure. Anytime a learning disabled child can have the experience of competence, he is developing the confidence to try new things and take new risks.

Any good teaching is diagnostic. The nature of a child's mistakes, difficulties, and confusions point out to a skilled teacher the areas of development that are lagging. We gain diagnostic information by analyzing a child's approach to a task. With spelling, we need to notice the child's body in relation to the paper, his posture, how he holds a pencil, how quickly he writes, how he forms the letters, whether he scratches out or erases continually, sounds out every letter, closes his eyes and tries to see the letters and writes in the air first. We need to look at his face as well as at each hand, where he starts on the page, how much of the page he covers, at what point he becomes frustrated, and how he handles his distress.

THE ARTIST'S CONTRIBUTION

Often an artist can make important diagnostic observations that alert a classroom teacher or reading specialist to a particular difficulty or can confirm a previous diagnosis. A woodwork teacher–sculptor observed that a child who could not hit a nail on the head with a hammer could not line up his body in a position that made it possible for the eye and hand to work together; the same child could not focus on a printed page. When the sculptor shared his observations, the reading teacher recognized that the position of the child's body in relation to the task of reading (much less writing) interfered with what he saw, and she was able to help him find a position for his body that helped him focus.

The art teacher who discovered an eleven-year-old's confusion between the colors blue and purple, and his trouble in differentiating pink from tan, added another dimension to the classroom teacher's picture of the child who was stumped by all nuances and inferences in language and thinking. It is often said that learning disabled children can't understand subtleties. The drama teacher who observed that a ten-year-old child could not pretend to stir a pot and speak like a witch at the same time underlined the teacher's analysis that this child could not integrate several functions at once; he could manage one thing at a time, but other components must be added slowly. This actress identified which children could not focus on the main point and were continually lost in details.

A dance teacher found that four of his eleven-year-olds could not move backward. Their classroom teacher discovered that they were the same four who were unable to do subtraction. Together the dancer and the teacher recognized that these same four could not use the past tense in their language.

The music teacher listed all the children in her class who could not discriminate differences in pitch; the list tallied with those having auditory difficulty recognizing vowels. The musician found that some students were excellent in discriminating sounds but that they could not link sounds with visual symbols. In filmmaking, the children who had a hard time focusing the camera on a particular object and framing it in the viewfinder or who had trouble distinguishing foreground from background were all demonstrating visual perceptual difficulties. The filmmaker also identified the children who could not organize the content of their Super-8 film, when they edited it, as to which part came first, what should follow, and what came last. This observation agreed with the classroom teacher's diagnosis of sequencing difficulties for these particular children.

A child who cannot work easily in one art form but succeeds admirably in another is telling something significant about what he can do and indicating where his strengths and abilities lie. *An analysis of the art form in which he excels gives clues to the components needed for the child to learn most effectively.*

Although the arts at The Lab School have been used to ensure quality education and to teach academic readiness, they have sometimes unearthed artistic talents that become vocations or important leisure-time activities. One former Lab School student, now in his second year of college, is majoring in music, playing in the college orchestra, and making flutes on the side. Another is a drummer in a band. One is a high-school student known for his artwork and cartooning. Another high-school student is heading for the stage. Several others have continued their filmmaking for pleasure and profit.

Practicing artists, art therapists, and art teachers are all needed in the field of learning disabilities, and they are often willing to make their time and talent available. But they must have that unusual spark that is excited by the challenge of trying to reach and teach the children who puzzle most adults. When that spark is present, their unorthodox approaches, originality, and ability to create with whatever is on hand make them uniquely suited to teach children who defy usual school practices.

Artists working part-time in a school bring freshness and relief to regular teachers. Learning disabled children consume their teachers, as anybody who has dealt with them knows. One teacher cannot possibly give her best to these youngsters five hours a day, find time to develop individualized materials for each child, and use her resourcefulness to the fullest.

Educators and artists share many common goals. Joining together means a pooling of talent and techniques. When it passed the Education for All Handicapped Children Act in 1975, Congress intended that the arts should be an important part of the education of handicapped children. The Senate Committee on Labor and Public Welfare stated:

> *The use of the arts as a teaching tool for the handicapped has long been recognized as a viable, effective way, not only of teaching special skills, but also of reaching youngsters who had otherwise been unteachable. The Committee envisions that programs under this bill could well include an arts component and, indeed, urges that local educational agencies include the arts in programs for the handicapped under this Act. Such a program could cover both appreciation of the arts by the handicapped youngsters and the utilization of the arts as a teaching tool per se. [Senate Report 94-169]*

The developing of organization skills helps strengthen memory, which in turn helps language development. All the arts offer opportunities for the child to talk about what he is doing or expects to do; verbalization comes naturally in the arts. Drama works specifically on language. However, woodwork, the graphic arts, music, filmmaking, and dance can be taught in ways that make the children describe what they have done, tell the order in which they did it, and then summarize the experience. All the arts work on helping a child to visualize. Frequently a learning disabled child cannot create a picture in his mind—a picture of a toy, a product he wants to make, an experience he had. No wonder that it is hard for him to visualize letters and word configurations. To visualize helps a child to remember vocabulary, which helps his language development.

A child with part-whole confusion may become quickly fatigued while working on syllables of words in the classroom; but he may pick up energy and motivation in the music room as he taps out the syllables of a musical phrase with a different teacher. The child with poor auditory discrimination may find such intrinsic pleasure in linking color to sound that he is spurred on toward linking sounds to letters and the ultimate goal of reading.

At The Lab School, we have found that even straight academic content—mathematical functions, grammar, syntax, spelling—can be taught effectively to learning disabled children through the arts. A vowel can dance between two consonants. Computing methods can be "invented" to save a flock of sheep in a make-believe encampment of ancient Assyria. The whole social science curriculum of The Lab School is carried on through an academic club method that I designed in 1965 and that employs all of the arts.

THE ACADEMIC CLUB METHOD

When Tom first came to The Lab School, he joined the youngest children in the Caveman Club, never thinking of it as a social science class. He and his classmates met for fifty minutes every day in the dramatic setting of the "cave" (a basement storeroom where simple decorations and props made the make-believe come alive). The children wore their "wild animal skins" (lengths of leopard-print cloth), and they threw themselves with gusto into their roles, calling each other by their cave names. It was a perfect place for Tom (who was quite prehistoric himself in many ways!).

The Cavemen whispered a secret password to their teacher, the

Cave Lady or "Wise Elder," as they crept in order through the narrow entrance of the cave. (The vocabulary-building password might be *fossil* for a couple of weeks, until every child learned it.) The stylized entry warded off distractions and brought the children around the "fire" (flashlights covered with red material) fully focused and ready to begin. The Cavemen soaked up knowledge of archaeology, paleontology, toolmaking, and the formation of early societies through their own experience and involvement. For most of them, it was the best period of the day.

The following year, Tom's group was placed in the next developmental sequence in the Gods Club, where they were steeped in the mythology, history, lawmaking, and governing principles of ancient Egypt, Greece, and Rome. Pictures and symbols were beginning to have some meaning for Tom. He could enjoy studying hieroglyphics and practiced his own on papyrus. Developmentally he was ready for more work in symbols, patterns, and relationships. He liked being an all-powerful god, symbolizing wisdom or immortality or one of the elements of nature. In the third year, Tom's club tallied with his own love of adventure, mystery, miracles, and rituals. The Knights and Ladies of the Middle Ages Club was centered in a period when magic was truth; this was the time of chivalry, alchemy, feudalism, Beowulf, and King Arthur. Tom was so taken with the story of Beowulf that he and the rest of the group made a Super-8 film of the story, a combination of animation and acting set to rock-and-roll music.

A JUDGMENT ON HISTORY

Tom liked the Renaissance Club best, when he was around eleven, because that age of discovery and enlightenment matched the stage of his own development. Truth was the magic of the Renaissance. He relished learning how the council in Florence made decisions about ownership of property or declarations of war; Tom and his classmates examined the problem before the council, decided on the best course of action, and then compared their own judgments with the verdict of history. For example, centuries ago near the village of Voltera, ruled by Lorenzo de' Medici, then only nineteen years old, discovery was made of a metal called alum. When mined and processed, this metal could be used to keep dyes from washing out of wool cloth. But there developed a conflict over how to exploit the valuable new metal. Lorenzo wanted to run the mines himself and collect the profits directly. The villagers preferred to mine, process, and sell the alum themselves and send the revenues to Lorenzo. When the question was presented to Tom and his fellow council members, they debated it and voted to let the villagers run the mines. Then Tom and his classmates consulted the history books to see what had actually happened. Their teacher read the text to them. They found, much to their delight, that the real Council of Florence had voted just as they had, but Lorenzo took over the mines anyway. The children were furious, as no doubt the villagers of Voltera had been too. But delving further into history, they were somewhat mollified to find that Lorenzo learned from his youthful mistakes and in later life did not so easily defy the will of the council.

My son, a classmate of Tom, went to the National Gallery and told his father as they were leaving that he had just seen a painting by Lippi. "You know, Dad—Lippi, the Renaissance painter. One of the first guys to use perspective." His father asked him how he knew about perspective. "Oh, Mrs. Lorenzo de' Medici [as the children called the artist who taught the Renaissance Club] has us line up on the street and look at street lamps. When you're farther away the lamp is tiny and it's large when you're close and that's perspective. And we've seen it in pictures. Tom and I had a great time on that street." The Renaissance so profoundly affected him that he used his understanding as a basis for judgment on other matters. When we were off to a showing of Matisse paintings, he asked, "Would Lorenzo de' Medici have sponsored him? Then he must be a great artist!"

The fifth year, Tom was Galileo in the Philosophical Society in a room decorated to represent a timeless tavern. Great philosophers, such as Socrates, Newton, Locke, Diderot, Rousseau, and Voltaire, joined Galileo around the beat-up circular picnic table; each had a concrete object representing his main theme as a way to trigger memory. Voltaire carried a paper chain as a reminder of his belief that people had the right to break the chains of their own mental and political bondage; Galileo carried a pendulum as a reminder of his experimental investigations of natural laws that enlarged man's vision and conception of the universe. There was a pictorial time line on the wall, with each philosopher's period clearly represented. Each philosopher also had his geographical place marked with a flag on a large wall map. Each had his main ideas listed on a colorful poster, and each one gave a birthday party for himself, featuring food from his country. Galileo brought pizza on his day, and Voltaire (and his mother) produced a chocolate mousse for his.

The philosophers took great interest and enjoyment in learning how each one of them had influenced the founding fathers of America, seeing which of their ideas appeared in the thinking of Jefferson, Adams, Franklin, Madison, and Hamilton. Had Tom been in The Lab School this year, he would have been a museum curator. We replaced the Philosophical Society with the Living Museum of History, which reviews the studies of the previous four years, from the Old Stone Age up through the ancient civilizations, East and West, on to the Renaissance around 1492, then on to the great explorers of the 1500s and 1600s. This serves as preparation for the study of modern history. Our current student body has more severe language problems than previous years' students, and the Museum of History Club is a better vehicle for teaching them social studies and developing their language skills.

American history is always introduced in the sixth year, and its theme is derived from the special interests of the group. In different years, the children have been American Pioneers, American Explorers, American Revolutionaries, and American Immigrants. Tom and his buddies were fascinated with money, so I set up the American Industrialists Club. They studied how America's wealth was built up, who benefited and who lost out in the process, and how the accumulation of wealth affected the westward development of America. Tom, Mr. Du Pont, sat in the parlor car of a train moving across America with Rockefeller, Carnegie, Vanderbilt, Guggenheim, Ford, J. P. Morgan, Gould, and others. They not only counted their millions but studied the map to decide on investments and probed the life of early America to see how they had changed it. A historical period was evoked, as it was in the other academic clubs, painting a picture in Tom's mind.

In the junior high the next year, Tom was one of the orphans in the Charles Dickens Club, one day forced to eat "pretend" gruel and obey every command; another day he examined Victorian life and compared it with modern life. Oliver Twist, David Copperfield, Pip, and Scrooge became familiar friends because Tom heard these wondrous tales and experienced them.

In the junior high, clubs must adapt to teenage interests and take on new forms. Tom was in the Restaurant Program, the Commercial Enterprise Group, and the Corporation, where organization and life skills—such as cooking, keeping inventories, filling out forms, using the telephone, learning to be interviewed, and learning the different rights of employers and employees—were stressed.

When he was in the elementary school, Tom had been Agent 007 in the Secret Agents Club in The Lab School's six-week summer sessions. He learned reading readiness skills by detecting sounds, pairing fingerprints, discriminating among disguises and learning codes. He also enjoyed similar activities that made exciting use of distances, directions, and maps in the Pirates Club, and variants of both detective work and use of space in the Keystone

Cops Club. He learned math skills in the Storekeepers Club and the Carnival Club, and worked on expressive language in the Broadcasters Club.

Each Lab School summer session has a theme and clubs are designed to fit the theme. Each summer club has twelve youngsters. The clubs meet daily for an hour. In the winter curriculum, Tom followed a developmental sequence in history. They meet daily at The Lab School for forty-five minutes per session throughout the school year. Usually there are no more than eight to ten severely learning disabled students per club.

The club approach is designed to lure the child, to capture imagination and enthusiasm, to build on love of imaginary play, and to offer fun and success in learning by immersing the child in the atmosphere of a given historical period or plunging the child into the situation of a real-life experience.

THE DEVELOPMENT OF THE CLUB METHOD

I designed the academic club method based on the theory that we can teach children what they need to know through the very things that interest them most, what they like to do and want to do. The first questions to ask are: What do they need to know? What, specifically, am I aiming to teach them? The answer depends on the children being taught, but it can cover the entire range of academic subject matter and all forms of remedial work, including readiness and academic skills. The second set of questions is: What dramatic framework, what theme, will serve as a vehicle to convey what I want to teach? What will act as an enticing dramatic theme? This means searching out the special interests and concerns of the children. Then ask: What do they

do when they play? What do they talk about? What television programs do they watch?

I first recognized the power of this approach by watching one
child who was intelligent but failing at school. This child was not
unique; there were many others like him who didn't seem to learn at
school. Yet all of them were learning in one way or another at home. I
asked what was going on at home, in their backyards, and on the
streets. How were they learning there? From keen observation, it
became evident that they were learning a great deal through play,
through making things, by pretending, reenacting what they saw,
heard, and touched. They were learning through the arts, although
nobody called it that, using the arts to make sense out of all the things
that interested them, learning ways to organize their world and function in it. The arts were serving as supreme teaching tools. Children's
play is, in fact, serious learning, demanding their total involvement.

The idea of clubs grew out of a series of my three children's
birthday parties, all revolving around a main theme, such as secret
agents, pirates, Civil War heroes, or moon men, that created a mar-
velous environment for learning a whole world of academic skills.
One year we had an Indian party. All guests wore appropriate costumes, and all decorations conveyed American Indian life. Drumbeats
accompanied Indian games, such as "Follow the Tracks," table favors
were homemade Indian drums and feathered hats, and the birthday
cake I made was a recognizable tepee. My children and I spent weeks
preparing and planning for the party: reading about American Indians, listening to records, visiting museums, and looking at films,
slides, and photographs of Indian life. Our explorations covered
history, geography, government, science, art, music, dance, literature,
and drama. Choices for the celebration had to be made constantly, so
decision making was an important part of the experience.

When I designed a teaching approach of this sort, I chose the
word *club* carefully. It implies membership, belonging, ownership.
Clubs are groups where each person has a recognized place. There is

much room for individualization built into group activities in a club. By its very nature, a club is noncompartmentalized; the arts, the subject matter, the concepts, and the ideas all bear on one another, reinforce one another, and funnel toward the same objectives while the children are immersed in the dimensions of their play. Schools need to pick up on the ingenuity that children use in their play on the streets, in the backyards, and bring it into the classroom for serious academic purpose. Unfortunately, our Calvinist background seems to resist the idea that children can have fun while learning. When they have fun at school, parents—and sometimes teachers—worry that they are not learning. Parents of children who have been in academic clubs at The Lab School and elsewhere are converts; they are overwhelmed by how much their children learn. The club approach was first tried out in summer projects with children who were failing at school. It was then made the core of The Lab School social science curriculum. In the summer program, the academic clubs teach reading readiness, expressive language, and math skills. Other schools have seen the method work and have followed suit. The clubs can be developed with twenty-five youngsters in a club. Obviously learning disabled children need smaller groups for maximum impact.

PLANNING THE CLUBS

Any subject can be taught through a club. It is gently woven into a dramatic framework and approached through all the arts, literature, science, logic, history, geography, and civics. All the senses, the body, and the mind come alive in a club; creative problem solving is demanded from both teacher and students. Although the teaching may look very informal, academic objectives for a club are carefully programmed and continually reviewed. Club leaders plan their club activities with the greatest of care and keep files for future club leaders on available resources—museums, book lists, reference works—that they have discovered. They outline the basic concepts and objectives and plan precisely for the details of special projects. They build the necessary limits into their ingenious curricula so that the experience can be handled by these over-stimulated children. The academic step-by-step teaching is reflected in the ongoing reporting that is part of the club record-keeping procedure. The objectives, activities, materials used, and concepts and vocabulary presented, as well as comments on individual and group behavior, are also documented by the teacher in daily reports that are used constantly for reference.

An artist or teacher who becomes a club leader begins by immersing himself or herself in the topic—the literature that exists on an adult level, the artifacts of a historical period, the art, architecture, music, dance, drama, poetry. The teacher follows his or her own interests and builds on his or her own strengths, be they the graphic arts, music, or political science. The teacher studies in depth the history, geography, and civics of the topic and as much as possible includes some knowledge of the scientific discoveries, inventions, and innovations of the period. The club leader's experience, and thus the presentation, needs to be multisensory so the teacher can better convey the information through means other than speech. It is important that club leaders feel an excitement in this new learning experience for themselves, for this feeling is contagious and children respond with enthusiasm.

Every facet of a club is highly structured, which is just what a learning disabled child needs. The club's use of space, its setting, costumes, seating arrangements, its routines, rituals, badges, passwords, and "coming in and going out" behavior, predetermined by the dramatic framework, are designed to meet a child's need for order. Discipline is handled within the same framework; the Secret Agents Club would have "agent rules," run by the captain; an Indian tribe would respect "its elders"; the Storekeepers, with their employee cards, are hired by the manager. The Renaissance Councillors Club would use "council" discipline. Cavemen have rules for survival; Knights have a strict code of chivalry. Dramatic cover is provided not only for the teacher, the subject matter, and discipline but also for the child. As a Caveman or Zeus or Galileo or Mr. Du Pont, Tom could dare to experiment and risk failure with a courage that he was unable to muster in the regular classroom because it is not he who might fail but his character. (Children often do this with puppets too.)

The academic club method is designed to involve the children fully so that they, who cannot read and have opted out of learning, become full participants in their own education. Drama, which is central to the academic club method, helps to screen out distractions and achieve focus. The entry procedure focuses the child. The props and room decorations give a picture in the mind of the particular subject under study and keep the focus on the topic, triggering memory. For children who need help locating their own bodies in space, arranged seating is a blessing. A Secret Agent sits on the chair with his 007 number marked on it; an Egyptian god sits beside his column, which is decorated with his own hieroglyphics; a Medieval Knight sits on a pillow with his heraldic symbol on it; a Star Trekker mans his control panel; a Disc Jockey sits by his record. Language is developed through immersion in the topic, through being read to, through discussing projects, and always through the password as well as a vocal dismissal procedure.

Deep involvement is attained through the child's experiencing this total environment approach. A club draws on the full range of children's experiences and relates subject matter to their lives, relates the past to today's world, and relates cause to effect and planning to action. For the ordinary child without learning disabilities, the academic club method is sheer pleasure in learning, and all kinds of research, reading, and writing activities can be built into it. A club works as well in a regular classroom as in special classes, and it can run for as little as a month or as long as a year. Brothers and sisters of Lab School children express great jealousy that The Lab School has academic clubs and their school does not. Not only does it look like fun to them, but their brother or sister knows so much sophisticated material.

Clubs can be run by regular staff or by part-time artists and teachers who come in to teach one hour a day. Parents or university students can serve as aides. All children, and especially learning disabled children, can be taught through things that they like to do and want to do, as well as through the exercises they need that require plain hard work. They can learn almost any subject an adult understands in depth. All the time they can be given readiness training. A profound understanding by artists and teachers of the underlying skills needed for reading, writing, spelling, arithmetic, language development, and abstract thinking will lead to success. These foundations must then be programmed systematically into every area of a child's life throughout the day. The whole panoply of art forms can be used as teaching tools for academic readiness. Starting in the preschool and continuing throughout education, the arts can teach skills that are needed in conjunction with the main work of the classroom.

The arts were central to Tom's schooling as they have been to all other Lab School students since 1967. In the academic clubs, in art, crafts, woodwork, dance, drama, music, and filmmaking, Tom was learning the very readiness and academic skills that he needed to help him forge ahead as a student. For the most part, he was a total participant, actively engaged in each endeavor and having fun. At the same time he was learning art forms that he could enjoy and appreciate. He was experiencing the sense of mastery that breeds the confidence to move on. All the arts were offering him information and insights that he could carry with him on his journey into knowledge. Tom is now happily married and works as a computer programmer and analyst for a large, well-known corporation.

ELEVEN

PARENTS: THEIR CONCERNS AND FEELINGS

Parents of children with learning disabilities often feel helpless and incompetent. There are no simple answers, formulas, or panaceas for them. No one product or one way of behaving for them to follow can fix what's wrong.

Some people, when they feel very uncertain,
give the appearance of being very certain.
Some people, when they feel helpless,
are attacking,
angry,
defensive,
mute,
and they give the appearance of being uncaring or
unhelpful.

A severely learning disabled child can affect husband-wife and a whole host of other family relationships. The following letter from a parent lets us view some of the pain that a family can feel. Professionals need to keep enough in touch with that pain to avoid increasing it; it is important to seek ways to lighten the load and give true support to parents.

July 17

Dearest Joan,

I can't tell you how much I'm looking forward to your visit—it's been eight years since the last one. I'm glad your family is growing well—I wish I could say the same.

Henry is almost nine, and I feel ninety. You remember how sick he was as a baby when you were here last? Well, he kept that up for two years—colds, croup, earaches, bronchitis—never properly getting over one before he came down with another. It seems like he never had time to just plain grow like other children. Bill was an angel—he did extra things with Rosie while I coped with Henry.

Once he walked, Henry always looked battered because he kept falling. I used to carry a silver fifty-cent piece to press on his bumps to keep them from turning black and blue. He walked and talked at the normal age, like Rosie, but he was different. There was a pain deep inside me that just ached for this child— and it still does. Everything seemed so hard for Henry, though he was full of smiles and spark. Too much spark. He was everywhere and into everything—still is. I could lose him in a flash. One time I ran upstairs to get a clean pair of pants, and, when I came down, the front door was open and Henry was in the middle of the street with a police car stopped and a policeman about to pick him up and look for the right house! Now he climbs way up high in trees and can't get down, and it terrifies me.

For eight years, Joanie, I've lived with a pit-of-the-stomach fear that something will happen to him. It's a desperate feeling

of "Oh my God—what will go wrong next?" I dread every time
the phone rings. Bill's folks say, "A few good spankings will set
him straight." Mother says I just need patience. Dad says,
"What are you trying to do—turn him into a sissy? He's all
boy." I'm trying everything I know how to do. I'm exhausted
from trying. But when I take Henry out, people look at me
askance and say, "Lady, do something about this child."

His nursery school teacher said I babied him because he
couldn't button or zip, and his clothes were forever falling off.
His kindergarten teacher said I should discipline him more
because he was too lazy to learn his letters and numbers. His
first-grade teacher called one parent conference after another. I
tried to help Henry sit still and learn his letters. At the same
time, Rosie complained that I was never that easy on her, and
she hassled Henry half to death, telling him, "Just try, Henry.
You're not trying!" Bill and Rosie and the neighbors all told me
I spoiled him, so I tried to be tougher. I took away the TV, which
was the only thing he enjoyed, but he cried all the time and
seemed more babyish than ever. I couldn't make him be more
independent because he had so little to be independent with!

The pediatrician says not to worry; he's a "late bloomer."
The eye doctor says he sees well. The Hearing Society gave some
routine tests at school and tried to tell me he was deaf—and it
took three ear specialists and an audiologist to prove that he
wasn't. Now we've been sent to a psychiatrist who makes both
Bill and me feel like the most inadequate parents in the world.
He's asking us if our marriage is okay, and I sometimes wonder
if it is! We've stopped going out or seeing friends. Henry is
repeating second grade, and Bill has a session with him every
night because he says I mollycoddle him. He shuts the door but I
hear his voice getting louder and more impatient, then Henry
crying and the books being slammed down on the table—and I
wonder if our life will ever be good again.

I'm angry. Joanie, I hate the world for doing this to us. I wish we could just pick up Henry, get on a boat, and take him clear away from it all. Do you understand that we love this handsome little boy and we don't know what to do? He doesn't sit still and he can't do his schoolwork. And yet he talks so intelligently (such a big vocabulary!), and he describes things wonderfully. He is intelligent. Do you know he's called "dumbhead," "retard," "spaz" by the other children! I don't know which of us is crying more—Henry or me. Bill is carrying so much responsibility at the office that I try not to burden him with too much of this.

It will be so good to have you to talk to, and I'll try to make your visit a good one. I promise.

Love,
Sue

Henry's mother feels:

Drained
Blamed
Guilty
Helpless
Overwhelmed
Confused
Hurt
Anxious
Uncertain
Attacked
Afraid
Almost all parents hurt when their children hurt.

Parents of children with learning disabilities are very apt to catch their youngsters' emotions. Feelings are as contagious as a cold. When their child feels depressed, they do too. When their child comes in brimming with anxiety, before they realize it, they too are anxious. Or perhaps they sense the deep injustice their child feels—the rage and the fury. We all tend to overidentify with our children and feel their bruises with them. When the child is failing at school, when he is being teased and bullied, when he is friendless or lonely, the hurt that a parent feels is almost unbearable. Sometimes a parent will take on the child's feelings, mix them with his or her own sense of the world's injustice, and then wildly overreact on his behalf. The parent knows from his child's gestures, the way he walks, the manner in which he enters the car, the way he asks what's for dinner, how school went that day. The parent of the learning disabled child, so worried anyway about his day at school, will attend even more to the youngster's demeanor.

A mother tends to be home more than a father is. She becomes more involved in the daily ups and downs; she has to cope more with the instant frustrations, the anger, and the sadness. She worries constantly. The learning disabled youngster has so many defeats that she tends to feel bad about herself, and the person on the front line, probably her mother, feels defeated too. Unfortunately a number of the professionals she goes to for help can make her feel worse.

A father may not come home until dinnertime, so he doesn't see the child so much. It's usual that at first he feels that his wife is exaggerating the child's difficulties and that she's overconcerned. Then it's typical for a father to feel that stricter controls, more rewards and punishments, and harder work will take care of the situation. When they don't and when the specter of learning disabilities raises its head, the father may have more difficulty than the mother in accepting it—particularly if a son is in trouble. The dreams of achievement, Little League, a better livelihood than his, and all the unmet hopes he had go into a father's pain. The defects of the child overwhelm many fathers (and plenty of mothers too), and they too feel defective.

A significant number of disabled youngsters are adopted. Presumably they were affected by maternal malnutrition, poor maternal care, not enough oxygen at birth, and many other such reasons. Their parents, who have suffered the anguish of not being able to conceive a child themselves, hurt even more when faced with the child's defects; they tend to feel even more inadequate. Sometimes, however, they feel less guilt because they did not give birth to the youngster and do not have to torment themselves looking for causes. When people are hurt, they react in different ways. They may eat a lot, or drink a lot; some work a lot or fight; others pity themselves or withdraw. And, worst, some reject what is hurting them.

Rejection can take many forms when the hurt is caused by a child: too little care, too much care, too little concern, too much concern. Pain makes people anxious and sometimes unreasonable. A whole lifetime of resentments can be dumped on a child. Fear for the future of a child can loom threateningly large and be dumped on the child. Most parents of learning disabled children have anxieties that are realistically based on their day-to-day experience. Parents frequently can't anticipate the behavior of their learning disabled child; they can't explain it in the light of their own childhood experience or their understanding of their other children. Since they don't know what to expect, they remain anxious and off balance.

ANXIETY AND OVERREACTION

Eleven-year-old Max was late coming home from school one day. Every other time he had been late, something disastrous had happened: he had gotten lost, had fallen down and been hurt, had gotten into a fight, or had been bullied by a group of children. His mother, nervous, was worried that there was an accident because Max didn't always look when he crossed the street. Then she heard an ambulance siren and stood frozen to the spot. A moment later she was running fearfully into the street, only to see Max ambling happily along,

tenderly stroking a wounded bird. She exploded at him. Max yelled a
bad word at her and stomped off with his bird while all the neighbors
watched. This sort of episode happens to many parents, but with a
learning disabled or ADHD child it happens more often, more in-
tensely, and for a longer period of time.

Parents' anxieties are just as catching as a child's and may cause a
youngster who hasn't been particularly worried about himself to
become suddenly terrified that something is dreadfully wrong with
him. A sudden increase in a child's anxiety may reflect a sudden
increase in his parents' anxiety. Professionals need to note not only
the child's anxiety and the form it takes but how parental anxiety is
expressed. The number of phone calls to the school, the number of
requests for appointments, the quality of the voice, and changes in
appearance are all signals.

A parent's overreaction to an admittedly uncomfortable or un-
pleasant situation can increase a child's worry about himself by leaps
and bounds. One vacation morning, ten-year-old Patrick woke early
and went down to the hotel dining room ahead of his parents. He
asked the waitress what was for breakfast.

"Read the menu," she replied curtly.

"Do you have scrambled eggs?" he pursued.

"What's the matter with you!" she snapped. "Can't you read the
menu, a great big boy like you? My, you're lazy! Kids today expect the
world to do everything for them. Now, just open your eyes, young
man, and read the menu!"

Patrick could not read the menu. His face was pale and tear-
stained when his mother joined him a few minutes later. He didn't
want to tell her what had happened, but when she coaxed the story
from him, she was absolutely furious. Over Patrick's protests, she
bawled out the waitress and called the manager. Patrick was mortified,
and his half-formed doubts about himself were devastatingly con-
firmed by his mother's overprotective overreaction. Patrick ran to his
room, locked the door, and refused to come out.

Another mother might never have given Patrick the freedom to go down to the dining room alone and take his chances with a bad-tempered waitress. She would have made certain that each step of his day was planned, made fully manageable to him, and supervised. By providing the organization and foresight that he lacked himself, by buffering him against the insensitivity of other adults or the cruelty of other children, by taking over, she could easily have created a world for him in which he had no initiative, no privacy, and no opportunity to make his own decisions. Teachers and doctors call this mother "intrusive." With the best of intentions, she leaves no room for a child to develop his own personality; she tries to absorb all of the child's problems and prolongs his infantilism. This damaging kind of emotional overprotection must not be confused with the well-prepared structure and organization that all learning disabled children need. A different mother might simply have said to Patrick, "Well, I wonder what happened to that lady today that made her take it out on you. Next time, tell a cranky lady like that, 'Look, I have reading problems and someday I'll be able to read, but I can't right now.' "

It's hard enough for parents to acknowledge that they have a learning disabled child; for some it becomes an almost overwhelming tragedy. This seems to be particularly true of families who are highly intellectual and whose world is tied up in abstractions—and the child is left out. It is often true of parents who are authors, journalists, or playwrights, whose lives depend on writing, whose pleasure lies in books, and who see their child excluded from the world of literature and words. It is true, frequently, of educators whose lives are devoted to academic excellence, who admire scholarship and value degrees, who feel that fate has slammed the door on their child's fulfillment. It seems especially hard for these families to accept the child at her own level, to nurture the areas of her intellect and imagination that are not defective, and to enjoy her for the qualities that lie outside her mind.

The problem seems especially poignant for the family of twins, where one twin is fine and a constant reminder of what the learning disabled one might have been. Parents suffer in a special way when their learning disabled child is the eldest one, and they find themselves holding the younger children back, trying to instill in them the need for respect for the eldest one, trying to gain time for the learning disabled one before he is inevitably overtaken and surpassed by the brothers and sisters. It is just as hard, in another way, when the learning disabled child is the middle one, the odd man out, surrounded and surpassed academically on both sides. Parents feel a special ache when their last child is learning disabled. In some ways, it is hardest for parents to bear when he is their only child, the repository of all their hopes and dreams. It is almost irresistible to push him a little more, tutor him a little longer, and urge him to try harder. Sometimes parents try consciously to avoid putting pressure on the child without realizing that the shape, the pace, and the tension of their lives are themselves a form of pressure.

THE FEELINGS OF BROTHERS AND SISTERS

A learning disabled child can provoke intense emotions in his brothers and sisters and complicate their lives in ways that they will inevitably resent at times. They had wanted a perfect brother or sister whom they could be proud of and stand with, shoulder to shoulder, against the world. Instead they are in the position of always having to explain the invisibly disabled child to other children. Just as parents are blamed for the unacceptable behavior of their learning disabled child by neighbors and shopkeepers, so brothers and sisters are often held responsible by their peers. A youngster may feel very resentful at being labeled "Weirdo's sister," or at having a child she scarcely knows come up and say, "Hey, do you know what your brother did?" or "Is your sister dumb or something? She can't read!"

Professionals need to know that the other children in a family may feel neglected, and they may envy the learning disabled child for the extra time and attention she gets from their parents. Her illnesses, her school problems, her messiness, and her incompetence may appear to brothers and sisters as an unfair source of privilege. They don't see that their mother makes concessions to the learning disabled child at certain times so that frustrations and commotion can be avoided, so dinner can be enjoyed, and the whole family can be at peace together.

They may feel put upon when they are urged to include the learning disabled sibling in their play and their free-time activities. She has few friends of her own, and it is natural for parents to seek occasional relief, to expect cooperation and a sharing of responsibility from their other children. But she can be such a burden! They have to watch her every minute to see she doesn't hurt herself, destroy someone else's possessions, or disappear. She wrecks any hope of making new friends that day. They can't go far or move fast. Or little sister may be perfectly behaved, but she doesn't understand the simplest things and they have to spend so much time explaining.

They may feel mean and guilty for feeling this way because they really do love their brother or sister. They care deeply about her underneath the irritations. It's a rare family where the siblings are not extraordinarily understanding at times and where they don't act appropriately in emergencies. We can't expect more. They must come to terms with the problem in much the same way their parents do.

Parents go through stages with their normal-looking, intelligent child who doesn't learn or behave as other children his age do.

It's a shock to see things going wrong.

It's a shock to hear that all is not well.

It's a shock to have to face up to these difficulties.

It's easier to deny the problem, and it's normal to begin with that reaction. Professionals must be aware that parents must face a whole gamut of emotions before they can grapple effectively with the stark

truth that their child has learning disabilities. There is no set order to
these feelings. Usually they start with denial and, most often, end with
acceptance and hope.

Denial

My child doesn't really have anything
    wrong with him.
He only needs more time, more under-
    standing neighbors, a better teacher,
    a better school.
These people don't understand him.
He's just the way I was.
There's nothing basically wrong.

> *Flight*
>
> These doctors jump to conclusions.
> We're going to see another specialist.
> They're only out to make money with
>   more tests and more examinations.
> They probably get a kickback from the
>   other doctors they recommend.
> We have to fly to the east [or the west].
> There's a new specialist with a good
>   reputation.

Isolation

Why doesn't anyone care?
Nobody seems to understand.
Why can't they make allowances?
He's much more interesting and unique
    than most other children.

> *Guilt*
>
> Why me?
> What did I do to him?
> Why is God punishing me?

How could I have made life better for
   him?

If only I hadn't let him bump his head.

If only I had kept him from catching
   measles.

If only I had played with him more.

If only I had been more strict.

If only I had talked with him more.

Anger

Doctors don't know anything! They
   should have caught it earlier!

That teacher is out of her mind!

These psychologists are for the birds!

I hate this neighborhood!

That child makes a monkey out of me!

Blame

You baby him.

You're the one who spoils him.

You don't make him take responsibility.

We never had anything like this on my
   side of the family!

This child is just perverse.

Fear

Maybe it's worse than they say.

Is he retarded and they won't tell me?

Is it a progressive disease?

Will he ever be able to marry? Have
   children? Hold a job?

Envy

Look at those other kids.

They don't know how lucky they are.

Everything comes easy to them.

How did they become so popular?

We're better parents.

It's not fair!

Bargaining

Maybe he'll be okay if we move.

Maybe he'll do fine in third grade.

Maybe if we stay home more he'll be okay.

Maybe if we send him to camp he'll shape up.

Maybe if I work with him every night he'll be okay.

Maybe if he goes to visit his grandparents he'll pick up.

Maybe if . . .

I'll do anything to help him.

Oh God, what can I do?

Maybe if . . .

Depression

I've failed him.

I'm no good.

No wonder he can't make it.

I can't either.

The world's no good.

I'm no good.

There's no hope.

Mourning

Think what could have been.

He might have . . .

Acceptance and hope

Okay.

So he's got learning disabilities.

What can I do to help?

How can I make him feel better about himself?

What are his strengths?

What are his interests?

We'll make it!

It will just take time and some concerted efforts.

When parents recognize that their child has learning disabilities, they have the same choices as the child: to pity themselves or to do the best with what the child has and work hard at it.

Most learning disabled youngsters grow up to be achievers. Many other youngsters never excel in reading, and a huge number are poor spellers, but they still become successful in business, mechanical fields, architecture, the arts, and many other occupations. Some are lawyers. A number of them become teachers. Some become exceptionally creative, imaginative problem solvers (while others, of course, do not). Some have become doctors, scientists, inventors, or generals. Bruce Jenner, athlete; Harvey Cushing, brain surgeon; Thomas Edison, inventor; Paul Ehrlich, bacteriologist; Whoopi Goldberg, actress; William James, psychologist; Wendy Wasserstein, playwright; President Woodrow Wilson; Vice President Nelson Rockefeller; Cher, singer/actress; General George S. Patton— all these famous men and women are known to have suffered from one or more learning disabilities that they overcame, compensated for, or learned to live with in adulthood. Artists such as Auguste Rodin, Leonardo da Vinci, poet Amy Lowell and Danish storyteller Hans Christian Andersen were also thought to be learning disabled.

DIAGNOSING LEARNING DISABILITIES

Today there is great hope that a learning disabled child will be able to function effectively in our society. More parents, as well as professionals, are becoming alert to the problems of the learning disabled child earlier in the child's life. In the past, a youngster's problems would not be recognized until the sixth grade unless they were very severe or unless they were combined with disruptive behavior. Now they are likely to be noticed in the first, second, or third grade, and it certainly should be no later. Most services are becoming available to both the children and their families.

There are pockets of ignorance all over the country. Parents should be encouraged to seek help from the Learning Disabilities Association of America (formerly ACLD) which has branches all over the nation. (For other organizations, see appendix 4).

Learning Disabilities Association of America (LDA) (formerly ACLD)

For parents, teachers, and professionals.

Purpose: To serve as a national membership organization of professionals and parents focused on advancing the education and well-being of children and adults with learning disabilities. Free information is available, which includes a listing of state learning disability associations and a bibliography of resources.

Location: Find the organization nearest to where you live by writing to LDA, 4156 Library Road, Pittsburgh, PA 15234. (412) 341-1515.

The Council for Exceptional Children (CEC)

For administrators, teachers, therapists, clinicians, students, and other interested persons.

Purpose: To provide an information center for general and specific information on learning disabilities and to publish information.

Location: CEC, 1920 Association Drive, Reston, VA 22091. (703) 620-3660.

The Orton Dyslexia Society (ODS)

For parents and professionals.

Purpose: To provide leadership in dyslexia-related language problems, research, and publications through a membership organization.

Location: ODS, 8600 La Salle Road, Chester Building, Suite 382,
             Towson, MD 21204. (800) 222-3123 or (410) 296-0232.

Children with Attention Deficit Disorder (CHADD)

For parents of children with attention deficit disorder.

Purpose: To offer support groups for parents who have children
             with attention deficit disorder (ADD) through its 215
             chapters across the country.

Location: CHADD, 499 N.W. 70th Avenue, Suite 308, Plantation,
             FL 33317. (305) 587-3700.

National Center for Learning Disabilities (NCLD)

For parents, educators, physicians, nurses, and mental health workers
in the United States and abroad.

Purpose: To increase awareness about learning disabilities through
             publications, *Their World* and *NCLD Guides*, grants, and
             legislative advocacy.

Location: NCLD, 381 Park Avenue South, Suite 1420, New York,
             NY 10016. (212) 545-7510.

Parents need information, as well as reassurance, about learning
disabilities. There are many good books that can clarify the complicated problems of this child who is so deceptive in terms of what he
can and cannot do. (See appendix 2.)

If a child is not doing well in school by second grade and shows
many of the traits I have described, it may be worthwhile to seek help
from the school system. Under the IDEA legislation, the states are
mandated to provide the proper education for each child with a
disability and this includes identifying them. The schools will have
psychologists do the testing. If parents are dissatisfied, they should be
encouraged to find a second opinion. Sometimes it helps to hear the
same opinion twice or have it explained more in depth; occasionally
there is a difference in opinion. If parents are still not satisfied, they

should find the diagnostic center near them that knows the most about learning disabilities and have the child tested there. Help in finding such a service might come from their nearest LDA chapter or the Orton Dyslexia Society.

If no diagnostic center is close by, they should find a psychologist whose specialty is testing and who knows the manifestations of learning disabilities. The results must be interpreted to them in detail. Here are some of the questions they should ask:

What are my child's strengths?

What are my child's weaknesses?

How much disparity is there between the two?

Is any further testing by medical specialists needed?

Is a neurological examination advised?

Will educational treatment alone be enough?

Does my child need a special class or special school?

Does my child need a tutor?

Does my child need an occupational therapist?

Does my child need a speech therapist?

Does my child, or do we as a total family, need psychological counseling?

Does my child need medication?

Which suggestion has top priority? And why?

What can the school do? And how can we tell them what to do?

What can we as parents do?

ORGANIZING THE CHILD'S LIFE

Professionals need to give to parents of learning disabled children advice about home management so they can provide structure in the child's life—order in his space and sequencing in his time. Everything in his room needs a place. If there are not too many things, it is easier to have a clear place where each thing can be put away. Shelves are often preferable to drawers because a child can see things in their proper places rather than having to visualize what is in a drawer. Parents need to know that structure can be introduced by making the child fully familiar with the parts of each of his usual routines—what comes first, next, and last. Less common events, like excursions, are explained by steps: "First we'll go to the store in the car; we'll buy the groceries at the store; then we'll stop at Aunt Ruth's house to say hello; then we will drive home again."

Parents need to know that it helps the child if the usual routines of the day occur at regular times, without too much deviation. It is worth the effort to keep mealtimes and bedtime as consistent as possible. Yet parents must not feel guilty for the occasional changes that have to take place in terms of the rhythm of the total family, outside demands, and emergencies.

Parents must learn that they not only have to take over the organization of space and time for the child until the child has the tools to do it, but they also have to be aware of how impossible democratic choices are for this child. "But I want him to think for himself!" is the typical response. "I don't want to run an autocratic family. That's against my principles." They must realize that just as structure gives the child a sense of security and safety in his disordered world, organizing his choices for him is allowing him to function. Only slowly is the child prepared for being a participant in a democracy and for taking the risks entailed.

The child's choices are best kept at a minimum, since the child's indiscriminate reactions prevent him from sorting out alternatives. At first a parent has to make all the choices, but the child can learn to handle limited choices even though many alternatives may still confuse him. If, when he is getting dressed, he is asked, "Would you prefer to wear your red soccer shirt or your blue T-shirt today?" he will probably be able to make a clear decision, whereas the question "What shirt do you want to wear today?" may produce total inaction or a tantrum.

Getting dressed is a struggle for many learning disabled children not only because of the choices involved but because of a need for sequencing and order. Here professionals need to help parents to place themselves in the place of the child who is trying to do the task. What steps are involved in putting on a pair of socks? In what order do the steps have to take place? What is involved in threading a belt through the loops on a pair of pants? What skills are needed?

STRUCTURING THE CHILD'S BEHAVIOR

Everyday behavior also requires structure. A learning disabled child needs to know more precisely than other children exactly what is expected of her. Her parents have to set clear limits for her and let her know what is acceptable and what is not, patiently but firmly, over and over again. Parents must learn that they have to structure the way they talk to her, using few words rather than many, being very specific when they give her instructions. "Put your puzzle back on the shelf now" will bring better results than "It's time to put your things away." Instructions that are given step-by-step are easier to follow than several instructions given all at once. "Go wash your face," followed by, "And now brush your teeth," followed by, "Now go get your pajamas on," will succeed, whereas "Run along and get your face washed and your teeth brushed and come back down when you have your pajamas on" will result only in confusion.

Normally parents watch a child go from solo play to parallel play to playing with one friend to playing with others and becoming part of a group. It is a natural process that we all take for granted, with occasional reminders: "You don't treat your friend like that. You let him go first in your house. You go first in his house. You serve your guest first." Professionals need to help parents recognize that with the learning disabled child, the way to play with another youngster must often be explicitly taught. Because of immaturity, a learning disabled child often cannot play in groups until he is much older than other children. In this case, parents need to provide imaginative and unusual playthings to entice other youngsters to come over and play and then structure the games that the children play together.

With careful forethought, parents need to plan for their learning disabled child to experience success. Sometimes they have to step in and save face for him when defeat or humiliation seems unavoidable. When he starts a project, it is important for his parents to hold his attention span through each step long enough to get him to finish the job and once more demonstrate to him that he can succeed. Leisure time, homework, and long-term projects are particularly demanding of a parent's imagination and patience. Professionals need to give parents as much assistance as possible in talking about these problems and brainstorming on how each particular family can best meet the child's needs.

Planning, foreseeing outcomes, avoiding debacles, applying a child's emotional brakes for him, providing structure in all areas—these take great stamina and perseverance. Parents of learning disabled children often find that they need more sleep than normal in order to keep their energy and equilibrium at a high level of efficiency. They need as much praise, as little unconstructive criticism, as many helpful hints as possible.

DEALING WITH AN ANGRY CHILD

With all the frustrations they experience, children with learning disabilities tend to feel angry at times. Parents can understand why they are angry but can also find their anger infuriating.

Tactics That Don't Work in the Long Run
use of force
use of threats that won't be carried out
shouting, screaming, yelling

lecturing and pointing fingers at them

making sweeping generalizations such as "You always . . . You never . . ." etc.

withholding affection

trying to reason with a child who is out of control

being a bully

using the silent treatment

dredging up every grievance from the past

making dire predictions about the future ("You will never be able . . .")

ripping up a child's work (equal to ripping up the child)

nagging incessantly

shaming them in front of others

setting a trap to catch a child in a lie to prove a point ("I talked with the gym teacher and you weren't good today.")

imposing excessive guilt ("You're killing me.")

scorekeeping ("That's the 47th time you yelled this week.")

sarcasm

comparing with successful siblings/friends

carrying on any restriction or punishment for too long

using anger to deal with anger

POSITIVE REINFORCEMENT CHANGES BEHAVIOR.
NEGATIVE REINFORCEMENT ONLY STOPS BEHAVIOR.
IT DOESN'T CHANGE BEHAVIOR.

Some Phrases to Help Parents Deal with Their Child's Anger

It's okay to be angry. It's what you do with it that counts.

I understand your being angry. I would be too if someone called me names. But it's the way you expressed it that was not okay.

What could you have done instead? What could you have said instead?

What other options did you have?

Do you know when you're angry? Do you know when it's coming on, before you get out of control?

*Do you know what made you feel angry? Then you can do
    something about it.*
Choose your battles carefully.
*Was it a big important issue or a little one? If it's a big issue, then
    you need to give it all your energy. Fight small battles with
    small weapons.*

SEEKING PROFESSIONAL HELP

All children need as much positive reinforcement for their good
efforts as they can get. They need to be rewarded with praise, a
gesture, or some other form of approval whenever they succeed. But
even the best parents cannot salvage the ego of a child who has failed
again and again in school, in the neighborhood, and on the athletic
field. Often a tutor, a special class, or a special school is necessary to
provide the therapy needed to make this child feel competent, to show
him that he is capable of doing something about himself, that he is the
master of his own destiny.

The defeat that is so often met by a learning disabled child can
make it hard for the child to develop a strong sense of self, and
sometimes it is necessary for parents to consult a psychologist or
psychiatrist. These professionals can help build the ego strength so
vitally needed for every child's development. Sometimes play therapy,
sometimes an individual therapist who talks with the child, sometimes group therapy can help. These methods can help the parents too
to cope with the reality of living with learning disabilities. The fears,
anger, guilt, and anxiety suffered by both the child and the parents can
become better understood and thereby eased. When a child feels
victimized by learning disabilities, or seems totally unmanageable or
very depressed, it is frequently necessary to consult a professional

counselor. To locate this person, one might begin by checking with the local Learning Disabilities Association.

Many psychologists and psychiatrists, even today, do not know much about learning disabilities. Parents need to be made aware of this situation because a learning disabled child needs structure in his therapy just as much as he needs it in other areas of his life. Parents can find out if a therapist understands the unique problems of learning disabled youngsters by asking questions like the following ones:

What do you look for to decide whether a learning disabled child needs therapy?

How would you explain the purpose of therapy to a learning disabled child?

How do you work with the child who has trouble expressing himself in words?

What can you do with a child who can't focus his attention?

Is it effective to work with a child without working with his parents?

How do you see the relationship of his low self-esteem to his learning disabilities?

Under what conditions do you recommend medication?

Can you explain to me the relationship of learning disabilities to my child's social problems?

For an evaluation, the therapist meets with the parents once or twice to take down the history and to understand their concerns, has one or two sessions with the child, and then sets up an interpretive session with the parents. After the diagnostic evaluation, parents have a right to ask the therapist or counselor some questions that will give them an impression of how he or she views their child and to see if the evaluation meshes with their own observations. Some new information should be provided from the evaluation, but they should also be

able to recognize their own child. Here are some questions they might
ask at this time:

> *Can you tell us what you see as our child's strengths and*
>   *weaknesses?*
> *What would be realistic goals for our child at this time?*
> *How can therapy help achieve the goals you describe?*
> *How would you explain this to our child? How would you help*
>   *him understand what's wrong and why he needs help?*

A therapist qualified to work with a learning disabled child must
be able to answer questions like these in clear, simple terms because he
will be dealing with a child who has difficulty in processing language.
If the therapist is vague, obscure, or full of technical jargon not
understandable to the parents, quite likely he will not be effective with
the child either. Like teachers, parents often feel that they are not
supposed to understand readily what a therapist is aiming to do, the
process he's using, and how he feels the therapy is going. Therapy
involves the art of communication; feelings must be communicated
and relationships established. Therefore the quality of the relationship established with the parents is crucial in order to gain their trust.
If the therapist does not have their trust, he will not be able to give
them the kind of support that they need. If parents do not feel
reassured by the answers they receive or do not feel positive toward
the therapist, they should be encouraged to find another therapist in
whom they can place their confidence.

If the parents are not sure of their own feelings, they should not
hesitate to talk over the situation with the prospective therapist once
more. A positive, supportive relationship is needed to proceed with
the difficult work ahead. Helping the learning disabled youngster is a
joint effort; trust in the therapist is necessary. The trust must be
established *before* starting the child's treatment because it is crucial
not to interrupt an ongoing therapeutic relationship. The therapist

who understands learning disabilities can make an enormous impact on the child's behavior at home and at school, and he can have a marked effect on the parents' attitudes and their ability to manage the child. The therapist can affect the comfort and well-being of the whole family. But parents must begin by feeling some comfort with the therapist.

PARENTS' OWN PROBLEMS

Great resourcefulness and planning are required from the parents of a child with learning disabilities, yet they are only human. Family life puts the same pressures on them as on anyone else, and there is no way they can do all they would like to do. Perhaps the most important place they can start work is in the area of their own attitudes.

Parents need to be helped to hold on to optimism regarding the child's strengths, building on whatever he likes to do best, and using the momentum of his enthusiasm—even if the only thing he likes is television. That too offers possibilities. (See chapter 9.) He must know that his abilities are much more important to his parents than his failings.

It is vital for parents to develop their sense of humor in every way they know how. Laughter helps surmount many hurdles, and it gives the child an important unspoken message: that life is basically sunny despite all his difficulties. Comical elements can be found in many situations, even though they are sometimes hard to see. When the whole family can see the humor in some of the experiences they go through together, the result is worth the effort.

Parents should try not to dwell on the future in their own minds. They can plan realistically for today, tomorrow, next week, even a few months ahead. But it is unrealistic to become preoccupied with the long-range future of a young child. There is not yet enough knowledge, there are too many variables, and there are too many unknown factors for this kind of worrying to be useful in any way. Instead of worrying if their seven-year-old will make it to college, they need to grab hold of the present and deal with it step-by-step, just as their child must. They need to know the problems and both the short-term and long-term objectives. False hopes will help no more than feelings of doom, and in due time, the college potential of their child can be discussed. Sometimes, however, a child may reach the age of sixteen or eighteen before this becomes entirely clear. In other cases, an experienced person who has worked with learning disabled children over many years can be fairly sure how the child will be able to handle adolescence.

If parents can face their problems truthfully, they will be able to talk to their child truthfully. They can emphasize that the child is smart but that he has problems. People can and will help him. They can acknowledge that progress will take time, that he will have to work harder than most other people, that there are no easy answers, and that both they and he know it feels unfair. Clearly they don't talk to a teenager the way they do to a seven-year-old, but the quality of honesty has to be the same.

The lack of talent in the learning disabled child can be recognized in the same way parents would recognize lack of artistic or musical talent or mechanical prowess in any other youngster. They can point out that they too have areas of incompetence. They would like to be talented, but lack of a certain ability does not make them any less whole persons.

Parents should be encouraged to give themselves permission to make mistakes and learn from them. This gives the child permission to make mistakes too, and survive. He must be shown that amends can be made for the mistake and things can be restored—perhaps not quite the same as before, perhaps better. When something gets broken—particularly by the child—it must be mended. (It must not be thrown out. The child himself feels broken and incompetent and needs to see broken things put back together. He has trouble seeing the parts that make up a whole. He needs as much help as possible in putting together his whole world.)

Parents must be helped to identify their own feelings and those of their child so they know when they are absorbing and expressing the child's feelings. Parents can be more help to the child when they isolate what his feelings are. If they follow his ups and downs in their own moods, their lives will be a veritable seesaw. They need their own attitudes and feelings intact in order to give the child the support he needs. And let's hope that these parents have caring families and friends who give them the support they need. They need all the emotional nourishment and sustenance that is available to them.

Parents need to trust themselves. Professionals working with parents of learning disabled children need to tap their own ingenuity to find as many ways as possible to help parents feel better about themselves, feel competent, and trust their own observations and judgment. Usually parents know their own child better than anyone else does. Usually they love their children very much. They need information, practical suggestions, and solid support.

TWELVE

PARENTS AND TEACHERS AND THE INDIVIDUALS WITH DISABILITIES EDUCATION ACT

Gilbert is not doing well in school. He's in the sixth grade and is struggling with reading, writing, and spelling. He is quick to figure out math problems in his head, but has trouble organizing them on paper. He doesn't pay attention to instructions and rarely follows them properly. He can't sit still and tends to wander around the classroom. Gilbert is confused about how to get started on projects, yet he asks excellent questions. His parents are not surprised to hear from his teacher that Gilbert is very sloppy, forgets where he's supposed to be, leaves a trail of belongings behind him, trips over his untied shoelaces, and talks incessantly.

Gilbert's parents are typical in that they hope whatever it is that's wrong will disappear—and quickly! They offer rewards to entice him to put out extra effort. Then they use admonitions and punishment. They don't allow him to watch TV during the week. They don't permit him to play outdoors with his friends. Gilbert's father starts working with him, then turns the task over to his older brother and sister so there will be fewer tears. All kinds of homemade remedies are tried— more sleep, a nutritious diet (with extra vitamin supplements), fewer sweets, no sweets, no soft drinks, then more exercise, extra hugs. But, unfortunately, Gilbert's problems do not go away; in fact, they get worse. He is taken to a pediatrician who proclaims that he is in good shape and should not be pressured, then to the eye doctor and hearing specialist, who also say he is fine.

Meanwhile, the sixth grade teacher, Miss Porter, is very confused by Gilbert. He can talk to her about the presidential elections, what it means to be a nonreader, the relationship between Greek myths and the Navaho Indians' rain dance. She decides that if he can think like that, he can certainly learn to read. She vacillates between feeling he isn't trying hard enough and feeling that something is drastically wrong. Gilbert can't even recognize familiar words no matter how often and in how many clever ways she tries to teach him. He can't keep his mind on his work.

Finally, Miss Porter and Gilbert's parents have a conference. There it is agreed that Gilbert is bright and that they obviously need more information as to why Gilbert can't read, write, or pay attention in class. Under the Individuals with Disabilities Education Act (IDEA), Gilbert, his parents, and his teacher may be able to receive appropriate help.

THE INDIVIDUALS WITH DISABILITIES EDUCATION ACT (IDEA)

In November 1975, the Ninety-fourth Congress adopted PL 94-142, the Education for All Handicapped Children Act. It became effective in October 1977, with the final phase taking effect in September 1980, to assure free and appropriate education for all handicapped persons aged three to twenty-one. Learning disabilities were recognized by

Congress as one of the handicapping conditions requiring appropriate education. Since that time the law has been amended several times, most recently in 1991. The act is now called the Individuals with Disabilities Education Act (IDEA) as amended by PL 101-476. Along with renaming the law, the 1990 Education of All Handicapped Children Act (EHA) mandated the change of the word *handicapped* to *disabilities*. The word *abilities* is contained in disabilities, which produces a different image than a person called handicapped with the image of a beggar, cap in hand. The disabled don't want to be pitied or have to beg. They want opportunities, accommodations, to enable them to be productive.

Public Law 94-142, now PL 101-476, is very exciting because it is truly child-centered. In the best tradition of American humanism, it aims to give each disabled child every opportunity to achieve his or her potential. It has resulted in regulations published by the U.S. Office of Education outlining a comprehensive system of special education procedures to be implemented by state and local education agencies throughout the nation. These regulations are available to the public.

> *The spirit of the law*
> > *dictates that the unique needs*
> > > *of each disabled child are to be served*
> > > > *by providing him with a free appropriate education.*
> *Unfortunately, the practice of law*
> > *frequently reflects the budgetary constraints*
> > > *of local and state agencies.*

Although Congress passed the law to provide incentives to the states to integrate the quiet minority of the disabled into our school systems, the monetary incentives are small, the responsibilities are huge, and the drain on state and local budgets is monstrous. The generosity of spirit shown by Congress in this legislation has not been matched by generosity of appropriation.

Nonetheless, as the desperate needs of disabled children become more understood, as it becomes evident that a proper education can make the difference in the quality of lives lived, new hopes have been raised and new pathways charted. School systems have attempted to tackle the individualized needs of youngsters who cannot learn in traditional ways. Because of this legislation, schools are spending far more than ever before on their disabled students. At the same time, however, school budgets are being drastically reduced due to dropping school enrollments, a poor economy, energy costs, and a myriad of local concerns. As a result, school systems and parents find themselves increasingly pitted against one another.

Parents cannot assume that the very existence of IDEA is going to mean that their child's needs will be served appropriately. However, as parents become acquainted with the law, they see that it gives them the right to challenge the school system at every point to make sure that their child receives the appropriate education he needs for his disabling condition. Parents of learning disabled youngsters have to be even more aware of their rights, not only because of the shortage of funds but because of the vast number of students who give evidence of some form of learning disability.

What is a learning disability? Unfortunately, even now, there is no agreement among specialists as to exactly what constitutes a learning disability, which battery or batteries of tests can properly diagnose neurological dysfunction, and how learning disabilities can best be treated. We do know that the learning disabled child needs to be taught in a special way: he needs to learn *how* to learn. Parents like Gilbert's have to find ways to use IDEA to make sure this happens.

Teachers like Miss Porter need to know the provisions of the law in order to advise parents about their child's right to a proper evaluation and an individualized educational program (IEP). Just as for a parent, there is nothing more frustrating to a teacher than to see a child's needs and not be able to meet them. Because the teacher is an employee of the school system, there is only so much he or she can do.

Teachers can voice their concerns and become advocates for the child up to a certain point. But it is the learning disabled child's parents or guardian who must be the permanent advocates for the child and who must translate the humane intent of the law into concrete, practical action.

Eight important aspects of this law are interrelated and need to be understood: (1) right to an appropriate education, (2) multidisciplinary evaluation, (3) confidentiality of a child's records, (4) individualized educational program (IEP), (5) least restrictive environment, (6) personnel development, (7) due process, and (8) parent participation.

RIGHT TO AN APPROPRIATE EDUCATION

Every child with a disability is entitled to a free and appropriate public education. This concept grew out of the civil rights movement of the 1960s in which unfair discrimination against minorities was challenged at every point. In this case, the minority is the disabled child!

Under IDEA, no child is uneducable. The beauty of the legislation is that it is committed to the belief that all children can learn, that it is up to educators to figure out how to teach them, and that education must be viewed not simply as an academic process, but as one that includes instruction in basic living and vocational skills.

For some disabled youngsters, special programs must be provided, and if they do not exist in the public schools, then school systems must pay private facilities to do the job.

For too long there has been a prejudice against the obviously disabled child. Often because of the way he looks and/or his problems in mobility, he has been excluded from regular public education when, in fact, he could learn in a regular classroom if he could get his wheelchair into the room or if he received some limited but specific aids. That child can no longer be excluded from the regular class-room. The right-to-education concept is for the disabled child what the 1954 Supreme Court decision was for the black child. And where equal educational opportunity is denied, each has redress under the law.

Whereas the child in a wheelchair with his very visible handicap, but no learning problems, does not need to be taught in a special way, the learning disabled child, who is usually invisibly handicapped, needs very special teaching techniques in order to survive in school. But the learning disabled youngster often falls between the cracks. "A little off, but he's not really disabled; he'll make it," said one school administrator, echoing many others. Often the invisibly disabled child is not served, even though he is as entitled to a free and appropriate education as is the child with obvious disabilities. Federal funding for the disabled will cover only a small percentage of local school enrollment. Although under the original legislation, the fed-eral government would cover 40 percent of the excess cost, the actual funding never exceeded 12 percent and has been closer to 8 percent in the late 1980s and early 1990s. Local and state funds must be used for any disabled students above that number. The visibly disabled are readily included, but too often the parents of a learning disabled child are forced to fight for their child to be educated properly. Gilbert's parents may well be faced with this problem because he doesn't look disabled, and because testing by itself may not reveal the severity of his disability.

MULTIDISCIPLINARY EVALUATION

Gilbert can receive an evaluation through the public school system at no cost to his parents. In this case, because Miss Porter and his parents have had a conference and agreed that more information is needed, it is likely that Miss Porter will suggest a meeting with the school principal. At this conference, Gilbert's parents will request that their son be evaluated to determine if he is eligible for special education placement. IDEA specifically states that a school may not formally evaluate a child without parental permission. Gilbert's parents must sign the appropriate evaluation referral forms and a separate form giving permission to the school system to test and evaluate their son. Copies of any previous assessments done privately or by other school districts are to be submitted with the forms. Miss Porter will also submit a statement describing Gilbert's problems in her classroom.

Parents who are unable to work through their child's teacher should call the school and ask to meet directly with the principal or school social worker to request an assessment of their child. Parents of children who do not attend public schools and have had no previous assessment by the public school system need to telephone the office of the superintendent of schools to make arrangements. All requests for an evaluation must be followed by a written request to ensure that the school system will respond within a reasonable length of time.

Parents and teachers must monitor what happens to their request. In many school districts there are delays of several months to a year until the testing is done. IDEA places a huge burden on local school districts to identify all disabled children aged zero to twenty-one. They must locate children in the public schools, as well as children in other public agencies, institutions, and private schools. School systems are charged with identifying all children from birth on. The number of necessary evaluations is staggering. Often there is a shortage of trained personnel to do the job. Some states cannot afford to hire additional personnel, and others feel they are already overcommitted. Some local school boards resist reallocating funds from their athletic or regular academic programs to special education when they see a disproportionate per-pupil expenditure already going to the disabled. Nevertheless, the child who is not evaluated within a reasonable period of time suffers unnecessarily. The teacher cannot give him the special help he needs; thus, not only is he confronted by failure for an inordinate amount of time, but his reaction to that defeat can also affect the entire tone of the classroom. Gilbert's parents, it turns out, had to wait two months and might have had to wait even longer had Miss Porter not joined them in applying pressure to the school system to speed up the date for evaluation.

IDEA mandates that a multidisciplinary evaluation be conducted by trained personnel. Group tests are not appropriate because they strike at the deficit areas of the learning disabled child— the inability to follow instructions in a group, to work at grade level, to work within specific time limits. Professionals tend to believe that an individual intelligence test is crucial to determine a child's true cognitive ability. Once the child's potential has been established through intelligence testing, educational diagnostic testing should continue to determine specific areas in which he cannot function.

The tests selected may not be racially or culturally biased; if English is a second language, tests must be provided and administered in the child's native language, unless it is clearly not feasible to do so.

IDEA requires that the evaluation team must be multidisciplinary and shall include the child's regular teacher or an appropriate substitute if this person is unavailable. The information about the child coming from parents, teachers, and other sources—his physical condition, cultural or social background, and adaptive behavior—must be documented and carefully considered by the team. At least one member of the team other than the child's teacher is required to observe the child suspected of having learning disabilities in his classroom setting. Parents need to make sure that as many members of the team as possible see their child personally and get a feel for what the child can and cannot do.

Parents have the right and need to ask the evaluation team or the team member they see such questions as:

What tests are being given to my child?
Why have these specific tests been chosen?
What can be learned from them?
Will you be looking for the strong points as well as weak areas?
Will you be able to tell me how my child seems to learn best?
How will the test information be used to help teach my child?

The present system for identifying learning disabilities is complicated because professionals do not always agree on what constitutes a proper battery of tests or how to interpret the test data obtained through the evaluation. (See appendix 6 for a list of the most frequently used tests and their descriptions.)

Under IDEA a child may be identified as learning disabled if the evaluation team finds a "severe discrepancy" between his age and his ability in one or more of the following seven areas:

1. oral expression
2. listening comprehension
3. written expression
4. basic reading skills
5. reading comprehension
6. mathematics calculation
7. mathematics reasoning

The term *severe discrepancy* was not defined by Congress; however, a discrepancy of one standard deviation (fifteen standard score points) or more is considered significant by most experts. Various school districts use their own criteria and diagnostic tools. The result is that in some districts, many children are found to have severe discrepancies and, therefore, are considered learning disabled, while other districts claim that only very small percentages of the children show discrepancies severe enough to be judged learning disabled. Although severe discrepancy is one criterion for determining a learning disability, other factors, such as classroom observation and a careful analysis of test results, must also be considered in determining eligibility for special education. This has been made clear in some court cases and by the Office of Special Education Programs in response to letters of inquiry.

The evaluation team may not identify a child as learning disabled if the severe discrepancy between ability and achievement is primarily the result of blindness, deafness, motor handicap, mental retardation, emotional disturbance, or "environmental, cultural, or economic disadvantage." There are some children, however, who have a physical disability such as blindness, deafness, or cerebral palsy and learning disabilities. The child who is economically disadvantaged is not automatically learning disabled; however, a high incidence of learning disability can be expected because of poor prenatal care, malnutrition, and a host of other factors that may contribute to the delayed development of the child's central nervous system.

In evaluating for possible learning disabilities, much depends upon the diagnostician's depth of experience with learning disabled youngsters and his or her ability to recognize the subtle constellation of difficulties and characteristics that point to a learning disability. The score differentials on tests are often not as meaningful as the type of errors and/or mistakes made in academic work, the erratic quality of the work, and the behavioral manifestations of learning disabilities. What the law doesn't deal with are the intangible aspects such as the learning disabled child's immaturity and the developmental lag that produces his inability to sustain selective attention. Hyperactive, hypoactive, and normally active learning disabled youngsters may all have attention-span difficulties. All may lack the tools to organize the information bombarding them through their senses, to make life more understandable and meaningful.

The daily challenge to teachers and principals is this: these are intelligent children *who are unable to cope adequately with classroom routine.* As noted in earlier chapters, learning disabled youngsters are

often disorganized, distractible, impulsive, perseverative, and emotionally labile, overreacting to the least little thing. They may be
egocentric and unable to work in a group. They may be able to pass a
test working alone with one adult but may not be able to do work in
a group. And what about the child who cannot find his way around a
building, who takes weeks to learn where his classroom is? Or the
child who has no sense of time and is late to every class? Every teacher
knows the child who can't deal with the slightest change in routine,
who falls apart when confronted with unfamiliar material such as a
new workbook, who takes months to adjust to a new teacher. Learning disabled youngsters cannot follow a simple set of directions,
particularly in the classroom setting. Many of them are so awkward
and clumsy that they cannot follow classroom routines within the
proper time limits, and they misinterpret social interactions. Recess
and lunch are troubled times because they involve so many choices, so
much decision making, so much organizing of time and space. How
are these subtle behavioral manifestations of learning disabilities to be
measured so that these children can receive the special education they
need?

*The inability to cope adequately with regular classroom academic
work* is the other area that the law does not touch unless the child
shows a severe discrepancy between his potential and achievement.
Many do display this discrepancy, but there are learning disabled
students who don't show it on tests. Their oral expression may be
immature and disorganized, but adequate in a testing situation; however, in a classroom, they can't organize information to ask a question,
are unable to communicate what they have learned, and miss the
main point of a discussion. They miss a great deal because they are
very concrete and literal, do not pick up on nuances, innuendos, and
multiple meanings of words. The children who are unable to begin
work without a teacher standing over them every moment, who can't
sustain work without constant teacher monitoring, and who don't
know how to finish a task are in trouble in a regular classroom; they

need to be taught the approach to a task while the other students simply need to be taught the material. It's exceedingly difficult to cope adequately with regular classroom work if you have attention difficulties, cannot process directions easily, and require repetition and/or interpretation of all instructions; the challenge is even greater if you are the "One-Way Kid" who has only one way of doing things, one answer, and cannot consider alternatives. The child who impulsively plunges into work, never proofreads, and needs slowing down may be considered just careless, but the patterns of his behavior spell out a form of learning disability to specialists in this field. The student who never finishes his work in the allotted time, who processes information slowly and works at a snail's pace, needs special teaching to learn to increase his speed. The youngster for whom the act of writing is a form of medieval torture may be able to write enough to pass a test but cannot keep up with written work in the classroom.

Children who are overwhelmed by the introduction of too much information at once and cannot tolerate a lot going on at once cannot function in a regular classroom. They need to have information and work broken down into small increments; they need to learn in very small groups. Many youngsters show enough discrepancies in test scores to qualify for special help, but those with the hidden handicap, who compensate because they are so bright, do not receive it.

Once the multidisciplinary evaluation team has concluded its assessment, the team is required to produce a written report of the results and recommendations and a copy must be sent to the parents. Fortunately, IDEA demands that the report be written in understandable language. If it is not, parents should insist upon clarity and feel free to ask for explanations. The report must include a statement as to whether or not the child has a learning disability and what tools and processes were used to make this determination. The problem areas of the learning disabled child are to be clearly identified and related to the test results and behavior observed. Finally, each team member has to sign the report. If there is a disagreement, a separate statement must be prepared by any dissenting members of the evaluation team.

Some parents who do not want their child to have to wait for an evaluation will opt for an alternative route: testing by an independent agency, hospital, university diagnostic clinic, or private diagnostician trained in learning disabilities. Some parents do not trust "the system" to take an objective look at their child. Others want a second opinion. Parents who are dissatisfied with the public school evaluation and recommendations can secure a private, independent evaluation at public expense unless the school system successfully demonstrates that its evaluation is appropriate. If the school system proves, before an impartial hearing officer, that its report is appropriate, the parents can still obtain a private evaluation, but at their own expense. In any case, IDEA requires the school system to consider and comment in writing on whatever outside evaluations are submitted.

Some diagnostic centers provide free services, others charge on a sliding scale, some provide full or partial scholarship, and others may charge anywhere from $400 to $1500 for an evaluation that includes a parent interview, a full battery of tests, a conference interpreting the results, and a detailed written report. Some clinics or collaborative groups also agree to act as a liaison between parents and the schools. Parents must ask private facilities in advance what the total cost will be, how soon the process can begin, how long the child will be tested (one morning, two mornings, a whole day, two whole days?), how many different professionals will be seeing their child, what their specialties are (i.e., educational diagnostician, psychologist, speech and language therapist, occupational therapist). Parents have a right to expect a good diagnostic report outlining the child's strengths, areas of difficulty, questions to explore further, ways in which the child seems to learn best and, thus, the most effective channels for teaching. A well-trained diagnostician is a keen observer and an astute listener. He or she notes how a child approaches a task, holds a pencil, sits in a chair, what questions he asks, as well as when a child becomes frustrated, with what kind of material, and how he deals with the frustration. All of the child's test behavior is treated as important diagnostic information to be stirred into the same pot with test scores, school reports, medical reports, and information given in parent interviews, to produce a comprehensive picture of a child's learning profile with very clear and specific recommendations for action. A diagnostician should be able to report to parents in as much detail as necessary the information gleaned, the way in which it was discovered, and its significance for the child's schooling and his life at home. Most diagnosticians will guide parents on how to interpret the information to their youngsters. And often the diagnosticians themselves will interpret the test information directly to an older child.

It is important for parents to sit down with their child before the child goes for testing and say something like:

> *"We know you're smart. We know you are having trouble learning certain things at school. We need, and you need, more information on how you learn best, how your teachers can help you the most. That's why tomorrow you will be seeing————."*

The learning disabled child needs to know that his parents are convinced he will learn, that they understand the problem is one of detecting the best ways to teach him, and that they have found a specialist who knows how to achieve this goal. The emphasis must be put on ways to help the child succeed, rather than concentrating on what's wrong with him. From the youngster, parents may still hear: "So you think I'm dumb?" "So you think I'm crazy?" The child's fears cannot be totally allayed, but they can be alleviated if parents make it vividly clear that they are seeking ways to help him learn better and will share what they discover with the child.

If a child is sent directly for diagnostic evaluation from his classroom at school, it helps if the teacher will take the time to reinforce what the parents have said at home and tell the child that he will be taking some tests so that "we can learn how you learn best. It will help all of us find ways to teach you better."

CONFIDENTIALITY OF A CHILD'S RECORDS

Parents have the right to see all the accumulated information concerning their child and to have a representative of their choosing inspect and review the records. Test materials, reports, teacher comments, correspondence with professionals, conferences held about the child are all to be made available. Students aged eighteen and over have the same rights with regard to seeing their records as do their parents, including the right to an explanation of anything they don't understand.

IDEA continually confirms that parents are a working part of the team that is to educate a handicapped child. The law guarantees parents the right to ask that misleading or inaccurate information be removed from their child's file or, at the very least, be amended with an explanatory statement. The records of a learning disabled child must be studied closely because his behavior and reactions can be misinterpreted by those who are not familiar with learning disabilities. For example, the learning disabled child's slow processing may mean that he responds in a very delayed fashion to a previous conversation. And it could be in his file that this behavior "had a schizoid quality." The social inappropriateness of the learning disabled child might have been labeled as emotional disturbance when it wasn't. A learning disabled teenager may have been called retarded because of being unable to count change. A parent would want to make sure that this is called "an area of retarded development" rather than a statement about the child. Many parents have discovered that the records are full of reports characterizing their child as lazy and unmotivated, when in fact it is the child's lack of focus and sense of defeat that are really being described. However, parents also need to know that there will always be things in a child's file that they may not like, but that may be true. No one, except for the child's teachers and other legitimate school personnel, has access to a child's records. Confidentiality is to be protected to such an extent that schools must write down the names of anyone who has looked at a child's file, why they did, and when. Before anyone else is given access to the records, a written consent form detailing the purpose and the name of the person must be signed and dated by the parents. The child's and the parents' rights are protected at every point.

Within forty-five days of their request, parents must be allowed to study their child's record. Becoming familiar with all of the information helps parents prepare for the meeting to design an individualized educational program and placement for their child.

INDIVIDUALIZED EDUCATIONAL PROGRAM (IEP)

Any individual, up to twenty-one years,
identified as disabled
is unique
and
must have
an *individualized* educational program (IEP).

An IEP is a written plan setting forth the specially designed instruction that the student needs for learning and the reasonable expectations for him that are measurable and can be monitored.

Within thirty days after a child like Gilbert has been identified as disabled, an IEP meeting must take place. The IEP is the mechanism by which a child receives the special services and instruction he needs; without it, he cannot receive special help. To write Gilbert's IEP his learning problems have to be known, as well as his strengths, and the ways he seems to learn best. The skills he needs to learn and their prerequisites have to be outlined in order to establish very specific goals for him to achieve in the areas that are disabling him. Based on how he seems to learn best, certain methods and techniques of instruction are recommended. Every IEP must include the following minimum components:

1. statement of the child's present levels of educational performance,
2. statement of annual goals or achievements expected by the end of the school year,
3. short-term objectives stated in instructional terms which are the steps leading to the mastery of annual goals,
4. statement of the specific special education and support services to be provided to the child,
5. statement of the extent to which a child will be able to participate in regular educational programs and justification for any special placement that is recommended,
6. projected dates for initiation of services and the anticipated duration of the services, and
7. statement of criteria and evaluation procedures to be used for determining, on at least an annual basis, whether short-term objectives are being achieved.

Gilbert's parents are an important part of the IEP development, as is Miss Porter. They meet with a representative of the public school system who is qualified to provide or to supervise special education. Since Gilbert has just been identified as learning disabled, a member of his multidisciplinary evaluation team would join the meeting too. If Gilbert were older, it might be appropriate for him to join this meeting, although this rarely happens except in secondary schools. Other individuals may participate in the IEP meeting at the request of the parents or the school system. Clearly, the results of Gilbert's assessment are central to the IEP meeting, because it is through the work of the evaluation team that a child's academic potential, performance, special needs, and best learning style are detailed.

Prior to the meeting, Gilbert had been tested by a psychologist, an educational specialist, and a social worker. The results showed that Gilbert gave evidence of average intelligence, and in some areas such as reasoning and vocabulary, he was in the superior range of his age group. His math ability proved to be extraordinary, although he could not do written math, and the examiners were impressed with his advanced knowledge of history and science. The evaluation demonstrated that he had some visual motor difficulties, and visual discrimination and visual memory problems. He showed a large discrepancy between his achievement and his age and ability level in two areas—written expression and basic reading skills. The report noted that he learned best through his auditory channel. Although they identified Gilbert as mildly disabled, the evaluation team concluded that Gilbert had so much talent that he could learn to compensate for many of his deficits and, therefore, could remain in the regular classroom. The team thought he could benefit from some tutoring and the use of special aids such as a tape recorder. These recommendations were discussed at the IEP meeting.

The school system representative on Gilbert's IEP team recommended that Gilbert remain in his regular classroom, but that he receive special services, including reading and handwriting tutoring one hour a day and the use of a tape recorder instead of having to write. Miss Porter said that Gilbert's gross motor skills also needed special services and that his short attention span was of concern to her. They agreed to add an adaptive physical education program twice a week.

Gilbert's parents were uncomfortable with these program suggestions. They didn't want to challenge the school system representatives,
for they didn't think they knew enough. But, on the other hand, the
degree of Gilbert's distractibility and disorganization didn't seem to
come out as serious problems needing specially designed instruction.

If the IEP meeting was uncomfortable for Gilbert's parents, who
were somewhat sophisticated, imagine what it must feel like for a
parent from the inner city or a parent from a foreign country for
whom the whole educational process is often overwhelming and
threatening. Many of these parents need convincing that their child is
not bad but has some learning problems, that the school system is not
bad and can provide some new kinds of teaching to help their child
learn. Frequently, once they are calmed and can feel some trust that
someone really wants to help their child, parents can offer important
diagnostic information and clues as to how their child succeeds best at
home. This information can be translated into effective teaching
techniques for use at school.

It took some time for Gilbert's parents to realize that they had
lived with him the most, probably knew him the best, and that the
evaluation team's report did not describe his needs as thoroughly as
they felt was necessary.

IDEA clearly states that every opportunity must be provided to
allow parents to have an active involvement in making decisions
regarding their child's IEP. Public school systems are required to
encourage parent participation, to provide detailed documentation of
all their efforts (including telephone calls, correspondence, home
visits), and to arrange a mutually convenient IEP meeting time. Only
if parents have rejected all attempts of the school to involve them may
an IEP meeting take place without them. Parents cannot be pressured
to give their consent to the IEP. They should sign the IEP document
only after they are genuinely satisfied that it represents the best
individually designed program for their child.

Parents need to ask for explanations of any educational terms
they don't understand and seek a description of the functions of the

various support service personnel that might be working with their child such as an occupational therapist or speech and language specialist. Parents need to feel free to ask a number of questions, such as:

1. Do you base your long-range goals on just test scores or on what he does in the classroom, or both?

2. What are my child's main problems? What would be the next layer of problems that are not as severe but for which she needs help? Are any of these problems included in the short-term objectives?

3. What approaches do you plan to use with my child, and why?

4. Will you use different approaches in different subjects? If so, what and why?

5. Can you explain to me why the approaches that you have selected are the best ones to teach my child? How much exposure do your teachers have to a wide variety of techniques and materials effective with learning disabled students? Do they have enough access to different methods and materials?

6. How large a class will he be in? If he's in a regular classroom, how can you assure that his IEP is carried out?

7. What training in learning disabilities has her teacher received? What about the special teachers who see her?

8. Are there aides in the class; if so, what are their duties and what is their training?

9. What special related services does my child need? Will they be provided in his school building or must my child go to another facility for them?

10. How many times per week will my child receive services? What is the present caseload of the personnel giving the support services? (The amount of service should be based on the child's needs, not on the service provider's caseload.)

11. When can we meet during the year to discuss my child's progress on her IEP?

Most school personnel genuinely want to clarify for parents the intent of their program. However, there are all kinds of ways these questions can be asked, from a genuine wish for information and assurance about a child's program to wanting to unload years of pent-up frustration and anger on a school. The focus must be kept on the best interests of the child at the present time. At least in the beginning, it helps if each party is receptive to the questions and comments of the other.

Ordinarily, most parents are satisfied with the answers to their questions and sign the IEP. Gilbert's parents were different in that they felt that their child's learning problem was more severe than the evaluation had demonstrated. On the advice of their local Learning Disabilities Association (LDA), they asked for a second evaluation, an independent private assessment, which can be secured at public expense unless the school system initiates a due process hearing where it successfully demonstrates that its evaluation is adequate. In Gilbert's case, the school system agreed to a second evaluation.

Within a few weeks Gilbert was evaluated again by a private agency whose report indicated that although he tested within the average range, there was evidence that he had the potential of nearly superior intelligence, which was mitigated by his severe perceptual handicaps. The report outlined his severe visual discrimination, visual memory, eye tracking, and visual motor problems; it pointed out his immaturity in organizing any task and in trying to integrate several things at once, and his inability to link visual symbols with specific sounds (decoding). This evaluation found that Gilbert had some fine auditory discrimination problems that affected how he heard the different vowel sounds. The examiners observed that this youngster was clumsy and awkward, demonstrated poor balance and coordination, did not know left from right, could not isolate one part of the body from another or plan his movements. They found that his visual motor skills were similar to those of the average child five years younger than Gilbert.

The second evaluation agreed with the first in terms of Gilbert's extraordinary vocabulary and reasoning, his vast knowledge of history, science, and other topics, but did not accept the finding that he could compensate for all his deficit areas with proper use of these talents. In fact, the second group of examiners indicated that the degree of hyperactivity, distractibility, impulsiveness, and perseveration shown by Gilbert in the testing would make it exceedingly difficult for him to learn in a large class. The judgment of the second set of examiners was that if Gilbert's learning needs were not addressed properly and promptly, it was likely that he would develop emotional problems beyond his existing lack of confidence and poor image of himself. Apparently Gilbert was becoming convinced that he was retarded; he was angry that people weren't telling him "the truth" about himself. The second evaluation recommended that Gilbert be placed in a self-contained classroom in order for him to develop the very elementary competencies he needed for academic work and to feel better about himself.

The IEP committee met again to review the information from the second evaluation. Gilbert's parents asked that he be placed in a self-contained classroom.

The school system representatives on the IEP committee felt that Gilbert was not disabled enough to be taken out of the regular education program completely, that putting him in a special class was tantamount to segregating him and violating his civil rights. Miss Porter took the lead in suggesting that the IEP committee change the original recommendation and have Gilbert spend part of the day in a resource room learning basic skills, but that he join her class for social studies, science, music, and recess; she also recommended that he receive occupational therapy twice a week.

The hesitancy of the school representatives on the IEP committee can be understood; this child did present an unusual profile and clearly could function, in some areas, on a high intellectual level. The school representatives made it clear that they had limited financial resources and had to place many children much more severely disabled than Gilbert in special classes. Special classes cost more than special services. Also, state systems are cautious because they have been flooded with requests by parents in many suburban communities seeking special education services for their bright and *not* learning disabled youngsters to help them in the race for better grades.

Most parents don't want their youngsters to be labeled as severely handicapped, or placed in a special class or special school, for they want their children to feel as normal as possible. However, Gilbert's parents and an adviser that they brought with them to the second IEP meeting contended that by keeping Gilbert in a regular classroom even part of the day, the system would be convincing him during that part of the day that he was inadequate and incompetent. They believed that with the new IEP there was still no way Gilbert could succeed academically, socially, or emotionally, so they refused to sign the IEP. Gilbert's parents used their rights of due process (to be discussed later in the chapter) to challenge the school system's recommended placement, and a third IEP meeting took place following the hearing, where Gilbert's parents and the school system finally agreed and signed off. Just as all parents are to receive a copy of the signed IEP, so, too, did Gilbert's parents.

An IEP must not contain general goals—e.g., "Gilbert will learn to read," but, rather, very specific objectives—e.g., "Gilbert will identify letters of the alphabet in sequence from a written model with 80 percent accuracy within the time period of 9/95 to 11/95." Teachers and parents of learning disabled students tend to chortle when they have to put a percentage figure on the consistency with which a task will be performed, since a prime characteristic of the learning disabled child is inconsistency.

Frequently parents ask for school advice on how they can most help their learning disabled children at home. Some parents like to design a very informal IEP for the home because it helps them to target very specific areas to help their child. Clearly all parents need to help promote any latent talents and the child's socialization needs and generally to help him feel better about himself. Just as there are disputes in many areas among specialists in learning disabilities, so there is no meeting of minds as to whether or not parents should work with their children in the very areas where the child is hurting. It really depends on the personalities of the parents, the personality of the child, the atmosphere in the home. A good rule of thumb would be that a parent should ask himself or herself, how much extra anxiety, confusion, frustration, or anger is my working with my child adding to our home life? Usually it is best for parents to work with a child on what he can do well, where he feels competency and can associate parental help with success and pleasure. Home should remain a safety zone where competencies are built and enjoyed since school too often treads on dangerous vulnerabilities.

The IEP is a commitment to the individualization of education. It forces adults to look at the whole child, target the areas in which she needs the most help, set goals for her to achieve, and teach her in the ways she learns best. This is a superb idea. In fact, every child in our school system would benefit from an IEP! Certainly, attention to individual learning styles is central to special education. It is The Lab School's experience that anything that works with learning disabled children works even faster and more effectively with inner-city students and children for whom English is a second language. *Standardization is the danger* to education in general and to learning disabled children in particular. More and more frequently, the IEP is being handled by standardized means. Unfortunately, too many teachers and specialists are using a computer program or looking in a book and copying down the goals, objectives, and techniques contained therein. Computers and other aids can expedite the process of designing an IEP as long as the child's individualized needs, interests, and learning style remain paramount.

There is no question that to create a proper IEP takes an

enormous amount of time, energy, and thought—an effort for which teachers receive no extra pay. The task can be overwhelming to many special education teachers (who are primarily responsible for developing and implementing the IEP once the child has been placed in their class). The sequential nature of academic programming has to be understood by the writer of the IEP in order to outline in detail which skills a child must master in order to reach a certain goal. The act of having to write an IEP can promote the best kind of diagnostic-prescriptive teaching. Many teachers feel a pride in the IEPs they draft, in the systematic way they are going about helping a youngster, and this leads to their feeling more positive about their work. And the learning disabled youngster can only benefit from those feelings!

If a learning disabled child does not show any measurable progress within the projected dates on an IEP, the IEP challenges the adults to seek out new ways, try different methods, and go back and look at the severity of the child's problems. The quality of the treatment plan varies according to the teacher's background, training, and exposure to a wide variety of techniques and materials. For the severely learning disabled, however, progress may be recorded in many areas, but the reading or spelling scores may not rise in a very significant manner for two or three years. IDEA does not hold teachers accountable for achieving every annual goal, but it does hold schools responsible for offering the services written down on the IEP.

What IDEA does not provide, and what seems to be needed, is a case manager from the IEP conference—one person responsible to protect and preserve the child's IEP—who keeps in touch with all the parties involved, who visits the school, checks on special services, raises appropriate questions, acts as the child's advocate within the system. Although expensive, such a system would mean that one person in the vast bureaucracy, where everything tends to become so impersonal, would be fully acquainted with the child and would thoroughly know his needs and the techniques that have been tried. Hopefully, the case manager would be a person whom parents could turn to with trust rather than treat as an adversary.

LEAST RESTRICTIVE ENVIRONMENT

The intent of IDEA is to ensure the growth of every student with a disability by providing an appropriate education in the least restrictive environment. It is at the IEP conference that the appropriate education is detailed along with the locale where special services are to take place. The least-restrictive-environment concept does not necessarily lead automatically to the inclusion of all disabled children in the regular program. If it did, it would have another name.

IDEA has often been called the "Mainstreaming Act." Yet the word *mainstreaming* never appears in any part of the legislation. However, the clear intent of Congress in using the three words *least restrictive environment* was to assure that disabled children be educated side by side with children who are not disabled to the greatest extent possible.

The impetus for this emanated from the fact that for too many years students with problems were dumped into catch-up classes where expectations for achievement were so low that poor performance was a natural result. Also, black students, rural students, and children for whom English was a second or third language often were mistakenly classified as retarded. Racial segregation was supported by this misuse of separate classes and facilities, so there was mounting pressure to end such practices. It then surfaced that handicapped children had been lumped together as a group that could not function in regular classrooms and had been segregated into special classes or facilities, often apart from regular school buildings, so that nobody would have to be reminded of their existence. Again, there was usually little expectation of achievement. Many of these students did not need special teaching techniques as much as they needed access to the regular classroom, and with a few special aids they could master the work.

School is a place where a child ordinarily experiences a sense of mastery and competence. If a child can be in a regular classroom with a minimum of services that are enough to help his handicapping condition, and if he can experience mastery in that situation, then that child is served appropriately. There are a number of learning disabled students who have mild handicaps who simply require special kinds of aids such as being allowed more time to do their work, more specific structure to help them organize their work, and the breaking down of instructions into smaller increments. Others can succeed in the regular classroom with the help of computers, calculators, tape recorders, and other such materials. There are other learning disabled youngsters who need one-on-one tutoring daily, but can feel competent in many activities of the regular classroom. Some learning disabled students need to spend part of the day in a resource room, where they receive special help in such areas as reading, spelling, and oral and written language, but join the regular classroom for all nonacademic programs and as many other academic programs as possible. Other learning disabled youngsters with greater difficulty may be in a special class in their neighborhood school for every period except lunch and sports. The severely learning disabled need to be in a self-contained classroom or learning center for the entire day or may need placement in a special school. For a very few, a residential school will best serve their needs. There exists this continuum of services that school systems must provide. An important facet of IDEA is that the least restrictive environment can change according to the needs of the child. Previously, once a child was in a special class or special school, he rarely got out. IDEA provides for reevaluation through annual reviews and interim reviews to determine if the placement continues to be appropriate.

The greatest controversies regarding the least restrictive environment center around a child like Gilbert. There are some classroom teachers who can help mildly to moderately learning disabled students find ways of functioning that minimize their disabilities and enable them to feel enough success each day to continue to believe that they can learn. However, students like Gilbert usually feel more inadequate and frustrated by remaining in classrooms with children who are not disabled. For Gilbert to be placed in a regular classroom when his needs cannot be met there is in fact a more restrictive environment than to be placed in a self-contained classroom where he is helped to learn and succeed. It was not the intent of Congress to plunge Gilbert into an environment where he feels more inadequate and more frustrated and is subject to teasing and social isolation because of his deficits. Since Gilbert is bright enough to see that others can easily do what he, with massive effort, cannot do, how can he feel better about himself as a person in a regular classroom? In that situation, Gilbert can feel so defeated that he may turn inward or he may act out and become the class clown, the negative influence, the vandal, the disrupter who keeps everyone from learning.

When a child is placed in a self-contained classroom, he does not have to be denied normal experiences. He can be introduced to exciting materials, challenged intellectually and creatively, taken on trips, and given opportunities to interact with the community. The self-contained classroom can allow the child to absorb the materials and the experiences by structuring them in ways so he *can* learn. Normal experiences belong in the self-contained classroom.

Many students like Gilbert belong in a self-contained classroom of nine to eleven severely learning disabled youngsters until they are ready to move into a resource room, and finally, with the proper support services, into a regular classroom. We would never think of throwing a preschooler who doesn't know how to swim into a large pool, telling him to swim. Yet every day we are throwing children who do not know how to learn into regular classrooms and often we watch them begin to drown. Parents need to be vigilant in regard to what is best for their child. This means looking closely at the child's needs and being able to face the disability courageously. There are some parents who lose sight of the needs of their own child and become involved in the stigma that they feel will taint them with their child's special placement. All parents want to see their child "make it" and not be isolated as "different," but the emotional complications that occur from a child failing day after day can become more severe than the learning disabilities themselves.

The severely learning disabled child is multihandicapped. As one teacher cogently said, "He's a little bit blind in that his eyes don't make sense out of what they see on a page; he's a little deaf in that he can't organize the information coming in from his ears. Frequently, he has touches of what could be called cerebral palsy in that his movement is disjointed and clumsy. Sometimes his speech is halting and he can't find the words that he needs. Emotionally, he tends to overreact or to act inappropriately. And yet he has many areas of competence. He's the hardest to teach."

Can Miss Porter, who has thirty-four sixth-graders in her class, among them one blind and one deaf child, give hyperactive, severely learning disabled Gilbert and two other moderately learning disabled students the help they need? She needs to help them learn to control themselves and teach them, step-by-step, the prerequisites in order for them to learn. Miss Porter might be able to serve Gilbert's needs systematically if she had only fifteen students in her class, a trained aide, and many support services available; even then it would be difficult.

INCLUSION

In 1993–94, school systems developed "the principle of inclusion," saying that all children, including the severely retarded, autistic, emotionally and physically ill, and learning disabled, belong in the regular classrooms. Inclusion makes it sound as though the child's civil rights are being violated if the child is placed in a resource room for part of a day, or in a contained classroom or special school. For the severely learning disabled students, their civil rights are being violated if they are forced to be in the regular classroom.

The Learning Disabilities Association of America wrote a position paper in February 1993 that states, "LDA believes that the placement of ALL children with disabilities in the regular education classroom is as great a violation of IDEA as is the placement of ALL children in separate classrooms on the basis of their disability."

Gilbert's parents feel that the state systems are pushing "inclusion," not because this model benefits every single child, but because the systems are

> BUDGET DRIVEN
>
> not
>
> CHILD DRIVEN

Marie's parents have always been embarrassed that Marie needed special education. They are delighted she has been put in an inclusive classroom, even though she cannot function effectively in it. Are Marie's parents thinking about their daughter or about their own social needs? Angela's parents are conflicted because she refuses to go to school and seems unhappy in her inclusive classroom. Yet they believe that constant contact with nondisabled children will make her behavior and learning better. Is that magical thinking? Craig's parents are worried because their son's ADHD combined with severe learning disabilities have made him "the bad boy" in his inclusive classroom; he is being sent to the principal continually. Craig's parents consider inclusion to be a form of academic child abuse.

According to IDEA, schools should "assure that, to the maximum extent *appropriate,* handicapped children . . . are educated with children who are not handicapped, and that special classes, separate schooling, or other removal of handicapped children from the regular educational environment occurs only when the nature or severity of the handicap is such that education in regular classes with the use of supplementary aids and services cannot be achieved satisfactorily." In other words, IDEA, legislated by Congress, does not say that *everybody* belongs in the mainstream. It says that all children with disabilities need individualized education and specialized teaching appropriate to their learning needs. It recognizes a continuum of services.

Inclusion has not reduced Miss Porter's class size of thirty-four. In fact, it has increased the class to forty and she is now responsible for three ADHD and learning disabled youngsters, two learning disabled, and one with a degenerative physical ailment. To compensate for this, she has been given a special education teacher who comes in a few hours a day, but she still feels unsuccessful and many of her students are feeling the same way.

Large classes rarely serve children's needs. All over the United States test scores are going down, discipline problems are soaring, children are not learning to read and write properly, yet not one school district is drastically reducing class sizes in order to give children and teachers a fighting chance to succeed. Why? Because citizens and their representatives decide that money must be allotted elsewhere. Yet we continue to wring our hands in despair at the poor quality of our schooling and too often blame the teachers.

Teachers are rarely given the support and training they need in order to work with youngsters with disabilities.

PERSONNEL DEVELOPMENT

There are extensive provisions in IDEA for states to develop comprehensive systems of personnel development with ongoing preservice and in-service training programs to be made available to all personnel who are engaged in the education of children with disabilities. Certainly all teachers working in inclusive classrooms need as much training as possible in working with students with disabilities.

Some states have indeed tried to carry this out, but most teachers complain that they have not received special training to work in a regular classroom setting with children with disabilities; they say they have at most attended one workshop or lecture or seen some films. In particular, most regular education teachers have not been trained in the special techniques that help learning disabled students. There is not enough special education included in the undergraduate programs training elementary- and secondary-school teachers. Some teacher training programs require one course (fifteen to sixteen lectures) studying all the disabilities that exist. Many programs don't even require that one course. All teachers in training need to be made aware of the many different ways students learn, their individual learning styles. Hardly any universities require a course on learning disabilities as part of the degree program for elementary- and secondary-school teachers, yet each regular classroom has about four or five students with learning disabilities in it.

Teachers of the learning disabled must first understand the normal perceptual and cognitive development in young children. Teachers need this information in order to understand the prerequisites of learning language, reading, handwriting, spelling, and arithmetic. This is necessary not only to understand the learning disabled child and his developmental stage, but also in order to write a proper IEP to meet this child's special needs.

Teachers who will be in charge of self-contained classrooms or who will be resource teachers, must study in depth the world of the learning disabled child, the means of teaching her how to learn, and basic principles of remediation. They need to have a year's daily practicum working with the learning disabled under a certified special-education master teacher. The individualized needs of teachers-in-training must be recognized and cared for if we want them to meet the individualized needs of children with learning disabilities. Exposure to a wide diversity of materials and techniques is mandatory as part of their education. Intensive training in diagnostic and remedial reading, language, perceptual-motor development, and arithmetic must be required for teachers of the learning disabled, along with courses on behavior management and psychoeducational assessment. It is important that their creativity is tapped so they will learn to use all their own personal resources; teachers in training need to be taught to make individualized materials and teaching games so that they will not rely solely on commercial materials to teach children.

Furthermore, all special education teachers need to learn to do task analysis. They have to analyze a task and understand all the steps a child must master in order to complete the task successfully. Task analysis is not only a key to good remedial teaching but it is the precise technique that helps teachers develop sequential objectives on a child's IEP. Developing IEPs must become part of every teacher's training.

University graduate programs have to train special education teachers to be able to provide appropriate education for a child like Gilbert. Teachers like Miss Porter, through their professional organizations, must demand the training and support services they need.

DUE PROCESS

Extensive due process provisions are contained in IDEA. Essentially this part of the law provides parents with the ways and means for challenging decisions or inactions of the school system with regard to:

1. notice of actions to be taken or refusals to act,
2. identification of their child as disabled,
3. evaluation of their child,
4. educational placement of their child,
5. specially designed instruction (appropriate education) being offered their child.

The school system also has its rights of due process. For example, the school can request a due process hearing on a parental refusal to consent to an evaluation or to placement. There are some parents who cannot tolerate or do not wish to accept the disabilities of their children. These are the people who say there's nothing wrong with the child, that the problems are caused by poor teaching and lack of discipline in the schools. If parents refuse help for their child, the school can and must take on an advocacy role for the student to allow him to learn.

Gilbert's parents did not know what to do after they had signed the forms to have an evaluation, and no action was taken over a two-month period. It was only because they attended a meeting of the local chapter of the Learning Disabilities Association (LDA) that they learned what legal steps could be taken on Gilbert's behalf. To begin with, the advocacy group advised the parents to buy a notebook to write down every phone call they made to the school system, the date of the call, and the person to whom they spoke. Gilbert's parents learned to request that all responses be made in writing and to write letters themselves to the school system confirming what had been said on the phone and in person.

Gilbert was evaluated shortly after the two-month period not only because the parents applied pressure to the school system, but because Miss Porter also continued to request that the child be evaluated. When Gilbert's parents were dissatisfied with the results, they knew, from studying IDEA, that they had the right to have an independent education evaluation and the right to be told where it could be obtained at little or no expense. They weren't sure whether the school system would pay for the evaluation. The school could also ask for a hearing in hopes of demonstrating that its evaluation was adequate. Had it gone to a hearing, the hearing officer, who must not be a part of the school system and must be impartial, might have ruled that Gilbert's parents had to raise the money independently.

If the school system had challenged Gilbert's parents' request for another evaluation, it could have requested mediation, another step for the school system to suggest before going to a hearing. While not mandated by the law, mediation is being used by many states to resolve differences. The advantage is that it is not a formal confrontation; the disadvantage is that it has been used by some states to delay taking any action for an interminable period. This delay can be avoided. Parents can request a due process hearing that requires that the mediation take no longer than forty-five days.

After Gilbert's parents had Gilbert evaluated a second time, they returned to an IEP meeting to discuss how the school system could provide the most appropriate education for their child. They disagreed with the school system's interpretation of the least restrictive environment, so they refused to sign the IEP and requested a hearing. At this point they turned to one of a number of advocacy groups for help. (See appendix 4 for suggestions on how parents can obtain free and low-cost assistance.) Law schools often have clinic programs; also, the federal government has given each state funds for protection and advocacy systems to protect the legal rights of developmentally disabled children. LDA chapters can help obtain legal assistance through this means. Also, the school system is required to inform parents in writing of any free or low-cost legal services available in their area.

Gilbert's parents were advised that they should hire an attorney, although they didn't have to. It is vital to find an attorney who is familiar with the law and relevant local and state statutes. They sought out a lawyer and asked these kinds of questions:

1. Are you familiar with IDEA and relevant local and state statutes?
2. Have you defended other parents in hearings?
3. Is there anything that can be done short of a hearing?
4. As a parent, what is my role in a hearing?
5. What are the possible repercussions for my child in having a due process hearing?
6. What sort of preparation must I do?
7. What kind of witnesses do we need?

8. What are the guidelines used by a hearing officer in making his decision?
9. How much will all of this cost?
10. What is our first step?

Attorneys study all the records relevant to identification, evaluation, and placement and then try to work out a reasonable agreement with school officials to avoid taking the case to a hearing or to court. Negotiations broke down in Gilbert's case. The school system adamantly insisted that it had many children who appeared to be more severely disabled than Gilbert and were more in need of a self-contained classroom. The school administration argued that the least restrictive environment for Gilbert was the regular classroom. If Gilbert's parents had been fighting for placement in a private school for the severely learning disabled, the same arguments would have applied, and the state would have had to pay the private school. Private schools usually cost more than a special class in a public school. And the parents would have had to prove that the local public school facilities definitely could not meet their child's special needs.

After the formal request for a hearing has been filed, both the hearing and the decision of the hearing officer must occur within forty-five days. Documents have to be submitted at least five days in advance of the hearing by both sides or they cannot be used, unless both sides agree to waive the rule. The list of witnesses (usually professionals with expertise in learning disabilities) also has to be presented at least five days in advance of the hearing. Parents have the right to obtain a written record or tape recording of the hearing. Hearings are closed to the public unless the parents ask for them to be open. If the parents wish, the child may be present. As with most parents, Gilbert's parents decided that Gilbert should not have to undergo such a procedure. Until his parents and the school system agreed on a placement, Gilbert was required to remain in Miss Porter's classroom.

There is no question that the wear and tear on parents can be emotionally draining, but Gilbert's parents figured the cost was worthwhile because his future was at stake. In Gilbert's hearing there was a minimum of unpleasantness, accusation, or pettiness. In some hearings, particularly when parents are attempting to win approval of private school or residential placement, the parents have been vilified by the school system's legal counsel, who must advocate for the school system's budget.

Gilbert's parents were at his hearing for a few hours. Some hearings go on for a number of hours or many days. The hearing officer gives both parties the chance to present evidence, allows cross-examination, and usually has a number of questions. The hearing officer has to provide a written decision with the forty-five-day limit of the initiation of the request and outline the facts upon which the decision was based.

In Gilbert's case, the hearing officer ruled that the school system's proposed placement was inappropriate and gave the administration twenty days to come up with a new IEP and the appropriate placement. Within days, Gilbert was placed in a self-contained classroom and one year later he was doing well; although still below grade level, he was reading better and doing some written math, but his writing skills, though improving, remained very immature. His self-esteem, a vital ingredient in learning, had been bolstered. He began to feel good about himself. All in all, he was becoming convinced that he would eventually be a good student. Gilbert's parents felt that their efforts had been worthwhile.

If Gilbert's parents had lost the hearing, they would have had the right to appeal to a state agency composed of impartial examiners. Their review of the hearing and subsequent decision must be made within thirty days of the appeal. The public school system has the same right of appeal for review of the hearing. Gilbert's parents or the public school can go on to appeal through civil action in a court if the state agency upholds the decision of the hearing officer.

There has been a rash of hearings, court suits, and class action suits, primarily concerning the placement of severely learning disabled students whose parents feel that state and local systems are not offering adequate facilities with well-trained teachers to educate their multihandicapped children appropriately. For the most part, the federal courts have been ruling for the children. The backlash, however, is growing among state and local officials and among citizens who deplore the outlay of the public money and administrative time that is involved in such litigation. A private school education at public school expense is deeply resented by some. School systems must have better facilities and trained teachers to meet the needs of severely learning disabled students, and advocacy groups need to help the public gain a better understanding of the serious issues involved.

TRANSITION SERVICES

A welcome addition to Public Law 94-142 that is an important part of IDEA is a provision for transition services. Students leaving school to go on to higher education or to the world of work require transition services that must be included in the IEP.

IDEA defines transitional services as

a coordinated set of activities for a student, designed within an outcome-oriented process, which promotes movement from school to post-school activities, including post-secondary education, vocational training, integrated employment (including supported employment), continuing and adult education, adult services, independent living, or community participation. The coordinated set of activities shall be based upon the individual student's needs, taking into account the student's preferences and interests, and shall include instruction, community experiences, the development of employment and other post-school adult living objectives, and when appropriate, acquisition of daily living skills and functional vocational evaluation.

Section 602 (a)(20) further specifies that the IEP shall include "a statement of the needed transition services for students beginning no later than age 16 and annually thereafter (and when determined appropriate for the individual, beginning at age 14 or younger), including, when appropriate, a statement of the Interagency responsibilities or linkages before the student leaves the school setting."

Junior-high and high-school special educators have to work with parents and the youngster with learning disabilities to do transition planning. Since its objectives are long-range, community agencies (i.e., Department of Rehabilitation) and postsecondary institutions (i.e., community colleges, trade schools) become part of the team. The individual transition plan (ITP) is based on individual needs, interests, talents, and dreams. It includes long-range goals such as:

- learning self-advocacy
- career-planning options
- social skills training
- learning to use local transportation
- learning to live independently
- postsecondary training

Learning self-advocacy is the most important transition skill when the destination is college or employment. Parents and teachers need to keep pointing out to the student with learning disabilities what the student is good at, where the student experiences difficulties, and what approaches and methods seem to work best. The ability to explain one's strengths and weaknesses, what helps or doesn't help, allows a person to receive the necessary accommodations under the Americans with Disabilities Act. (See chapter 13).

PARENT PARTICIPATION

Parent participation permeates all aspects of IDEA. The law acknowledges the importance of parents every step of the way and encourages their involvement in the development and approval of educational policy. Participation at public hearings and parent membership on local and state advisory panels on the education of children with disabilities allow parents not only to affect educational policy but also to influence procedural guidelines and ways of monitoring them.

The intent of the act is to best serve the individualized needs of each child with a disability by providing an appropriate education. Parents and teachers of learning disabled youngsters need to work together as much as possible to achieve this goal. If it could be possible for local systems to have a case manager who follows each disabled child through his education, then parents, teachers, and school administrators might all feel heard and supported, and as a result, might be able to work more closely together. Learning disabled youngsters need all the support they can get. Basically, it is in the child's best interests not to have schools and parents as adversaries, but as team members.

What we all share in common
  is a concern
    for a child who is disabled in learning.

What we all know
  is that the quality of teaching received
    can make a crucial difference
      in the quality of a learning disabled child's life.

What we all need to do
  is to use IDEA
    to give a learning disabled youngster
      the appropriate individualized education he or she
        deserves.

THIRTEEN

ADOLESCENCE: SOCIALIZATION AND ORGANIZATION

The parents of a teenager with learning disabilities are older and more tired than they were when he was a child. *Tomorrow has come.* Not only is he not cured, he is more difficult than ever to manage. He is still very dependent, while becoming harder to control and guide. He is bigger, stronger, more withdrawn yet more defiant, and his parents find that now, more than ever before, they need

> *more energy,*
> *more stamina,*
> *more patience,*
> *more tolerance,*
> *more hope that he will be able*
> *to manage effectively in the world.*

It is normal for the parents of learning disabled adolescents to want to give up sometimes. Their frustration and anxiety have increased. The future has to be reckoned with, and they are deeply concerned about it. Schooling, vocational possibilities, and social opportunities have to be studied carefully. They have to devise ways to help the learning disabled adolescent be able to learn to be self-sufficient. When the child was younger, his parents could use their ingenuity and problem-solving resources effectively, programming ways for their child to succeed and have fun, tempting other children to join in and be his friends. But teenagers are rarely lured by parental endeavors except in the form of tickets to football games or other exciting events, and not always by these.

Teenagers live by the rule of the pack. They band together against or, at least, apart from the adult world. This is a normal process, separating themselves temporarily into their own society, integrating the past—their childhood—with the present, getting ready to deal with the future. It is a time when peer relationships are crucial, and they are most often guided by one another through communications that may appear incomprehensible to adults.

Some learning disabled teenagers have the social maturity to keep up with the pack; they may feel defeated at school but not in the neighborhood. However, the majority of learning disabled adolescents do not have either the social maturity or the communications skills to gain solid membership in teenage groups, and they feel increasingly isolated. As Ms. Anthony put it, "I used to cry because Jim couldn't read and he and I had to watch his younger brothers and sisters surpass him at school. Now I am filled with tears because he is so alone, so isolated, hanging around the house more and more, glued to the TV."

Often the learning disabled adolescent doesn't know what to do with himself. His constant proximity to his parents increases the friction between them, increases his feeling of being picked on, and heightens everybody's unhappiness as all the people involved come to feel more and more inadequate. It is common for parents (and teachers) to say:

It's time for you to shape up.
You're too old for that!
When will you start growing up?
How long are you going to keep this up?
Won't you ever learn?
When will you stop acting like a two-year-old?
When will this end?

Everyone needs to realize that most of the time these things are not said to hurt the youngster, to be mean, or to get even. They are expressions of helplessness, frustration, fear, guilt, or anxiety. These words come spontaneously out of pain, out of not knowing what else to do. Yet while parents are struggling with these realities, the other children in the family may criticize them for not being tough enough, or kind enough, or helpful enough with the learning disabled brother. Often they scream at their parents, "Do something about him!" Almost every parent tries to do his or her best for a child, and when the best is not good enough to make things change, the parent may feel desperate.

The learning disabled adolescent feels the same desperation. He absorbs all the angry, guilty, frightened feelings that make him feel unworthy. He learned during his most formative and impressionable years that he couldn't do things, couldn't understand, and couldn't perform like other children, and the cumulative effect of repeated failure firmly established his poor self-image. His perception of his home is frequently that his parents nag him all the time because he can do nothing right. His perception of school is often one of nagging teachers. He feels he is being told he is "no good" all the time.

I can't do anything right.
  I'm no good.
    I'm dumb.
      I'm a retard.

Nobody likes me.
Everybody's picking on me.

These are some of the feelings that the learning disabled child shoulders as he grows up. He doesn't understand or he misunderstands many aspects of his life, and he receives correction or criticism, which he translates into "everybody's picking on me." It probably reflects his very real view of the situation because he doesn't interpret the correction or criticism as being helpful. Often he sees his world as a series of mistakes, one after another, all totaling personal disaster. It's hard to grow up feeling good about himself under these conditions. If he has special skills, a learning disabled child can feel good about his success in sports, his artistic talent, or his popularity with a group, but still has a gnawing feeling that something is wrong with him.

This is why straight talk is so important. It is vital that the child hear over and over again from different sources that he is intelligent but that he needs more time to learn than others and that he will make it in the world. He needs as much information about himself as he can handle, and he needs it frequently. He may still feel dumb. But at least he knows he is not retarded and does not have any progressive brain disease or whatever else he may secretly dread.

FEELINGS OF GUILT, ANXIETY, AND INCOMPETENCE

In many ways, life seems very unfair to the learning disabled child. He perceives the world in the only way he can, albeit incorrectly, and he meets rebuff or ridicule as a result of what he says or does based on that perception. This youngster is often brought into child guidance clinics because someone thinks he is an angry, willful, unmotivated, or spoiled child who is purposely not performing well at school. This very frightened child cannot, rather than will not, perform well at school.

If you are awkward and you are faced with the task of rewiring a delicate stereo set, the job has to be done by you and you alone, and you know you are not up to it, how do you feel? Suppose you don't know how to draw. You have tried drawing many times, and you know you are terrible at it, but you have been told by an implacable authority that you must draw a picture for public display. How do you feel?

When you feel incompetent, you can easily feel imposed upon, and this can lead to anger. "Why me?!" is a frequent rejoinder of a learning disabled child when he is asked to do something. Some say of this child, "He has a chip on his shoulder," or, "He has a mad on the world." To an extent, he does.

He's angry at the world's demands on him, demands he cannot meet. He's angry at himself for not being able to do what he wants to do. He's angry at his parents, teachers, brothers, sisters, neighbors, and classmates for seeing him in the act of not being able to do. He's angry at God or God's representatives in church or synagogue. He's angry at being what he is.

When a child is angry, she does a lot in excess by acting out or withdrawing. She frequently makes others into scapegoats. A learning disabled child, seeing her own inadequacies reflected in others, can be a terrible tease, picking on the flaws of her companions and then perseverating. A beautiful, blond boy of thirteen, who was very intelligent, had severe learning disabilities. He followed a pattern—in school, on the playground, and at camp—of finding the least attractive youngster in the crowd and asking, "How does it feel to be ugly?" This child did not feel attractive himself; he felt ugly, worthless, and inadequate, and he projected his feelings on others. As soon as he overcame his disabilities to a point where he felt better about himself, he no longer displayed this need. The amount of teasing, provoking, and bullying that goes on in special classes for the learning disabled can be overwhelming, and it is one of the biggest management problems for teachers. "Mary is always calling me stupid!" complains Alison. Why? Because Mary feels stupid. "Harry's called me *dumb fool* all week!" says Jerry. Why? Because Harry feels like a dumb fool.

Along with the anger is the accompanying helpless guilt. Placing blame on things undone and constant self-castigation are familiar ways of acting when one feels guilty for not meeting standards. Rituals are important to the learning disabled child not only because his inflexibility craves what is familiar and safe but also because of a primitive belief that wearing a certain sweater, sitting in a special seat, or using a red pen will make everything work. "If only I had worn my good luck ring and the blue ribbon I had in my hair the last time I got a good mark on the test, I could have done well today," mused Connie. It is typical of a very young child to count on magic to solve problems. The more profound the guilt a child feels, the more disparaging she feels about herself, the more she makes the people around her feel guilty and bad about themselves.

If a young person's nervous system has matured and if he has received sufficient remedial help to overcome the worst of his learning disabilities by the time he reaches adolescence, he will probably suffer no more than the normal stresses and strains of that period of life. Adolescence is the pathway from childhood to adulthood with much backward and forward movement. It's a time of identity crisis. Who am I? What do I believe in? Am I child? Am I a grown-up? If the turbulence of this period is combined with the profound self-doubt and confusion stemming from severe learning disabilities, the youngster faces a very painful and difficult time.

All children become less cute and endearing as they grow up, but this is normally offset by their developing sense of independence and responsibility. The learning disabled child, however, does not become much more independent as he grows older. His delayed maturation keeps him from acquiring the skills needed for independence. He has become a teenager by his number of years; he may have the physical size and puberty development of a teenager, but his neural development and his behavior are like those of a much younger child. Yet the world expects his behavior to fit with his appearance. The bigger the child, the more grown-up he looks, the harder it is for people to tolerate his immature behavior. The sixteen-year-old who is still small and baby-faced can get away with more than a gangly six-footer whose stubbly beard has begun to show.

NO SUBSTITUTES FOR ORGANIZATION

The learning disabled adolescent's disorganization infuriates her parents and teachers, for she is careless, untidy, messy, clumsy, forgetful, unthinking, and egocentric. Hank begins each day by sleeping through the clatter of his alarm clock; only his mother's strong will and strong arm finally get him up. He skids out of the house many minutes too late, leaving a trail of chaos in his wake—unmade bed, dumped-out drawers, forgotten books, spilled milk, and the front door standing open behind him. By the time he reaches school, he has missed the bell, and classes have started. He is angry, defensive, miserable, and embarrassed; he hates the way the day has begun, and he hates himself for being the way he is. To cover these feelings, he makes a grand entrance into his classroom: "Tadaaa! Superman is here!" He interrupts an interesting discussion, nobody thinks he is funny, and his teacher, thoroughly irritated, reprimands him sharply. Hank slinks to his seat, making an obscene gesture at an athletic classmate who clearly scorns him. He hears nothing that is said during the rest of the period, for he is preoccupied with his own inner turmoil, hurt feelings, helplessness, rage, and the firm conviction that nobody likes him—and never will—and that he cannot do anything right—and never will.

And so Hank's life goes. Untidy and disorganized, he forgets to take a bath, brush his teeth, and comb his hair. His bedroom smells awful, and he would never change his clothes if his mother did not take full responsibility for doing his laundry and laying out clean clothes. When other kids tell him his feet stink, he does not draw the conclusion that he should wash his feet and his socks; instead he thinks they are picking on him again because they don't like him. Instead of reforming, it is likely that he becomes even more disorganized, plowing through the morass of homework papers, dirty clothes, and unfinished projects all scattered around him. Most teenagers have a problem with messiness in varying degrees, but the learning disabled youngster has them more pronouncedly, in more areas, and they last longer. Usually they are combined with poor planning, a lack of punctuality, poor study habits, poor follow-through, and unproductive uses of his time.

A college developing a program for intelligent students with learning disabilities concentrated heavily on audiovisual equipment and other academic props for these young people who had difficulty with reading and writing. After spending great amounts of time and money planning for these academic problems, the directors found that the students couldn't get up in the morning, couldn't organize their homework, lost their belongings, couldn't find their classrooms, forgot their assignments, and in general were so hampered by their pervasive disorder that they could not benefit properly from the academic program. The college finally instituted a buddy system whereby a well-organized student was teamed up with each learning disabled one, and they began to work explicitly on the organizational problem so that the students could learn successfully.

The three Rs are not substitutes for organization. Organization needs to be taught, taught again, and reinforced by every available means until habits and procedures become routine or, if possible, automatic. The learning disabled adolescent must consciously program herself to stop, think, figure out what comes first, next, last, and then go back and check to make sure she did it. This process is very demanding and exhausting. The tendency of the learning disabled youngster to react indiscriminately and to have her attention all over the map uses up enormous amounts of energy. She fatigues easily, making every task that much harder. Frequently learning disabled people who are successful adults stress their fatigue. They will tell you that, even today, the hardest thing for them to combat is this fatigue that comes from the constant overloading of their senses, the ever-present clamor of stimuli on their attention, which they must consciously work to keep under control. They need to develop systems to help themselves with organization. They need to program for the fatigue by allowing more time and more intervals of rest or by obtaining extra help on certain aspects of their jobs. They must be more conscious than the average person of the slow processing in their brain and the resulting inefficiency that demands so much of them. They have to come to recognize their own patterns of fatigue (as they must know their deficit areas) and find ways to compensate.

From the time a child enters adolescence, school, parents, recreation centers, and all other adults who come in contact with the learning disabled need to center attention on the organizational skills that he will employ for his adult life. The youngster has to be taught explicitly how to gather up what he needs to work with, how to begin a project, and follow through to the end. Adolescence is the age when checklists have to be made up with the help of the child, outlining every stage of each task and each household chore. He has to be in on the planning to get an overall view of how to accomplish a task and to see what all the stages are, to check off what has been done, step-by-step, and eventually internalize the process so that it can be performed automatically. This system applies to mopping the floor, emptying the garbage, delivering newspapers, and making a project for school. It is hoped that this method of breaking down a task, systematically finishing each stage in order, and checking off a list will, with sufficient repetition, become a habit, transferable to all other areas of activity.

Learning disabled young people are delayed in development, often by two, three, or even as many as five years in certain areas. They are immature. Some parents realize this, and offer a great deal of protection and the guidance appropriate to a much younger child. Other parents take into account only the actual age and demand that their children act appropriately. One may encourage infantile behavior, while the other makes unrealistic demands. A fine line is needed to encourage independence at every step while giving necessary support—this is no easy task.

Independence usually relies on organizational skills. Self-sufficiency means taking responsibility for oneself. In areas where a learning disabled adolescent needs to learn specific, everyday skills to enhance his self-reliance, he can be taught to do many of these things, and the feelings of competence he derives from mastery set him up for more accomplishment. The following list taps some of the daily living skills the adolescent must master. They may cause great difficulty to many learning disabled teenagers for they involve organization, planning, memory, and a sense of time and place.

Use the Bus
Learn to go around town.
Know the bus insignias.
Know their destinations.

Set the Table
Lay out correct place settings.
Clear the table.
Wash and dry dishes.

Do Simple Cooking
Feed self.
Cook eggs and toast.
Heat soup.
Make hamburgers, hot dogs, frozen dinners.

Make a Bed
Know sequence of sheets, blankets, bedcovers.
Learn tucking-in techniques.

Use Newspapers
Know the organization.
Learn where to find the
    sports, amusements, want
    ads, etc.

Eat at Restaurants
Learn how a menu is
    organized.
Understand the check.
Learn to order.
Calculate the tip.

Use Money
Learn to count change.
Keep money in a systematic
    way.
Make simple accounts.
Learn to use cash machine.

Deal with Time
Learn to read the clock.
Make approximate schedules.
Learn the "feel" of intervals
    of time: how long is fifteen
    minutes? Half an hour?
    Two hours?

Do Shopping
Plan purchases.
Find the right store and
    department.
Make choices.

Use the Telephone
Know how to dial numbers.
Learn emergency numbers.
Learn how to ask clear
    questions.
Give and receive pertinent
    information.
Make an appointment.

Fill Out Forms
Learn to fill out job
    applications and
    questionnaires.
Understand bank forms (use
    enlarged forms and go
    slowly, step-by-step, from
    simple forms to more
    complex ones).

Coping with daily life demands developing strategies. Learning to live
effectively with certain disabilities employs strategic thinking. Educators as well as parents need to teach strategies to teenagers.

Games are important for learning disabled adolescents for more reasons than the social know-how of playing chess, checkers, bingo, backgammon, Monopoly, Ping-Pong, pool, pinball, or video games. Games also develop nonverbal reasoning and logic. They demand strategies just as life does, and these are of vital importance to the learning disabled teenager.

Because of his good intelligence, this child learns the strategies of con men at an early age, plus all kinds of strategies of avoidance and denial. The adults around him can provide the learning disabled teenager with the experience he needs to invent strategies as he needs them, ways to get through situations when he does not know what to do. Using games of confrontation can help him to confront his own battles and talk about them. There are ways to win, and he needs to know them.

DEVELOPING SURVIVAL STRATEGIES

The important educational job for both teachers and parents is to help teenagers and young adults develop survival strategies. These young people have to recognize their needs and develop their own survival techniques, for school in the short run, for adult life and job holding in the long run. They need tricks to help them to stick with a problem until it can be solved or successfully bypassed. They need conscious devices to trigger memory. Whether it's by using magnetic letters or simply magnets holding notes on a refrigerator, or their own bulletin boards, or a special hook near the door where they can hang notes to themselves, they need concrete help in remembering what they have to do. A special place has to be found for homework to be put in order to help them remember to take it back to school. Name tapes on all clothes, book bags, eyeglasses, and notebooks help the disorganized to hold on to his or her belongings. A special place or container for keys must be provided in order to prevent their loss.

Poor memories demand smart, practical strategies. Seymour learned to control his habit of speaking impulsively and thoughtlessly by chewing gum. Another student achieved the same result by keeping his finger pressed to his chin. Mildly learning disabled youngsters who cannot take fast dictation, for instance, might learn to use a tape recorder or work out an arrangement with another student to take the notes in exchange for typing them. Professionals may need to provide some of the strategies, but it is more important for a youngster to learn to devise his own.

When the nervous system is overstimulated, both the brain and the body work inefficiently, wasting energy on indiscriminate matter. This is compounded by, or produces, slow processing. The result is fatigue. Strategies to deal with that fatigue must be invented by the student and by the parents and professionals who advise her. To begin with, she must recognize when the fatigue sets in so that she can do something about it. Leota found that by moving her body position frequently and by breaking her assignments into short periods, she could minimize the effects of fatigue. She found ways to maintain her focus when her mind wandered by moving small objects about on her desk. And she found it essential, from time to time, to retreat to a place where she could find silence and solitude as a relief from the perpetual overload on her senses. What worked for Leota did not work for her friend Vanessa, who had to find other ways of dealing with fatigue.

CONCENTRATION ON LANGUAGE SKILLS

No system can compensate for a dearth of basic language skills that make for easy communication. Solid language training has to take place for the adolescent who has poor language skills. These skills need special concentration not only to help him get along with people but as preparation for finding a job. In a job interview, he has to be able to answer questions on demand, and performance on demand may be his nemesis. He must know how to listen carefully to questions and stick to the point in answering them. He has to remember to have eye contact with the interviewer, to be appealing as a person, to be attractive and clean in appearance, and to give indications of his reliability and sense of responsibility. Talking about these things is not nearly as effective as role playing, in which the teenager can play the role of both the interviewer and the job hunter while an adult takes the other part.

SOCIALIZATION PROBLEMS

The learning disabled adolescent frequently finds himself shut off from young people his own age, not only because of his appearance (which advertises his own opinion, "I am not worth knowing") or his inappropriate behavior, but because he really can't share with other youngsters. He isn't yet capable of sharing ideas or feelings or even belongings with any degree of give-and-take. Often he has difficulty with communication. His language does not flow. Words are not useful tools for him at an age when young people like to talk about themselves a great deal. Words become a burden to him because they create confusion rather than clarity and understanding. When he tries to take part in group activities, he feels himself to be odd man out, and this feeling invites others to reject him. His personality, the total of his behavior, which was tolerated when he was younger or excused because he was just a child, now turns people off. They are made edgy by his unreliability and impulsiveness. They get fed up when he perseverates, going on and on about his favorite subject. They become bored by his gullibility, impatient

with his inability to do two things at once, threatened by his disor-
derliness, and exasperated by his self-centeredness and stereotyped
responses. Furthermore a young person like Hank does not make
people feel good about themselves when he is with them. He, like his
classmates Christine and Arthur, frequently make people feel ha-
rassed and overwhelmed, which, unfortunately, is the way Hank,
Christine, and Arthur feel.

Christine doesn't look at the person who is shaking her hand
effusively. Arthur pushes right between two adults who are actively
engaged in conversation. Christine demonstrates her social ineptitude
by barging into a private office without an "excuse me"; so does Hank
by throwing his books on the table where the guest is drinking coffee,
and Alice, by pulling at the teacher's sleeve and talking to her a mile a
minute while the teacher is settling down the class.

Christine, Arthur, Hank, and Alice are not stopping to look,
listen, and feel what's going on. Not one of them takes a look at a
person's face to see if the expression is one of sadness, anger, fear, or
embarrassment. Not one looks to see if people are involved with one
another. Not one listens to what's going on. It is extremely hard to size
up a situation under these conditions, yet we know that the learning
disabled child is a poor judge of size, shape, and direction and doesn't
perceive more than his own wants and goals as of that moment. The
learning disabled child is immature and egocentric; he is not inten-
tionally unconcerned about others, but he is not yet ready to focus on
their needs.

Christine, Arthur, Hank, or Alice might demonstrate social clumsiness at the dinner table or in a school discussion by interrupting
constantly and usually with inappropriate remarks. Without a good
sense of timing, conversation is virtually impossible, and the tendency
to monopolize the conversation is far too easy. This is an immature
pattern, understood when it occurs with the very young child but
unacceptable to society in the older child.

Most children learn decorum and polite behavior not only by

being taught rules but by copying their parents and others. The learning disabled child has trouble copying and does not absorb the family's behavior. Furthermore there are several ways of behaving in a given situation, and our One-Way Kid cannot deal with alternatives. When he sticks to one stereotyped way, his social clumsiness makes others feel uncomfortable and irritated.

He often feels picked on and bullied, and he often is because of his awkwardness and disruptive effect on others. He can wreck a group activity that depends on teamwork and cooperation. He can't wait, can't take turns, doesn't understand rules, misses the point. He may dampen the group's enthusiasm, convinced that any deviation from a familiar method won't work. He may try too hard, injecting discomfort into the group by his loud laughter at jokes he doesn't understand, his overeagerness, his tenseness. He is forever doing too much or too little. His problem is not misbehavior but miscalculation. He is clumsy and makes inappropriate responses. Later in life, he finds out he can't keep a job because his behavior is inappropriate. Or perhaps he loses his job and never recognizes that the real cause was his own behavior.

TEACHING SOCIAL BEHAVIOR

Professionals working with learning disabled teenagers and adults need to teach them how to pay attention to feedback, how to recognize it, and then how to use it. Socialization for many severely learning disabled youngsters has to be taught step-by-step, just as the tasks in reading and math are broken down and accomplished one step at a time.

Tina was thought to be a most unfriendly young lady. She brusquely pushed past adults she met in the hallway at school, and she was barely civil to her parents' friends at home. She felt as unliked by grown-ups as she did by her classmates. Her parents wondered why Tina couldn't see what she was doing and observe what impact her behavior had on other people. They talked to her endlessly about this, but to no avail. Fortunately she was one of a small group of teenage girls at school who were invited to take a grooming class. In fact, the class was designed explicitly to teach teenagers like Tina how to behave appropriately.

The teacher of the class asked one of the students to play the role of the hostess. The teacher then played the part of a guest. She barged into this imaginary situation, not looking at the girl playing hostess and brushing right past her. The teacher then entered again, this time offering her hand, looking the hostess in the eye, and saying, "Hi! It's so nice of you to invite me." She then discussed with the girls which of these two entries they preferred. Clearly it was the latter, and the students analyzed why. They each took a turn playing both hostess and guest in a variety of similar situations, and talked over the effects together.

Parents can reenact situations like this with younger children, but for teenagers, the schools, recreation groups, and church groups are needed to do this kind of teaching. Learning disabled youngsters cannot fathom these very simple ways to make people enjoy being with them. Eye contact, a smile, a reassuring pat, a firm handshake, a pleasant greeting, a gently phrased question, a polite interruption, a thoughtful inquiry, and sometimes a needed silence—all these are social skills that must be taught, each for its own place, one by one. Videotape machines can be enormously helpful for a young person to help him see himself as others do. The use of the absurd can also be an effective way to begin this kind of training, with the adult doing some most inappropriate and comical things. The exaggeration begins to define what is inappropriate, and from there the adult and the adolescent can move together toward understanding subtler behaviors.

The art of socialization is highly complex. Many learning disabled children have mastered it. Some have not, but they can, in time. No child has all the problems listed below, but even a few of them impede socialization.

What works against learning disabled youngsters using good judgment in social situations?

Disorder, disorganization, scatter.

Lack of impulse control (acting without thinking).

Low tolerance of frustration and need for immediate gratification.

Body and spatial problems (difficulties in judging size, shape, distance, direction).

Poor concepts of time and timing.

Perseveration (repeating an action or phrase or topic over and over again).

Difficulty in shifting from one situation to another.

Emotional lability (overreacting, moodiness, changeability).

Poor listening skills, poor memory, poor grasp of sequence (forgetting what they are doing and what they are supposed to do next).

Inability to look at what is going on and to visualize.

Giving as much weight to the most minute detail as to the key point.

Difficulty in making choices of any kind.

Concrete, literal comprehension, missing subtleties and nuances.

Egocentric outlook (the inability to put themselves in others' shoes).

Inability to relate cause and effect, and to generalize from social experiences (the inability to predict).

How do learning disabled youngsters demonstrate poor judgment in social situations?

Barging thoughtlessly into situations and interrupting without looking.

Having trouble taking turns.

Acting belligerent (when in reality they do not comprehend directions).

Making inappropriate remarks, gestures, actions, poorly timed responses.

Misreading the social signals given by others (not understanding facial expressions, posture, or symbolic movements that indicate fear, anger, guilt, complicity, irritation, sadness, etc.).

Missing the point of what other people are doing, off target.

Letting others take advantage of them; carrying out destructive acts for others.

Blowing up at the slightest hint of criticism, tiny mistakes, postponements, or delays; overreacting to mild teasing.

Telling jokes that are not funny; not understanding the jokes, puns, riddles of others.

Picking on everything that is different from last time (appearing uncooperative and intransigent by seeing only one way to do things).

Being bossy (the need to organize others stemming from their own internal disorganization).

Planning poorly.

Quitting, running away, or making fools of themselves when they cannot explain their failure to perform competently.

Placing blame on others (denial of their own role in a situation that has gone wrong).

Needing to win at all costs (this can lead to lying, cheating, destroying the game).

A NEED FOR ACCEPTANCE

Rafael is desperately lonely; he would do almost anything to feel accepted and liked by other youngsters. Because of his loneliness, he is in greater danger of being led astray by others than is his fourteen-year-old neighbor, a boy who is fortunate enough to have developed normally, with good judgment, self-confidence, and a clear understanding of right and wrong. When Rafael was little, other children found it was easy to take his toys. Now they find they can get his money. Where he used to give them cookies in exchange for "friendship," now he gives them money. Or he may give them alcohol or drugs, which can lead to stealing if he hasn't money of his own with which to buy them. He'll cheat, lie, tattle, take on a new friend's values and prejudices (which may be alien to his own), or he may become a "slave" to a person, following any command in order to gain friendship. He'll do anything to make a friend and to belong. Because he feels unwanted, he may be drawn to fringe groups that harbor other lonely, alienated people—religious cults or groups embracing bizarre food fads and diets. He may be drawn into vandalism or other delinquent behavior that he did not think up but for which he will invariably get caught. He may be lured into trying hard drugs, alcohol, or sex in all forms as a social route. The activity itself is not important. The warding away of loneliness and the embracing of companionship in any form is what matters.

He tends to be off balance here as in physical activities: overdoing, timing badly, judging incorrectly. Once more, he falls flat on his face and has to learn, one step at a time, how to cope with these situations. Too often he tends to retreat to the television, to become glued . . . or to the icebox, to become fat . . . to the bar, to become drunk . . . to the motorcycle or car, to race away . . . or to playing with the mother and baby next door, because he has become weary. Social clumsiness isolates the learning disabled youngster even more than his physical clumsiness. "It's not fair" is a frequent rejoinder of the learning disabled adolescent—and it isn't.

This same isolation, the lonely longing to belong, if channeled and trained, can draw a learning disabled adolescent into groups that can greatly help him. These can range from chess clubs to bowling teams to amateur theatrical groups. Where such groups don't exist, parents, teachers, or community organizations can *and must* create them. There is a need for group activities where learning disabled teenagers can learn the skills of daily life and acquire the know-how and the social "passports" to allow them to move confidently in the grown-up world of everyday living. There are many young Americans who do not know how to make constructive use of leisure time. Imagine what it is like for learning disabled teenagers! They must be taught explicitly the resources in their neighborhood and in their community. They need help to discover what they like to do and how to go about doing it. They have to be taught how to organize themselves to engage in satisfying activities, or they may opt for the TV because it is there, safe, and does not require any organized action. In order to learn that their voice counts and that our democracy depends upon involvement and active participation, an adolescent needs to be taught how to vote, learn about candidates and the positions they stand for, and how to form opinions and choose one candidate over another—an exceedingly difficult task for all of us, but particularly for the young person who has trouble assigning priorities. They need to be shown the value of asking questions, perhaps by supplying them with the questions at first and then helping them form their own. These are life skills that help them feel they can better their own lives and validate their stake in the world.

DEVELOPING A SPECIAL TALENT

Many successful learning disabled adults have had one area of special competence that allowed them to shine, to have a goal, and to build confidence. It is crucial for a learning disabled youngster to find one talent or one skill on which he can concentrate, if at all possible. Once such an interest is identified, it can be encouraged and trained by parents, teachers, and all other professionals who work with this child. If the youngster learns well by demonstration, he should have a chance to become apprenticed to somebody who is already skilled. Suppose a boy has a knack with machines; find a mechanic who will let the boy work in his garage as an assistant or pay the mechanic as you would any other tutor. Senior citizens are a great untapped resource in our society. Through church groups and interest clubs, they have a great deal that they could offer in working individually with learning disabled teenagers. Their calm manner and organization, their experience with life, and their available time can make a difference in the life of a learning disabled adolescent.

Sports can open up a whole world, even to an unathletic boy or girl. By dint of hard work with their learning disabled child, parents can bring alive sports that they love themselves. Step-by-step, they can build up an understanding and appreciation of football, soccer, baseball, basketball, golf, tennis, or almost any spectator sport. The ritual and procedure of stadium behavior can be learned and enjoyed. A learning disabled youngster with a keen interest in a sport may find purpose and satisfaction as a manager's assistant on a team—taking care of many routine but vital details, like towels and jackets, and earning the right to wear the team's uniform. He might become an expert on facts and figures concerning his favorite sport or simply have fun attending games with his father.

The learning disabled person needs a realistic view of his strengths and capabilities as well as his weaknesses and disabilities, to make the most of what he has. Nothing is more pathetic than the person who pretends to be what he is not, who chases after impossible goals, destroying himself along the way. This is not to say that the learning disabled adolescent should settle for the lowest practical opportunities without aiming higher. For many, a college education is possible and attainable. Community colleges are becoming a haven for young learning disabled adults after they leave high school. The time they spend there often gives them the opportunity to mature, to find a specialty, to develop organization, discipline, and study habits that will enable them to succeed in a competitive four-year college or to hold a job. Vocational schools are the answer for others who have no particular bent but who are especially good with their hands.

Some learning disabled children, through neural maturation and systematic special education, grow out of almost every learning disability. The majority grow out of most of their disabilities and learn to compensate for the rest. Others carry the baggage of many learning disabilities with them through life, grappling with them, using strategies to overcome or get around the deficient areas. Given a good bit of extra time and skilled teaching, they can learn to function independently in adult life.

Unfortunately, many people with learning disabilities do not receive the help they need to become productive. They need the same kind of highly individualized instructional programming for success in vocational areas that they needed in special education. Their strengths and weaknesses need to be matched to job categories. What's required on a particular job demands task analysis—the sequence of steps needed to be learned to perform the task effectively. The learning disabled require step-by-step teaching through their strengths to achieve mastery. Parents and teachers are helped by the new legislation, IDEA, which demands that transition services be written into the IEP. The highly individualized and specialized attention needed by the severely learning disabled adolescent (as incredibly expensive as it is) is *less* expensive than paying for welfare because of joblessness, psychiatric clinics, courts, and prisons. And what about the devastation of the entire family unit when an intelligent young person with potential falls by the wayside because of lack of necessary support services?

FEDERAL LAWS PROTECTING COLLEGE STUDENTS AND EMPLOYEES WITH LEARNING DISABILITIES

There are federal laws that protect the rights of the disabled, including the learning disabled, in the workforce and in college or university settings. These laws, along with PL 101-476, have opened doors to learning and employment that had previously remained locked. Opportunities abound for the learning disabled.

The Rehabilitation Act of 1973, section 504, makes it illegal for companies or organizations receiving federal monies to discriminate against someone solely by reason of his disability. Colleges and universities that receive federal funding cannot discriminate against a student based solely on his learning disability. In all cases, the law mandates that "reasonable accommodations" be made for individuals with learning disabilities, such as letting them use taped books in college.

In July 1990, the Americans with Disabilities Act (ADA), Public Law 101-336, was passed, extending the conditions of section 504. ADA, unlike section 504, is not limited to companies or organizations receiving federal aid or participating in federally connected programs. With ADA in effect, it is now illegal for employers to discriminate against workers with physical, mental, or learning disabilities, and those who do can be taken to court.

ADA prohibits discrimination against "otherwise qualified" disabled persons who apply for jobs and uses two factors to determine whether an individual is a "qualified person":

1.   Does the person possess the requisite skill, experience, education, and other job-related requirements of the position?

2. Can the person perform the fundamental job duties of the position, either with or without reasonable accommodations?

In addition to being required to hire disabled workers, employers may not refuse to promote or provide training to workers who are or become disabled; they must pay employees with disabilities the same salaries they would pay nondisabled workers holding the same or similar jobs.

Perhaps the most difficult term to define for the learning disabled is "reasonable accommodations." Many learning disabled workers do not require any accommodations in the workplace, and those who do need assistance require differing degrees of support on the job. Types of accommodations that a learning disabled worker might need include:

- A demonstration of the required task with written and verbal instruction
- Tests on the job to be given verbally, not in writing
- The use of computers, calculators, tape recorders and computing cash registers
- Having a mentor on the job until necessary skills are mastered.

One of the most difficult issues in obtaining reasonable accommodations for a person with a learning disability is telling the employer about the learning problem. The person with a disability does not have to disclose his disability during the interview, nor can an employer ask the person about his disability. Suggestions for how to handle disclosure are:

1. If the prospective employee is qualified for the job and is almost certain he will not need accommodations, he can

accept the job without telling the employer about his learning disability. The employee must consider all facets of the job and be sure accommodations will not be needed for any of them.

2. If the person takes the job and does so well that he is considered for promotion but must take a written test in order to be promoted, under the law, he can now tell his employer about his learning disability and ask for test-taking accommodations. He will want and need untimed tests.

3. If a person with a learning disability realizes that accommodations will be necessary, either from the beginning of the job or as responsibilities increase, he has to discuss this with the employer. The prospective employee must focus on his qualifications and special skills, noting specific areas that might need accommodations. For example, a person applying for a job as a secretary who has trouble spelling would need to have a computer with Spell Check.

PREPARING FOR WORK

Rehabilitation counselors find the severely learning disabled adult especially difficult to help. They say, "Give me any other handicap but LD" because the learning disabled are such a jumble of inexplicable behaviors marked by extremes of competencies and incompetencies. "They are bright, so they get bored with repetitive tasks, but they are inefficient and can't do the simplest of things. They oversleep, don't allow enough time to arrive at work on time, have no time sense." Another counselor says, "He loses his way everywhere, even within a building, and he would forget where his head was if it wasn't attached to his body." Another vocational rehabilitation counselor stated, "They are messy, unmotivated, and don't care!"

The learning disabled adolescent usually does care. In fact, he is often trying his heart out! He breaks fifty-two dishes at the restaurant because his motor skills are so poor. It's not for lack of trying but for lack of coordination and organization. A very perspicacious young adult with learning disabilities stated that parents and teachers must *instruct learning disabled adolescents to show that they are trying.* They need to gain the support of their fellow workers, supervisors, and also customers, by being able to talk about their difficulties, and to be savvy, as was the learning disabled adolescent who, each day, told her customers, "It's my first day waitressing and I'm nervous." For some, it is an impossible task to be a waiter, and finding more suitable employment is necessary.

We know from talking with learning disabled students and young adults that they put in double or quadruple the time that others do to learn something and master it. Their effort is massive. It is courageous. *But their hidden handicap prevents them from receiving positive feedback for their determination and stamina.* How can they be helped to let the world know what they are going through, without asking for pity?

Originality, ingenuity, a fresh eye, and an unconventional approach have led many learning disabled youngsters into the arts. Not held back by their learning disabilities, many thrive creatively in fields like montage, cartooning, window display, filmmaking, architecture, interior decorating, ceramics, fashion design, and landscaping. Tony made a flute and learned to play it in a special class when he was fourteen, and something inside him caught fire. By sheer perseverance, he graduated from college, majoring in music. He became a first-rate musician, and today he plays in an orchestra. Tom was a hyperactive boy who annoyed his teachers by drumming his fingers on the desk. He took up drums seriously in high school and, after he graduated, joined a band, which is now touring the country. The building of boats, sailing, and teaching these skills have been a source of great satisfaction and employment to some. To others, marine biology, oceanography, or the environmental sciences become a passion. The field of computers has opened up new exciting opportunities for many visual thinkers who happen to be learning disabled.

Too often in the past, an intelligent young person who doesn't spell well, who may be disorganized, who reads with difficulty, and who does not make it to college has ended up as a short-order cook or a grocery bagger in a supermarket, or has been relegated to some other unimaginative job that he does not do well and where his talents are wasted. His abilities would qualify him for many useful, challenging occupations if suitable training programs existed. There is a need for more systematic work-study programs in the helping professions such as hospital work, as nurses' aides, or physical and recreational therapists; in day-care centers and children's recreation programs; in work with growing plants in nurseries, at plant farms, and with landscape architects; in jobs in hotels, stores, and banks.

Even if a learning disabled young adult is fortunate enough to find the appropriate job, this person may still have difficulty socializing and taking care of himself. Independent living skills must be fostered with learning disabled young people. Parents and teachers have to program tasks so young people can perform them independently and feel self-reliant. Situations need to be set up where constant peer interaction is a normal experience. For the severely learning disabled, neighborhood halfway houses and group homes are taking over where parents and teachers leave off. In a few states, group homes established for no more than six to ten learning disabled young adults have been effective in helping provide the transition from home to independent living. Their aim is to help young adults learn to take care of themselves, share responsibility, and function effectively in the community as well as at work. Unfortunately, because these homes with qualified personnel are so expensive to run, there are very few of them to meet the needs of thousands upon thousands of learning disabled young adults. More of these are desperately needed throughout the country with the necessary components of mental health workers, vocational counselors, and special educators as staff providing the lifelines to the flourishing of healthy relationships and satisfying living.

HUMAN QUALITIES

In the end, what counts are human qualities. A person's sense of himself, his feeling of comfort with himself, and thus his ease with others are what matters. How many adults do you know whose knowledge of spelling or trigonometry makes any difference to you? Does it matter how good your friend's handwriting is or how many historical facts he can recite? Is it important that your friends be very athletic plus very scholarly, as well as talented in some artistic field? The chances are that you want to be with a person you enjoy, someone with whom you have easy communication to share interests and concerns, someone who is fun and caring. You want a friend who laughs with you, not at you, who can share your worries as well as your pleasures. A friend does not have to be fashionable, but a certain amount of cleanliness, neatness, and attractiveness matters. You want someone you can count on, whose word is good, who comes through on promises, who doesn't keep score on favors given and received.

To be a good friend, to be a fine mate, to become a good parent—these are crucial goals in our society, yet we do not educate our young people to fulfill them. We study, we plan, and we prepare for almost everything in life except our relationships. And what do we spend our whole lives doing except relating to other human beings? Most of us pick up enough clues, by tuning in to what is going on around us, to get along well with other people. But there are many among us—and a number of them are hampered by learning disabilities—who do not unconsciously absorb what happens around them and apply it to their own lives. They need to be taught these skills explicitly.

So socialization joins organization as top priorities for the learning disabled adolescent. As much as the learning disabled child needs systematic instruction in reading, spelling, math, and other academic areas, whether she will be a successful adult really revolves around socialization and organization. This is the great challenge to parents and professionals working with the learning disabled adolescent.

FOURTEEN

THE KEY IS ORGANIZATION

There is order in the universe.
There is order in life.
There is order in growth, from one step to the other.
The body develops its own order.
The mind develops its own order.
Ordered movement of the body brings
  ordered growth of the mind.

When the nervous system matures naturally, it orders the messages coming into the brain from all the senses and prepares the way for the master organizational job: developing groupings, patterns, and systems of thought. The organizing system within us lets us relate one person, one object, one situation, one set of feelings to another. If ideas are not related, then each experience is unique, unrelated to everything else, with the result of fragmentation. When every single thing has to be dealt with separately, energy is used inefficiently and wastefully. Part of growth is the making of connections producing patterns and systems for faster, more efficient performance.

The toddler flails his arms and screws up his face as he tries to run. He grows up to be a twelve-year-old who runs gracefully and fast, relating his movements to each other, using his body as a unified, coordinated whole. The learning disabled youngster, because of his immaturity, makes life much more difficult for himself and others. Teachers and parents are often heard to say:

Why can't he make life simple for himself?
She makes a mountain out of a molehill.
He does everything the hard way.
She makes easy things complicated.
He always finds a roundabout way to do things.

The learning disabled schoolboy who brings one six-pack of Coke at a time from the kitchen to the living room and the learning disabled teenager who loads the car one item at a time are inefficient; they use an excess amount of energy for a simple task. They have not organized themselves to look at the job, picture in their mind what it demands, and develop a system to get the work done effectively in as short a time as possible. The same is true with remembering a series of numbers, facts, or ideas. They have to be grouped to facilitate memory. To remember important American explorers, a student has to have learned the facts, isolated the prime characteristics of explorers, grouped these together with names and dates, and stored them in his mind to be pulled out as a category when necessary.

Humphrey, who became sidetracked by details when looking at a picture, studying a lesson, or exploring great ideas, could not make sense of the statement "Aristotle, Plato, and Socrates all had one thing in common. They were searching for the _____." He did not see how Aristotle's way of logically categorizing reality, Plato's approach to unity through ideals, and Socrates' method of asking questions could all be ways of seeking the truth. Humphrey's teacher gave him three pieces of paper and asked him to fold them in three different ways. She then asked him to look at the ways they were similar. From his seeing that all three were of the same color, shape, size, and texture, she slowly extracted from him that Aristotle, Plato, and Socrates were all searching for the truth although they went about it very differently.

> *As we mature,*
> *we relate more and more ideas,*
> *on higher and higher levels,*
> *adding, substituting, refining, regrouping,*
> *boiling things down to their simplest elements.*

Organization and reorganization produce simplicity. Formulation and reformulation produce clarity. We continue to order our existence as long as we live, simplifying it through increased organization. The difference between adults and children lies in the amount and degree of planning, preparing, and setting of priorities that adults do. Adults have to build organization into every aspect of a learning disabled youngster's life until he can take it over for himself. They have to set the boundaries, carefully establish limits, and provide order for the child with disorder until he can begin to establish his own borders and simplify his existence.

Sort, sort, sort. The child has to be given every possible opportunity to sort things—from buttons to toy cars to pictures to lotto cards, eventually to symbols, to words, to ideas. He needs training in groupings, categorizing, and systematizing numbers, facts, and ideas. Even with the best provisions, neural maturation cannot be hastened. A youngster's growth can be encouraged by the systematic learning of readiness skills rather than impeded by the pressure of unfair demands to learn at his age level. He can be given the undergirdings so that when neural maturation does take place, he has the foundations to leap ahead academically. He has to be helped to create an inner voice to order him. Strategies to help him build on his strengths and to help him get around some of his areas of weakness can be taught to him. Learning tricks to trigger memory, aids to help him focus, and ways to keep himself on a task until it is completed are a necessary part of schooling for the learning disabled child.

Everything she does well is a jewel to be treasured.
Every sense of accomplishment she feels is a deposit to success.
Every adult she trusts is an investment that will pay off.
Every opportunity she has to enjoy herself, to have fun, to feel
*   good about herself, is a form of savings bond.*

Lives have been saved and made productive when people feel good about themselves. This comes about through the mastering of tasks and through the establishing and maintaining of relationships. It comes about through very hard work on the part of the learning disabled youngster and all the important adults who share his life.

The needs of learning disabled youngsters are at last beginning to be recognized. The child who was previously incorrectly labeled as retarded or emotionally disturbed can now receive the appropriate help. There is greater hope today than ever before. We know more. Legislation is forcing states and counties to do their job. Parents and teachers are more on the alert so the child with difficulties is spotted earlier. There are many resources. More can be done.

Still the major responsibility sits squarely on the shoulders of the parents of each learning disabled youngster, followed by her teachers. The job is immense; the demands are constant.

The continual providing of order,
*   the continual planning ahead,*
*   the continual programming for a child's pleasure*
*   and success,*
*   the continuing training for independence*
*   mean*
*   continually putting a child's needs first,*
*   and*
*   that is not always possible or*
*   always desirable.*

Adults have needs. Adults have pressures put upon them not only by their children but by other adults, their employers, neighbors, coworkers, community, church, and their own parents. Adults have their ups and downs. They are only human.

One cannot serve the needs of even the most needy youngster every single moment. One can do only his or her best. A teacher cannot give all her attention to one or two learning disabled youngsters in her class to meet their needs, while neglecting twenty-eight others.

She can give as much structure as possible. She can attempt to obtain the best education for each child and to unearth the needed services. She can join parent and community groups to apply pressure on officials to help with the job. This much must be done for these intelligent young people who have so much potential.

Whether it is at home, in the church or synagogue, at the recreation center, in youth groups, or in school, we know there will be times when the learning disabled child inevitably becomes frustrated, despairing, angry, anxious, guilty, and fearful. Big ups and huge downs—rarely a middle ground—characterize this child. The adults around this child are very susceptible to the same feelings, and if they allow themselves to take part in the ups and downs, their life can become a seesaw.

It is normal to feel angry with a learning disabled child. What is important is to find the cause of the anger and analyze it. See what can be done to prevent the situation or the set of circumstances from happening again next time. Sometimes simple exhaustion from the ever-present demands causes anger, and a good night's sleep takes care of it. Sometimes the anger is deeper. The frustration of helplessness, of being unable by any human power to "make it all be all right" for a child can produce many varieties of anger.

All teachers and parents share the experience of failing at times, particularly when they are surrounded by uncertainty, unpredictability, inconsistency—the climate of the learning disabled child.

Any adult who is intensively involved with this child is unavoidably going to make many mistakes. Jean Piaget points out that a child's misunderstandings and mistakes are the most revealing source of information about his progress and development. Perhaps the same principle can be applied to adults.

We can learn from our mistakes and our confusions, not only about the child himself but about where we, the adults, stand in relation to him. The more we know about the nature of the learning disabled child and the more we know about ourselves, the better we will be able to separate our feelings and reactions from his. There are times when this is very difficult. We are affected because we care deeply about him, and that makes us vulnerable. Yet it is clearly in the child's best interest that we not identify too closely with him.

A toughness, as well as a sensitivity, is required of adults who work with learning disabled youngsters. The child must be kept to standards, held to finish each reasonable task she begins, and helped to learn to monitor herself to be sure she is picking up the feedback from materials and people that will tell her whether she is doing a task correctly and appropriately. The learning disabled child must be helped all along the way to know as much as possible about how she learns, the aids she must have, and the strategies she must use to help herself. Along with sympathy and understanding, the adult must resolutely help the learning disabled youngster to establish attainable goals for himself and stick to them.

The teacher has the crucial task of teaching the three Rs to this child—systematically, doggedly, imaginatively—until she has learned them. Into this curriculum, at every point, must be incorporated the teaching of socialization. The key to both is teaching organization. The child needs to be taught how to organize herself for learning. When she can finally hold this key in her own hands, she will have the means to open the doors to new worlds of learning and living.

CONCLUSION

EDUCATING THE LEARNING DISABLED FOR THE FUTURE

Leaders of industry tell us that they will need intelligent, clever problem solvers in the workforce in the year 2000. They will want people who are original, ingenious, imaginative. The future beckons to the person who knows what he can do and how to creatively circumvent what he cannot do.

The person of the future will need to know his own learning style, how to go about actively seeking information, how to solve problems, how to use teachers, experts, selected people, libraries, and data systems as resources in solving problems. The acquisition of these skills is far more complex than learning to decode words or manipulate numbers. Schooling for our children must be pointed purposefully to cognitive growth, to the art of thinking. Still, the skills of reading, arithmetic, and writing remain important foundations and must not be neglected.

Educators must rise to the challenge of educating the learning disabled and giving them the attention they need. Early detection and intervention are extremely important. Children can be saved from the pain of being asked to meet unattainable standards. The frustration caused by ineffective teaching can be reduced. The devastation of failure at school, of feeling stupid, of bearing the teasing, the many layers of emotional hurt can be avoided for the most part. Early intervention can eliminate the need to build up strong defenses to cover the insecurities caused by learning disabilities.

Parents of the learning disabled must assume new responsibilities, learning all they can about their children, teaching their children and advocating in school, in the neighborhood, in religious classes, and on the playground for their success. The children must then learn to advocate for themselves.

- Children with learning disabilities need help using their unique thought processes and developing their own styles of learning.
- The learning disabled need help working on organization, self-monitoring skills, and self-regulation.
- The learning disabled need to have strong support systems in place (i.e., mates, family, friends, tutors, mental health services) and use them regularly, not just in crisis.

The world of the future will require all kinds of problem solving, all varieties of intelligence to explore the unknown. To prepare for this challenge, we need to prize diversity today.

Parents and teachers must encourage different styles and untraditional approaches to learning. They must recognize the importance of hands-on learning. Visual thinkers, many of whom are dyslexic, will make good use of computers that rely on graphics and aid in the development of scientific visualization. Having to accept their own differences in learning, the learning disabled need to be helped to

prize diversity. Empathy for the unfamiliar ways of people from
diverse cultures will be needed as international contacts expand; they
are expanding rapidly now as the world's communication and transportation systems bring us closer.

AUTOMATION

The world of the future will be even more automated than that of the
1990s. Classrooms, workplaces, the library, and public transportation
will all be more machine-operated than they are today. More diverse
and complex technologies will have to be mastered. Education must
train the future workforce for technological advancement.

Let none of us forget that teachers, not computers, teach our
students. Teachers prepare, design, and choose the programs that
computers offer, and teachers, as well as students, must be able to use
computers today as easily as pencils. Teachers must know exactly how
the computer can free the learning disabled to learn and create. Word-
processing programs are important for helping the learning disabled
realize their creativity. For some, Spell Check and Grammar Check
make journalistic efforts possible, although others find these programs difficult to master. Interactive videodisc technology gives us an
exciting taste of the future world. Compact-disc technology will give
the student access to a catalog of multimedia activities; a student will
be able to read words and follow directions, or pick up a phone
attached to the left side of the console and ask verbally for help.

The thoughtful and inventive use of technology should enable
people with learning disabilities to learn more efficiently. With individualized planning, the teacher will have to decide which software
package is most effective for each student. Soon children will use
portable computers at home and in transit to do homework. The

sophisticated technology of the next ten to twenty years may be able to alleviate serious reading problems by allowing users to mix videos, photo-quality graphics, voices, sounds, and textual input. Optical discs will become storage units of huge volumes of information. The learning disabled of today will need to be able to operate these amazing devices, and to ask the right questions. Asking the right questions, keen problem solving, incredible resourcefulness, and creativity will be required in the world of the future.

THE NEED TO EDUCATE DIFFERENTLY

High schools will have to prepare students to join the workforce with as much effort as they now expend on the favored segment heading for college. The purpose of schooling must be success in life for all students.

A student's inability to learn indicates that we have not yet found the techniques to teach him. Success for a student at school comes through teachers, reaching for excellence, studying and knowing their students, programming appropriately, making sure that each student is able to achieve his goals, and teaching each one in the way that he learns.

Through much of America's history, the purpose of schooling was to pass on the values of its white, Anglo-Saxon, Protestant majority, including literacy, which was thought necessary to function in a dynamic society. In the process, it Americanized a stream of immigrant children. Industry flourished, and as standards were set up in factories to regulate manufactured goods, so standards were established by the states in their public schools. But children are not mass-produced; they require individualized attention.

Out on the frontier and in rural areas, students in one-room schoolhouses fared better. In these settings, the teacher had to deal with all age groups. She was forced to individualize for each student, to let older students help younger ones, to encourage small groups to solve problems together. Even though teachers were not highly trained, the underlying attitude seemed to be that everyone could learn. The teacher just needed to discover what worked and then provide each student with the tools to do the job.

Today, as more school districts become consolidated in order to save money, students are herded into huge classes in mammoth public schools. Strict standardization of urban schools sacrificed individual learning styles. While it brought success and opportunity to many children, it also brought disastrous failure to others. The effort to apply uniform performance standards introduced ferocious competition, dividing students into winners and losers, the rewarded and the punished. Undoubtedly there were failures in the little red schoolhouses too, but the prevailing attitude then was, "Well, we have to find another way," and usually they did. A student was not labeled unteachable or hopeless because he was unable to learn certain things. He was allowed more time to catch up. He was encouraged to seek the help he needed. Unfortunately, today many of our educational institutions are too good at making children feel terrible about themselves as learners.

Teacher training institutions need to educate teachers to be imaginative in seeking out alternative forms of instruction. If the old lecture method doesn't work for some students, then it must be adapted or replaced. Standard, timeworn methods are not good enough for nonstandard students, the ones whose mother tongue is not English, the ones who grow up in poverty, the tragic new generation of "crack babies" and those with fetal alcohol syndrome, as well as the learning disabled. They all require help in establishing the pegs in their brains on which to hang information. They all require more experiential education.

Their resourcefulness must be tapped, their interests must be explored, and visual, concrete methods and materials must be employed. The learning disabled need excellent teaching in order to succeed in school. The adept learner can tolerate poor teaching. The child with learning disabilities cannot.

Our society in the 1990s is beginning to respect teachers a bit more than in the past, although this respect is not reflected in financial support. We still seem to assume, as our early settler ancestors did, that teachers need to be part angels, selflessly dedicated to their students in an almost religious manner, without any mundane thoughts of earning a decent wage. This too must change if we want to draw more talented people into teaching and keep them there.

Children in many schools feel licensed to be disrespectful because too often parents do not respect teachers. Changing parents' attitudes is not simple, because their attitudes mirror national values. In America, money means power. Teachers are willing to work for very little money, and therefore they are not valued. An entry-level sanitation worker in the District of Columbia earns far more money than an entry-level teacher with a master's degree in special education: learning disabilities at The Lab School of Washington. If garbage is not picked up twice a week, the neighborhood is offended by the odor and it rebels. Good pay is needed to keep sanitation workers doing this odious job. Teachers have a higher social status, but that's no comfort.

Just as virtue is supposed to bring its own reward, so the job of teaching forty-five students in an overcrowded classroom (five of them with ADD, ADHD, and LD) is supposed to bring sufficient reward in itself to a teacher. No way! America, the land of instant gratification, needs to look forward. The investment in teachers today will pay off tenfold. When will America start looking ahead? How can the shortsighted attitude of a nation be changed?

A NEW LOOK AT PARENTAL RESPONSIBILITIES

Parents are not expected to be saints, but parents of children with learning disabilities often must have the patience of saints and be as nonjudgmental and all-loving. Children with learning disabilities tax parental souls and tap previously unused wells of resourcefulness. Children with ADHD (with or without learning disabilities) demand even more of their parents. Complaining, whining, and blaming can be discussed in a support group or a therapy group, but negative energy must be turned into positive action for the health of the whole family.

In the world of the future where both parents work, extended families are rare, and machines take over menial jobs (such as housework), the complexity of life will be staggering. Parents will need to be even more organized to deal with their families and to program all the technology (and fix it when it inevitably breaks down). Parents need to trust their gut reactions, to know their values, to fight for what they believe in. With a child who has ADHD with or without learning disabilities, a parent's job as an advocate must have top priority. First, parents must fight for their children to be treated and taught properly. Then children must be taught to fight for themselves.

Every parent knows that every child in a family has different strengths and weaknesses. What makes parenthood so tough is struggling to accept all this diversity without judging "very different" as "bad." Keeping an eye on the soul of the child, on what's working, on the progress that's been made in any area, Mom and Dad can give the child with learning disabilities what that child needs. Being able to laugh at clumsy mistakes, talk about your own errors, and keep a balanced perspective creates a happier home life. Parents must aim for reasonable expectations. If parents aim too high for a child, the child fails before she begins; if they aim too low, the message to the child is one of defeat.

It is not easy to be a parent, much less a parent of a child with learning disabilities with or without ADHD. It's one of the most complex jobs a human being can have. A parent is always thinking ahead, anticipating trouble, and planning for success for every member of the family. Exhaustion sets in too often. Parents are people and people who are exhausted are often impossible to deal with: angry, irritable, frustrated. Parents need to take care of themselves, have regular time out of the house. They need time for having fun, finding ways to recharge their batteries so that when they come home, they can give more to their child. When parents bring new energy to their parenting job, children respond with alacrity.

Moderate to severe learning disabilities are multidisabling conditions that can usually be overcome given enough time and attention. Some of the condition remains for a lifetime. Frequently it takes the form of a spelling problem, an organizational difficulty, or the social manifestations of a learning disability. But people with learning disabilities can soar to almost any height if they receive the proper accommodations and support and if they learn to apply the strategies they need for success.

- Parents need to cheer when any form of progress is made.
- Parents need to be grateful for the good times.
- Parents need to watch for signals of trouble and jump in before the situation becomes impossible.
- Parents need to plan ahead with their children.

The constant giving by parents of children with learning disabilities is depleting. And it goes on much longer for these children than for others since they remain immature for a longer time.

Adolescents and young adults with learning disabilities and ADHD often depend on their parents for support many years beyond others in their age group. This is why parents need to cultivate the joys, the hobbies, the sports, the social activities that can nourish their minds and spirits. They need to develop resources within themselves other than the skills of being parents to this special child.

> *Self-esteem*
> *is*
> *the core.*
> *Self-esteem*
> *must begin*
> *with the parent*
> *who helps*
> *self-esteem*
> *begin*
> *within the child.*

Specific praise for doing what is expected, such as, "I like the way you are sitting, Harold," and praise for effort, "I can see how hard you're trying, Emily" help build self-esteem. Photographs and videos of previous successful performances, projects, and events help remind a child there are things he can do. Specific praise rather than the global praise of "How well you are doing!" helps build self-confidence. Pointing out the excellent thinking of the child instead of criticizing the poor spelling, repeating the beautiful phrasing of something a child said instead of correcting a grammatical error, are both simple ways to increase self-esteem. Carefully placing a child in situations and classes where he has a good chance of success helps him feel better about himself. Putting him on a soccer team when he falls over his own two feet or placing him in a debating class when his language disability is fairly severe will not build confidence. Parents have to do a lot of critical thinking. They must really look at the individual child, analyze what he can and cannot do, and match his abilities to an appropriate class or situation. This same process applies to the selection of an appropriate college or possible career for the adolescent with learning disabilities with or without ADHD.

No matter what the world of the future brings (bigger schools, smaller schools, part-time schools) parenthood remains a massive responsibility. That's why parents need strong support systems. Parenthood is hard work! Sometimes it seems futile because the progress of students with learning disabilities is often so uneven, slow, unpredictable.

CRITICAL THINKING

How seriously do schools promote thinking? To prepare for life twenty years from now we need to offer fewer pat recipes, no simple solutions, and more tools for problem solving!

As mass media invade our lives, so propaganda designed to manipulate public opinion creeps in, disguised as facts. The citizen of the twenty-first century will have to think through what he is being told. More critical thinking will be needed to sort out what is essential from what is not and to set priorities. Our democratic society will depend on its citizens thinking critically, asking questions, checking sources, discussing their ideas with others. Bombarded as we will be with far more data, facts, figures, and opinions than we receive today, sharpened thinking skills will be needed to sift through it all.

As America's farmers have used scientific advances to increase our country's food production dramatically, so businesspeople have discovered that by applying information systems to commerce, they can greatly increase economic productivity. Many fewer people are needed to do the job, and there is little room for marginal employees. Projections from the business world indicate that future employees will have to work well in the realm of ideas, symbols, and theories. Rote memory has been relegated to computers, even though many schools still award high grades on tests to the students who can give back information in the exact form received, with or without comprehension. Those schools are not preparing youngsters for the fast-paced future, in which they will need to process masses of information in order to improve living and health standards, and to increase prosperity. Technological advances will play an important part, but the management and use of knowledge will guide them.

ORGANIZATION AND SYSTEMS APPROACH

The learning disabled population struggles with organization, developing systems for remembering material, putting facts and ideas into a manageable form, and the management of time and space.

- In the future, information will have to be sifted.
- More analyses will be required to evaluate information.
- More systems for organizing, remembering, and retrieving information will be needed.

Starting in kindergarten, there needs to be a time, a space, and a place for all things. Study skills need to be taught as early as first grade. Games of logic and strategy, exercises that encourage the development of unique thought systems, and the teaching of organization must be part of the daily curriculum of the learning disabled. It would not hurt other students to be exposed to these strategies too, though most tend to develop workable systems on their own with ease.

The learning disabled must be taught explicitly. Children who learn to organize their work and work space, to manipulate symbols, and to deal with ideas and solve problems will be in a far better position to benefit from the opportunities made available by technological advances than will their less-educated peers.

Parents have to set
reasonable goals
for themselves,
for and with their children
to help them organize themselves
to achieve
the goals
even if a goal
for many months is as simple
as remembering to bring homework to school.
The setting of reasonable goals
and checking on whether or not the goals have been met
helps organization skills to develop.

MAKING DECISIONS

Another area of difficulty for the learning disabled, closely related to their problems with organization and memory, is decision making. They either rush impulsively into decisions without thinking them through, or procrastinate so long that they avoid making any decisions at all. In the world of the future, more decisions will have to be made rapidly and constantly.

Parents can work with their children from an early age making simple decisions, starting with choices of food, toys, even alternative ways to spend a Saturday. Parents and teachers can help through experiential education at home and at school, through activities such as setting up a lemonade stand or a message booth. These activities require constant decision making, and the consequences of good or poor decisions are learned firsthand. Considering that we can choose from well over one hundred TV channels to watch in 1995, what will it be in the year 2020? Will every minute of the day require incredible choices and decision making?

Colleges have been required by law to accommodate many more students with learning disabilities; they now have modified curriculum and specifications to meet the needs of the learning disabled and have realized that they did not sacrifice standards of excellence in doing so. The students have proved their quality, and shown the academic community that it was worthwhile to make the effort. The Americans with Disabilities Act, passed in the summer of 1990, is helping the learning disabled to gain access to parts of the workforce previously unavailable to them where they can succeed.

INTERPERSONAL RELATIONS

What is precious in this world to most people is the emotional richness of close, loving relationships that bring us boundless joy, as well as sorrow, pride, frustration, and anger. Our mates, our children, our parents, relatives, and friends are the foundations of our emotional life, and will continue to be so. For this reason, relationships are as important as the three Rs. Parents and teachers need to ensure that the learning disabled have social lives, that they establish and maintain relationships. Adults with learning disabilities tell us that the loneliness of not having friends and meaningful relationships produces pain that is frequently far more insidious than the inability to read. Strong, close interpersonal relations in an automated world will be even more necessary to give warmth, joy, and meaning to life.

Children with learning disabilities who have poor social skills *can* be taught the fourth R—Relationships—through role-playing, video recordings of their own socialization, and constant feedback from the adults around them and their peers. Learning social skills can be as slow a process as the neurological process of learning to read. It is one thing to know what is required, but another thing to transfer that knowledge into action and behavior. Transfer of knowledge is one of the big problems of the learning disabled.

We will lose a productive slice of our country's workforce if we don't start educating and socializing the learning disabled properly for the future. American education needs to be of outstanding quality. Only through quality education can the learning disabled learn, and every other student will benefit too! The American Dream is not only what we ourselves can accomplish; it is what we can make possible for the next generation. There are many diverse paths toward progress but no easy answers.

APPENDIX 1

GLOSSARY

Abstract Thinking The ability to use categories and classifications; to grasp relationships such as cause-effect, part-whole; to generalize; to see similarities and differences; to analyze and synthesize; to deal with words and concepts that have no concrete referents, that can't be known directly through the senses (for example, democracy). The opposite of concrete and literal thinking.

Adaptive Behavior The ability of an individual to cope effectively, appropriately, and flexibly in a situation.

Apraxia The inability to motor-plan, to make an appropriate body response.

Auditory Discrimination The ability to perceive the difference between sounds or sequences of sounds. Example: hearing the difference in the final consonant of *can* and *cat*.

Auditory Perception The ability to understand and put meaning to sound; the brain organizes what is heard into something meaningful.

Body Awareness, Body Schema   The awareness of one's own body and the parts that make up the whole.

Body Image   Feelings and perceptions about one's own body, including body schema; feelings of attractiveness or ugliness, or fatness or thinness, for example.

Catastrophic Reaction   A sudden loss of control, an overflow emotional response to a relatively minor frustration or demand; it is out of proportion and seemingly unwarranted.

Cognitive Style   The unique way a person perceives the world, reasons, and thinks.

Concreteness   The need to see or touch in order to understand, plus the tendency to treat every situation as unique, unrelated to previous experience.

Constancy   The ability to perceive the essential quality of an object regardless of its presentation, such as changes of size, color, or position. Example: the letter *a* is always the same no matter what its color, typeface, or position on the page.

Decoding Problems   Problems of associating sound with symbol.

Developmental Lag   Delayed maturity in one or several areas of development.

Developmental Tasks   A series of tasks (or skills) related to mastery, normally accomplished by a growing child in a predictable sequence. Often the learning disabled child needs to be taught these tasks explicitly because his deficits prevent him from acquiring them automatically.

Directionality   The ability to perceive and label directions, such as up-down, in-out, front-back, left-right, north-south.

Distractibility   Easily sidetracked, often unable to focus and concentrate on a given task. It happens usually because the nervous system is unable to screen out extraneous sensory stimuli. The distractible child is unable to select certain stimuli and exclude others.

DSM IV   Diagnostic and Statistical Manual of Mental Disorders, Fourth Edition, Revised, describing the diagnostic classification system officially adopted and used by the American Psychiatric Association.

Dyscalculia   A medical term associated with neurological dysfunction, indicating an inability to perform mathematical functions.

Dysgraphia   A medical term associated with neurological dysfunction indicating the inability to perform properly the motor movements required for handwriting.

Dyslexia   A medical term associated with neurological dysfunction indicating a moderate to severe reading disorder.

Dysnomia   A medical term associated with neurological dysfunction indicating a deficiency in remembering and saying words. Children with dysnomia often talk around a subject or substitute a word like *thing* when they cannot remember the name of an object.

Emotional Lability   A tendency to sudden swings of mood. Related to organic difficulties in inhibiting behavior and manifested by quick changes of emotional behavior, from laughing to crying, gaiety to sadness, tranquillity to temper tantrum.

Encoding Problems   Problems in converting oral language into written symbols.

Expressive Language   The ability to communicate with others. The opposite of receptive language.

Eye-Hand Coordination   Coordinated movements of eye and hand in which the eye guides the hand to the accurate completion of a task.

Eye Tracking Difficulty   The inability of the eye to maintain focus and move smoothly, as in reading a line left to right across a page or following a moving object.

Faulty Body Image   The inability to integrate the various perceptions concerning the body and its relationship to the world. Makes the child unsure of where various parts of the body are; the shape and size of parts of the body are confused in the mind, and this affects the way the child moves. A child may be unable to imitate a simple posture of movement because of faulty body image.

Faulty Checking Mechanism   The inability to refrain from acting on an impulse (see impulsivity).

Figure-Ground Perception   The ability to focus on one thing (figure), allowing all else to drop into the background (ground).

Fine Motor Difficulty   Problems with the use and coordination of small muscles for activities such as writing or sewing.

Gross Motor Difficulty   Trouble with movement through space in which large muscles are used and in which balance is important, for activities such as running, walking, chalkboard writing.

Hard Signs   In neurological terms, evidence of brain injury that can be seen with medical technology (i.e., MRIs).

Hyperactivity, Hyperkinesis   Unorganized purposeless action, excess, random movement, inappropriate motor response, stemming from immaturity of the central nervous system.

Hypoactivity   Underactivity, sluggishness, failure to respond when response is appropriate. Like hyperactivity, it stems from immaturity of the central nervous system.

Impulsivity   The inability to inhibit, control, check, or even delay inner impulses for organic reasons; the child is driven to act on impulse without stopping to think through the consequences. The child's difficulty in postponing pleasure or gratification, waiting in line, and waiting to speak is related to this.

Kinesthetic Perception   The perception of movement that comes through the sensations of muscular activity.

Laterality   The awareness within the body of the difference between right and left; it is the conscious awareness that one side differs from the other, correctly labeled as the right side and the left side.

Lateralization   The tendency for certain processes to be handled more efficiently on one side of the brain than on the other. In most people, the right hemisphere becomes more efficient in processing spatial information, while the left hemisphere specializes in verbal and logical processes.

Low Frustration Tolerance   The inability to withstand much frustration without either blowing up or withdrawing.

Maturation Lag   A delay in the development of the central nervous system. A child's behavior, perceptions, and cognitive development resemble those of a much younger child.

Midline Difficulty   A tendency to avoid moving any one part of the body (arm, for instance) across the midline of the body.

Motor Plan (Praxis)   The ability of the brain to conceive of, organize, and carry out a sequence of unfamiliar actions. Motor planning is dependent upon adequate integration of information from all sensory systems and can affect skill development in all motor areas, especially handwriting.

Organicity   A term referring to some impairment of the central nervous system.

Overload   The result of too many sensations bombarding the nervous system at once. Results in the inability to respond to one stimulus and exclude the others, as though three people were talking to you at once; you cannot hear any one of them clearly, and you are not able to respond appropriately to any of them.

Part-Whole Difficulty   The inability to perceive the parts that make up a whole or to break down the whole into its components.

Perception   The process by which the brain organizes, integrates, and makes sense out of the stimuli coming from the eyes, ears, nose, and taste buds and from sensations in the muscles and the skin.

Perceptual Deficits, Perceptual Handicaps   An inability of the brain to order correctly or use effectively the data one perceives. These difficulties stem from damage to the parts of the brain that control movements, vision, audition, and impulses. Often doctors can find no evidence of damage to the central nervous system, so they cannot say that it is damage or injury, but the constellation of difficulties that the child shows tells the doctor that there are perceptual deficits. When the child cannot perceive effectively, he cannot sort out and screen the stimuli he is receiving, so he has a hard time making sense out of his environment.

Perseveration   The persistent repetition or seemingly senseless continuance of an activity that the child cannot stop when he wants to because he's not able to put on the brakes and/or does not realize what he's doing. Also manifested in the child's problems with shifting from one activity to another, accepting changes in routine, and postponing activities.

Processing Difficulty   The inability to integrate, organize, and make sense out of sensory information. It is organizational rather than interpretational breakdown.

Receptive Language   The ability to comprehend the spoken word.

Scatter Performance   Uneven development, which produces strong abilities and high performance in certain areas, failures or poor performance in others. One's total performance appears erratic, unpredictable, and inconsistent, known as scatter or scattered achievement.

Sensory Defensiveness   A condition in which a person is oversensitive to input from more than one sensory system (i.e., touch, sound, smell, movement).

Sensory Input   Electrical impulses flowing from the sense receptors in the body to the spinal cord and brain.

Sensory Integration   The organization of sensory input to help a person interact effectively with the environment and feel more in control of him/herself.

Sensory Integrative Dysfunction   A disorder in brain function that makes it difficult to integrate sensory input. Sensory integrative dysfunctions are at the base of many learning disabilities.

Sequencing Difficulty   The inability to remember a series in its proper order; for instance, letters in a word, days of the week, months of the year, following directions involving more than one action.

Soft Signs   In neurological terms, a lack of evidence of brain damage in a child, but specific learning disabilities seem to exist because of the constellation of difficulties the child experiences (poor attention span, uneven performance, distractibility, poor coordination, time and space problems, impulsivity, and perseveration).

Structure   Carefully planned, guided, sequenced activity. Not synonymous with rigidity, it encourages growth.

Tactile   The sense of touch on any surface of the body, including hair.

Tactile Defensiveness   A sensory integrative dysfunction in which light touch can cause excessive negative emotional reactions such as hitting somebody or running away (*fight or flight*). A lack of tactile discrimination makes every touch threatening.

Tactile Perception   The ability and process by which the brain organizes data perceived through touch and makes effective use of it. When a child has tactile perceptual difficulties, he cannot tactually discriminate textures and shapes and therefore cannot identify what he touches.

Task Analysis   The ability to analyze a task, break it down to the smallest steps, and know the sequences so it may be learned step-by-step.

Vestibular System   The balancing system of the inner ear that regulates the adjustment of body movement to gravity.

Visual Discrimination   The ability to perceive visual differences accurately. The learning disabled child frequently confuses *b, d, p,* and *q.*

Visual Perception   The ability to understand and put meaning to what one sees.

APPENDIX 2

RECOMMENDED BOOKS

LEARNING DISABILITIES IN GENERAL

Ariel, A. *Education of Children and Adolescents with Learning Disabilities*. New York: Merrill Publishing Co., 1992.

Benton, Arthur L., and David Pearl. *Dyslexia: An Appraisal of Current Knowledge*. New York: Oxford University Press, 1980.

*Bos, C. and S. Vaughn. *Strategies for Teaching Students with Learning and Behavior Problems*. Boston: Allyn & Bacon, 1991.

Brutten, Milton, Sylvia Richardson, and Charles Mangel. *Something's Wrong with My Child*. New York: Harcourt Brace Jovanovich, 1979. For parents, about children with learning disabilities; mentions the social problems stemming from learning disabilities.

*Bryan, Tanis H., and J. H. Bryan. *Understanding Learning Disabilities*. Palo Alto, CA: Mayfield Publishing, 1986.

---

* Asterisked entries are especially recommended.

Critchley, Macdonald. *The Dyslexic Child.* 2d ed. London: William Heinemann Medical Books, 1970.

Critchley, Macdonald, and Eileen Critchley. *Dyslexia Defined.* Springfield, IL: Charles C. Thomas, 1978.

Cruickshank, W. M. *Brain-Injured Child in Home, School, and Community.* Syracuse: Syracuse University Press, 1967.

Cummings, Rhoda, and Cleborne Maddox. *Parenting the Learning Disabled: A Realistic Approach.* Springfield, IL: Charles C. Thomas, 1985.

Dane, Elizabeth. *Painful Passages: Working with Children with Learning Disabilities.* Silver Spring, MD: NASW Press, 1990. A social worker's view of how to work with children with learning disabilities and their families.

Ellingson, Careth. *The Shadow Children.* Chicago: Topaz Books, 1967. A good beginning for lay readers. Describes learning disabled children and reviews their problems.

Featherstone, Helen. *A Difference in the Family: Living with a Disabled Child.* New York: Penguin Books, 1981.

Frierson, E. C., and W. B. Barbe, eds. *Educating Children with Learning Disabilities.* New York: Appleton-Century-Crofts, 1967. Comprehensive textbook including articles by Clements, Strauss, Myklebust, Eisenberg, and others.

Gearhart, William R. *Learning Disabilities: Educational Strategies.* 5th ed. Columbus, OH: Merrill Publishing Co., 1989.

Gearhart, William R., Carol Gearhart, and Mel Weishahm. *The Exceptional Student in the Regular Classroom.* 5th ed. New York: Merrill Publishing Co., 1992.

Goldberg, Herman K., and Gilbert Schiffman. *Dyslexia: Problems of Reading Disabilities.* New York: Grune & Stratton, 1972.

Hallahan, D. P., and J. M. Kauffman. *Introduction to Learning Disabilities: A Psycho-behavioral Approach.* Englewood Cliffs, NJ: Prentice-Hall, 1985.

*Hammill, Donald, and Nettie Bartel. *Teaching Students with Learning and Behavior Problems.* 2d ed. Boston: Allyn & Bacon, 1990.

Huston, Anne Marshall. *Common Sense About Dyslexia.* Lanham, MD: Madison Books, 1987. Includes many practical suggestions for parents as well as tips to classroom teachers.

*Johnson, Doris, and Helmer Myklebust. *Learning Disabilities: Educational Principles and Practices.* New York: Grune & Stratton, 1967. Excellent language, math, and behavior section.

*Kephart, Newell. *The Slow Learner in the Classroom.* Columbus, OH: Charles E. Merrill, 1971. Classic textbook.

*Kronick, Doreen. *A Word or Two About Learning Disabilities.* San Rafael, CA: Academic Therapy Publications, 1973. Social-psychological implications of learning disabilities for child and family. Discusses the socialization process, the family in the community, and recreation and camping for learning disabled children.

————. *New Approaches to Learning Disabilities.* Philadelphia: Grune & Stratton, 1988.

*Lerner, Janet. *Learning Disabilities: Theories, Diagnosis and Teaching Strategies.* 6th ed. Boston: Houghton Mifflin, 1993. Outstanding presentation of theoretical approaches to learning disabilities: sensory-motor, perceptual-motor, perceptual-linguistic-cognitive; also stresses role of maturation.

Levine, Melvin. *Developmental Variations and Learning Disabilities.* Cambridge, MA: Educator's Publishing Service, 1987.

Levy, Harold B. *Square Pegs, Round Holes: The Learning Disabled Child in the Classroom and at Home.* Boston: Little, Brown, 1974. Excellent beginning book for parents, as well as professionals; gives solid understanding of the many facets of learning disabilities.

*Lewis, Richard S., Alfred Strauss, and Laura Lehtinen. *The Other Child: The Brain-injured Child.* New York: Grune & Stratton, 1960. Outstanding book for laymen, details some of the conceptual confusions of learning disabled youngsters and describes fully their learning problems.

Lynn, Roa. *Learning Disabilities: An Overview of Theories, Approaches, and Politics.* New York: The Free Press, 1979.

McCarthy, James, and Joan McCarthy. *Learning Disabilities.* Boston: Allyn & Bacon, 1969. A good guide for understanding the broader field of learning disabilities.

Mercer, Cecil D. *Students with Learning Disabilities.* 4th ed. Columbus, OH: Charles E. Merrill, 1992.

Orton, Samuel Torrey. *Reading, Writing and Speech Problems in Children.* New York: W. W. Norton, 1937. One of the earliest books in the field and very perceptive.

*Osman, Betty. *Learning Disabilities: A Family Affair.* New York: Warner Books, 1988.

———. *No One to Play With: The Social Side of Learning Disabilities.* New York: Random House, 1982. Excellent on social skills.

Siegel, Ernest. *Helping the Brain-injured Child.* New York: Association for Brain Injured Children, 1962. Outstanding book for the lay reader and the professional, giving very concrete aids and practical advice on helping the children educationally and behaviorally.

Siegel, Ernest, Rita Siegel, and Paul Siegel. *Help for the Lonely Child.* New York: E. P. Dutton, 1978.

*Silver, A., and Rose A. Hagin. *Disorders of Learning in Childhood.* New York: John Wiley, 1990. Extremely thorough, written by two masters in the field.

*Silver, Larry. *The Misunderstood Child: A Guide for Parents of Learning Disabled Children.* New York: McGraw-Hill, 1992. Excellent on social skills.

Smith, C. R. *Learning Disabilities: The Interaction of Learner, Task and Setting.* Boston: Allyn & Bacon, 1990.

*Smith, Sally L. *Succeeding Against the Odds: How the Learning Disabled Can Realize Their Promise.* New York: Jeremy P. Tarcher/ Perigee, 1992.

*Stevens, Suzanne H. *Classroom Success for the Learning Disabled.* Winston-Salem, NC: John F. Blair, 1984.

————. *The Learning Disabled Child: Ways That Parents Can Help.* Winston-Salem, NC: John F. Blair, 1980.

Torgesen, Joseph. *Cognitive and Behavioral Characteristics of Children with Learning Disabilities.* Austin, TX: Pro-Ed, 1990.

Ungerleider, Dorothy. *Reading, Writing and Rage.* Rolling Hills Estates, CA: Jalmar Press, 1985.

*Vail, Priscilla L. *Smart Kids with School Problems: Things to Know and Ways to Help.* New York: Dutton, 1989.

————. *Unraveling the Myth.* Rosemont, NJ: Modern Learning Press, 1990. A forty-seven-page pamphlet that does a good job of introducing people to the subject of learning disabilities.

Wallace, G., and J. M. Kauffman. *Teaching Children with Learning Problems.* 2d ed. Columbus, OH: Charles E. Merrill, 1978.

Warner, Joan Marie, *Learning Disabilities: Activities for Remediation 5.* 2d ed. Danville, IL: Inter-State Printers & Publishers, 1978.

Weiss, Helen, and Martin Weiss. *Home Is a Learning Place: A Parent's Guide to Learning Disabilities.* Boston: Little, Brown, 1976.

Wender, Paul. *Minimal Brain Dysfunction in Children.* New York: John Wiley, 1971. Discussion of causes of minimal brain dysfunction covers medical and biochemical aspects; includes a good section on management and usefulness of medication for certain children.

Westman, Jack C. *Handbook of Learning Disabilities: A Multisystem Approach.* Boston: Allyn & Bacon, 1990.

ADOLESCENTS AND YOUNG ADULTS

Alley, Gordon, and Gordon Deshler. *Teaching the Learning Disabled Adolescent: Strategies and Methods.* Denver: Love Publishing Co., 1979.

Anderson, L. E. *Helping the Adolescent with the Hidden Handicap.* San Rafael, CA: Academic Therapy Publications, 1970.

Cordoni, Barbara. *Living with a Learning Disability.* Carbondale, IL: Southern Illinois University Press, 1990.

Cruickshank, William, William Morse, and Jeannie Johns. *Learning Disabilities: The Struggle from Adolescence Toward Adulthood.* Syracuse: Syracuse University Press, 1980.

Gerber, Paul, and Henry Reiff. *Speaking for Themselves: Ethnographic Interviews with Adults with Learning Disabilities.* Ann Arbor, MI: University of Michigan Press, 1991.

Johnson, Doris, and Jane Blalock. *Adults with Learning Disabilities: Clinical Studies.* Orlando, FL: Grune & Stratton, 1987.

Lewis, Richard S. *The Other Child Grows Up.* New York: Times Books, 1977.

Masters, L. F., B. A. Mori, and A. A. Mori. *Teaching Secondary Students with Mild Learning and Behavior Problems.* Austin, TX: Pro-Ed, 1993.

*Rawson, Margaret B. *Developmental Language and Disability: Adult Accomplishments of Dyslexic Boys.* Baltimore: Johns Hopkins Press, 1968.

Rogan, L., and L. Hartman. *A Follow-up Study of Learning Disabled Children and Adults.* Final Report. Project #443CH60010 Grant #OEG-0-74-7453. Washington, D.C.: Bureau of Education for the Handicapped, U.S. Department of HEW, 1976.

*Siegel, Ernest. *The Exceptional Child Grows Up.* New York: E. P. Dutton, 1974. Outstanding book gives guidelines for understanding and helping the brain-injured adolescent and young adult.

Siegel, S., M. Robert, K. Greener, G. Meyer, W. Halloran, and R. Gaylor-Ross. *Career Ladders for Challenged Youths in Transition from School to Adult Life.* Austin, TX: Pro-Ed, 1993.

Silver, A. and R. Hagin. "Specific Reading Disability. Follow-up Studies." *American Journal of Orthopsychiatry* (24), 1964, pp. 95–101.

*Smith, Sally L. *Succeeding Against the Odds: How the Learning Disabled Can Realize Their Promise.* New York: Jeremy P. Tarcher/Perigee, 1992.

Woodward, Delores, and Delores Peters. *The Learning Disabled Adolescent: Learning Success in Content Areas.* Rockville, MD: Aspen Systems, 1983.

Personal Stories

Anderson, Camilla. *Jan, My Brain-damaged Daughter*. Portland, OR: Durham Press, 1963. Story of a psychiatrist's daughter, her unusually severe health and learning problems, her problems relating to others, overreactions, and frustrations.

Evans, James. *An Uncommon Gift*. Philadelphia: Westminster Press, 1983. Describes well the problems and progress of a gifted child with learning disabilities.

Hampshire, Susan. *Susan's Story*. London: Sidgwick & Jackson, 1983. Excellent description of a gifted child with learning disabilities.

*Jones, Beverly, and Jane Hart. *Where's Hannah?* New York: Penguin Books, 1980. An inspiring story for parents and teachers of learning disabled children of a child lost in space and time who cannot trust her own senses.

*Keller, Helen. *The Story of My Life*. New York: Scholastic, Inc., 1991. Many of the techniques Annie Sullivan used for teaching Helen Keller are also extremely effective with children with learning disabilities. Parents and teachers can employ these very same techniques.

Lee, Christopher, and Rosemary Jackson. *Faking It: A Look into the Mind of a Creative Learner*. Heinemann, NH: Boynton Cook Publishers, 1992. A young adult describes what it was like before he received help and then receiving help through college.

*Lyman, Donald. *Making the Words Stand Still*. Boston: Houghton Mifflin, 1988. The best description of concrete thinking.

*MacCracken, Mary. *Turnabout Children*. Boston: Little, Brown, 1986. Five children with different profiles of learning disabilities are helped by their gifted teacher.

*Simpson, Eileen B. *Reversals: A Personal Account of Victory Over Dyslexia*. New York: Noonday Press, 1991. An inspiring story of a woman who discovers in her thirties that she is not stupid, but gifted with learning disabilities. Written in a compelling way.

ADHD

*Barkley, R. A. *Attention Deficit Hyperactivity Disorder: A Handbook for Diagnosis and Treatment*. New York: Guilford Press, 1990.

Cruickshank, W. M. *A Teaching Method for Brain-injured and Hyperactive Children: A Demonstrative-Pilot Study*. Westport, CT: Greenwood Press, 1981. Classic text. One of the first, most helpful, descriptive books.

*Gordon, Michael. *ADD/Hyperactivity: A Consumer's Guide*. DeWitt, NY: GSI Publications, 1991.

*Ingersoll, Barbara. *Your Hyperactive Child: A Parent's Guide to Coping with Attention Deficit Disorder*. New York: Doubleday, 1988.

Jordan, Dale R. *Attention Deficit Disorder: ADD Syndrome*. Austin, TX: Pro-Ed, 1988.

Kendall, P., and L. Braswell. *Training Impulsive Children in Self-Control*. New York: Guilford Press, 1984.

*Moss, Robert A., M.D. *Why Johnny Can't Concentrate: Coping with Attention Deficit Problems*. New York: Bantam Books, 1990.

Parker, H. *The ADD Hyperactivity Handbook for Schools: Effective Strategies for Identifying and Teaching Students with Attention Deficit Disorder in Elementary and Secondary Schools*. Plantation, FL: Impact Publications, 1992.

Spreen, Otfried. *Learning Disabled Children Growing Up: A Follow-up into Adulthood*. New York: Oxford University Press, 1988.

*Wender, Paul H. *The Hyperactive Child, Adolescent and Adult: Attention Deficit Disorder Through the Lifespan*. 3d ed. New York: Oxford University Press, 1987. An excellent introduction for parents.

THE BRAIN—HOW IT WORKS

Blakeslee, Thomas R. *The Right Brain*. Garden City, NY: Anchor Books/Doubleday, 1980.

Buzan, T. *Use Both Sides of Your Brain*. 3d ed. New York: E. P. Dutton, 1991.

Calvin, W. H., and George A. Ojemann. *Inside the Brain*. New York: New American Library, 1987.

De Bono, Edward. *Lateral Thinking: Creativity Step by Step*. New York: Harper & Row, 1973.

Gardner, Howard. *Frames of Mind: The Theory of Multiple Intelligences*. New York: Basic Books, 1983.

*Healy, Jane. *Endangered Minds: Why Children Don't Think and What We Can Do About It*. New York: Simon & Schuster, 1991. Eminently readable. Explores TV's effects on the brain.

Houston, Jean. *The Possible Human: A Course in Extending Your Physical, Mental, and Creative Abilities*. Los Angeles: Jeremy P. Tarcher, 1982.

Restak, R. M. *The Brain*. New York: Warner Books, 1988.

Samuels, M., and N. Samuels. *Seeing with the Mind's Eye*. New York: Random House, 1975.

Vitale, Barbara M. *Unicorns Are Real: A Right-Brained Approach to Learning*. New York: Warner Books, 1986.

West, Thomas G. *In The Mind's Eye.* Buffalo, NY: Prometheus Publishers, 1991. Describes the visual thinker and the number of dyslexics who think that way.

READING

Auckerman, Robert C. *Approaches to Beginning Reading.* 2d ed. New York: Macmillan, 1984. Annotated compendium of methods, materials, background history, and related research.

Barron, Marlene. *I Learn to Read and Write the Way I Learn to Talk: A Very First Book About Whole Language.* Katonah, NY: Richard C. Owens Publishers, 1990.

Bloomfield, Leonard, and Clarence Barnhart. *Let's Read: A Linguistic Approach.* Detroit: Wayne State University Press, 1961. A structured way to teach reading to learning disabled students.

Bond, Guy, and Miles A. Tinker. *Reading Difficulties.* 6th ed. New York: Prentice-Hall, 1989.

Chall, Jeanne S. *Learning to Read: The Great Debate.* Updated ed. New York: McGraw-Hill, 1983.

*Collins, M., and E. A. Cheek. *Diagnostic Prescriptive Reading Instruction.* Dubuque, IA: Brown & Benchmark, 1989.

Dechant, Emerald V. *Diagnosis and Remediation of Reading Disability.* Englewood Cliffs, NJ: Prentice-Hall, 1981.

De Hirsh, Katrina. *Predicting Reading Failure.* New York: Harper & Row, 1966. Excellent presentations of screening procedures and reading readiness prerequisites.

Durkin, Dolores. *Strategies for Identifying Words: A Workbook for Teachers and Those Preparing to Teach.* 2d ed. Boston: Allyn & Bacon, 1980.

Earle, Richard A. *Teaching Reading and Mathematics.* Newark, DE: International Reading Association, 1976.

Englemann, Siegfried. *Preventing Failure in the Primary Grades.* Chicago: Science Research Associates, 1969.

*Fernald, Grace. *Remedial Techniques in Basic School Subjects.* New York: McGraw-Hill, 1943; ed. by Lorna Idol. Austin, TX: Pro-Ed, 1988. A classic to read and reread. It describes the Fernald technique, which often helps the severely learning disabled.

Glazer, Susan Mandel. *Creating Readers and Writers.* Newark, DE: International Reading Association, 1990.

Herber, Harold. *Teaching in Content Areas with Reading, Writing and Reasoning.* Boston: Allyn & Bacon, 1992. Guidebook for elementary- and secondary-school teachers of basic subjects. Discusses methods of teaching learning skills along with content.

Johns, Jerry L. *Handbook for Remediation of Reading Difficulties.* Englewood Cliffs, NJ: Prentice-Hall, 1986.

Language and Learning to Read: What Teachers Should Know about Language. Richard E. Hodges and E. Hugh Rudorf, eds. Lanham, MD: University Press of America, 1985. Report of conference held in conjunction with the annual meeting of the International Reading Association.

Language by Ear and by Eye: The Relationships Between Speech and Reading. James F. Kavanagh and Ignatius G. Mattingly, eds. Cambridge, MA: The MIT Press, 1972. Conference proceedings.

McGee, Lea, and Donald Richgels. *Literacy's Beginnings: Supporting Young Readers & Writers.* Boston: Allyn & Bacon, 1990.

Money, John, ed. *The Disabled Reader: Education of the Dyslexic Child.* Baltimore: Johns Hopkins Press, 1966. A comprehensive look at reading disorders; the last section details specific remedial techniques.

Raines, Shirley C., and Robert J. Canady. *The Whole Language Kindergarten.* New York: Teachers College Press, 1990.

*Richek, Margaret Ann, Lynn K. List, and Janet W. Lerner. *Reading Problems: Assessment and Teaching Strategies.* Englewood Cliffs, NJ: Prentice-Hall, 1989.

Robinson, Alan H. *Teaching Reading and Study Strategies: The Content Areas.* 3d ed. Boston: Allyn & Bacon, 1983.

Roswell, Florence. *Reading Disability: A Human Approach to Evaluation and Treatment of Reading and Writing Difficulties.* 4th ed. revised and expanded. New York: Basic Books, 1989.

Shefelbine, John. *Encouraging Your Junior High Student to Read.* (Pamphlet) Newark, DE: International Reading Association, 1991.

Spache, George D. *Toward Better Reading.* Champaign, IL: Garrard, 1963.

Stauffer, Russell G., Jules C. Abrams, and John J. Pikulski. *Diagnosis, Correction, and Prevention of Reading Disabilities.* New York: Harper & Row, 1978.

————. *Directing Reading Maturity As a Cognitive Process.* New York: Harper & Row, 1969.

————. *Teaching Reading As a Thinking Process.* New York: Harper & Row, 1969.

*Stern, Catherine, and Toni Gould. *Children Discover Reading.* New York: Singer & Co., 1965.

*Tierney, Robert J., John E. Readence, and Ernest K. Diskner. *Reading Strategies and Practice: A Compendium.* Boston: Allyn & Bacon, 1990.

Vogel, Susan Ann. *Syntactic Abilities in Normal and Dyslexic Children.* Baltimore: University Park Press, 1975.

Wilson, Robert M. *Diagnostic and Remedial Reading for Classroom Teaching.* 6th ed. Columbus, OH: Merrill Publishing Co., 1989.

Wilson, Robert M., and Linda Gambrell. *Reading Comprehension in the Elementary School.* Boston: Allyn & Bacon, 1988.

MATH

Ashlock, Robert B. *Error Patterns in Computation.* 5th ed. Columbus, OH: Charles E. Merrill, 1990.

*Bley, Nancy, and Carol Thornton. *Teaching Mathematics to the Learning Disabled.* Austin, TX: Pro-Ed, 1989.

Burns, Marilyn. *About Teaching Mathematics: A K–8 Resource.* White Plains, NY: Cuisinaire Co. of America, 1992.

————. *A Collection of Math Lessons.* New Rochelle, NY: Math Solutions Publications, 1987.

*Cawley, John. *Developmental Teaching of Mathematics for the Learning Disabled.* Rockville, MD: Aspen Systems Corporation, 1984.

————. *Cognitive Strategies and Mathematics for the Learning Disabled.* Rockville, MD: Aspen Systems Corporation, 1985.

Collier, Calhoun C., and Harold H. Leech. *Teaching Mathematics in the Modern Elementary School.* London: Macmillan Co., 1969.

*Copeland, Richard. *How Children Learn Mathematics: Teaching Implications of Piaget's Research.* 4th ed. London: Macmillan Co., 1984.

*————. *Mathematics Activities for Children: A Diagnostic and Developmental Approach.* Columbus, OH: Merrill Publishing Co., 1979.

Ginsberg, Herbert. *Children's Arithmetic: How They Learn It and How You Teach It.* Austin, TX: Pro-Ed, 1989.

Golick, Margaret. *Deal Me In!* New York: Jeffrey Norton Publisher, 1988. Math games.

*Herold, Persis J. *Math Teaching Handbook.* Newton, MA: Selective Educational Equipment, 1978. An extremely practical guide for teaching mathematics to learning disabled children with "hands-on" materials.

Laylock, Mary. *Mathematics for Meaning.* Hillsborough, CA: Nueva Learning Center, 1977.

Lovell, Kennedy. *The Growth of Understanding in Mathematics: Kindergarten Through Grade Three.* New York: Holt, Rinehart & Winston, 1971.

Mathematics Learning in Early Childhood. Joseph Payne, ed. 37th Yearbook. Reston, VA: National Council of Teachers of Mathematics, 1975. A collection of papers on teaching math to slow learners; a useful reference.

Piaget, Jean. *A Child's Conception of Numbers.* New York: W. W. Norton & Co., 1965.

Piaget, Jean, and B. Inhelder. *The Child's Conception of Space.* New York: W. W. Norton and Co., 1967.

Problem Solving: A Basic Mathematics Goal. Columbus, OH: Ohio Department of Education, 1980.

Problem Solving in School Mathematics. Stephen Krulik and Robert Reys, eds. 1980 NCTM Yearbook. Reston, VA: NCTM, 1978.

Stenmark, Jean K., Virginia Thompson, and Ruth Cossey. *Family Math.* Berkeley, CA: EQUALS, Lawrence Hall of Science, 1986.

*Stern, Catherine, and Margaret Stern. *Helping Children Discover Arithmetic.* New York: Harper & Row, 1971.

Reys, Robert E., et al. *Helping Children Learn Mathematics.* 3d ed. Englewood Cliffs, NJ: Prentice-Hall, 1992.

Van de Walle, John A. *Elementary School Mathematics: Teaching Developmentally.* White Plains, NY: Longman, 1990.

LANGUAGE

*Baron, Naomi S. *Growing Up with Language: How Children Learn to Talk.* Reading, MA: Addison-Wesley, 1992.

Britton, James. *Language and Learning.* Coral Gables, FL: University of Miami Press, 1971. A general discussion of language and language development in relationship to learning.

Chukovsky, Kornei. *From Two to Five.* Berkeley, CA: University of California Press, 1963. Excellent, warm introduction to normal language development.

El Fey, Mark E. *Language Intervention with Young Children.* San Diego: University of Western Ontario, College Hill Press, 1987.

*Farb, Peter. *A Word Play.* New York: Bantam Books, 1984. Provocative book analyzes language according to theories of play and games; shows how personalities are shaped by language.

Greene, Harry, and Walter Petty. *Developing Language Skills in the Elementary Schools.* 5th ed. Boston: Allyn & Bacon, 1975. Good chapters on written expression, handwriting, and spelling with expectations at grade level for development of written expression.

Hodges, Richard, and Hugh Rudolph. *Language and Learning to Read: What Teachers Should Know About Language.* University Press of America, 1985. A collection of papers on the significance of language to the development of reading skills.

Stuttering and Your Child: Questions and Answers No. 22. Jane Fraser and Edward G. Conture, eds. Memphis, TN: Stuttering Foundation of America, 1989.

Vygotskii, L. S. *Thought and Language.* Revised and edited by Alexey Kozulin. Cambridge, MA: MIT Press, 1986.

*Wiig, Elisabeth, and Eleanor Semel. *Language Disabilities in Children and Adolescents.* Columbus, OH: Charles E. Merrill, 1976. This book is a classic.

Sensory Motor

A Parent's Guide to Understanding Sensory Integration. Torrance, CA: Sensory Integration International, 1986.

Arena, John I., ed. *Teaching Through Sensory Motor Experiences.* San Rafael, CA: Academic Therapy Publications, 1969. Excellent resource for teachers.

*Ayres, Jean. *Sensory Integration and the Child.* Los Angeles: Western Psychological Services, 1990. Brilliant but difficult; for persons with intensive background in the field.

Barsch, Ray H. *Enriching Perception and Cognition.* Seattle: Special and Child Publications, 1968. Difficult reading. Barsch is a neurologist and stresses the role of the body in learning.

Bissell, Julie, Jean Fisher, Carol Owens, and Patricia Polycyn. *Sensory Motor Handbook: A Guide for Implementing and Modifying Activities in the Classroom.* Torrance, CA: Sensory Integration International, 1988.

Cratty, Bryant J. *Active Learning: Games to Enhance Academic Abilities*. 2d ed. Englewood Cliffs, NJ: Prentice-Hall, 1985.

Montagu, Ashley. *Touching: The Human Significance of the Skin*. New York: Harper & Row, 1986.

*Sears, Carol. "The Tactilely Defensive Child," *Academic Therapy* (16:5), 1981, pp. 563–569.

*Van Witsen, Betty. *Perceptual Training and Activities Handbook*. New York: Teacher's College Press, 1979. Excellent for teachers or tutors.

GENERAL DEVELOPMENT AND CULTURE

*Beadle, Muriel. *A Child's Mind: How Children Learn During the Critical Years from Birth to Age Five*. New York: Doubleday, 1971. A good introduction to normal stages of learning in the early years.

*Fraiberg, Selma H. *The Magic Years: Childhood*. New York: Macmillan, 1981. Outstanding book that tunes in to children's fears and how they learn to cope with the world and themselves.

*Gardner, Howard. *Creating Minds: An Anatomy of Creativity Seen Through the Lives of Freud, Einstein, Picasso, Stravinsky, Eliot, Graham, and Gandhi*. New York: Basic Books, 1993.

*Hall, Edward T. *The Silent Language*. New York: Anchor Books/ Doubleday, 1990. The language subtleties and cultural values that affect our daily lives.

Smith, Sally Liberman. *Nobody Said It's Easy*. New York: Macmillan, 1965. A practical guide to feelings and relationships for young people and their parents.

DIAGNOSTIC TESTING

Anastasi, Anne. *Psychological Testing*. 6th ed. New York: Macmillan, 1989.

Boehm, A. E., and M. A. White. *The Parents' Handbook on School Testing*. New York: Teacher's College Press, 1982.

Bush, Wilma Jo. *Diagnosing Learning Problems*. 3d ed. Columbus, OH: Charles E. Merrill, 1982. Excellent introduction to diagnosis.

Frierson, Edward C., and Walter Barbe. *Educating Children with Learning Disabilities*. New York: Appleton-Century-Crofts, 1967. Chapter 3, "Diagnosing Learning Disorders," is particularly important.

Hirsch, Ernest. *The Troubled Adolescent As He Emerges on Psychological Tests*. New York: International Universities Press, 1970.

Ingram, Cregg F. *Fundamentals of Educational Assessment*. New York: D. Van Nostrand Co., 1980.

Pennington, Bruce F. *Diagnosing Learning Disorders: A Neuropsychological Framework*. New York: Guilford Press, 1991.

Salvia, John, and James Ysseldyke. *Assessment in Special and Remedial Education*. 5th ed. Boston: Houghton Mifflin, 1991.

Samuda, Ronald J. *Psychological Testing of American Minorities*. New York: Dodd Mead, 1975.

Swanson, H. Lee. *Handbook on the Assessment of Learning Disabilities: Theory, Research and Practice*. Austin, TX: Pro-Ed, 1991.

Wallace, Gerald, and Stephen Larsen. *Educational Assessment of Learning Problems: Testing for Teaching*. 2d ed. Boston: Allyn & Bacon, 1992.

Wiig, Elisabeth, and Eleanor Semel. *Language Assessment and Intervention for the Learning Disabled.* Columbus, OH: Charles E. Merrill, 1984.

EDUCATIONAL THEORY

Boyer, E. L. *High School: A Report on Secondary Education in America.* Carnegie Foundation for the Advancement of Teaching Staff & Ernest L. Boyer. New York: Harper & Row, 1985.

*Bruner, Jerome S. *Toward a Theory of Instruction.* Cambridge, MA: Belknap Press of Harvard University, 1966. Need for and how to teach structure of school subjects.

*———. *The Process of Education.* New York: Random House, 1960.

———. *Beyond the Information Given: Studies in the Psychology of Knowing.* New York: W. W. Norton, 1973.

———. *Actual Minds, Possible Worlds.* Cambridge, MA: Harvard University Press, 1986.

Caine, Renate Nummela, and Geoffrey Caine. *Making Connections: Teaching and the Human Brain.* Alexandria, VA: Banta Company, 1991.

*Dewey, John. *Experience and Education.* New York: Collier Books, 1963.

Alexander, Thomas M. *John Dewey's Theory of Art, Experience and Nature: The Horizons of Feeling.* Albany, NY: State University of New York Press, 1987.

———. *The Essential Writings of John Dewey.* New York: Harper & Row, 1977.

———. *The School and Society.* Carbondale, IL: Southern Illinois Press, 1980.

Furth, Hans G., and H. Wachs. *Thinking Goes to School: Piaget's Theory in Practice with Additional Thoughts.* New York: Oxford University Press, 1974. Examines need for stimulating reason and thinking in depth and gives concrete practical activities.

*Gardner, Howard. *Frames of Mind: The Theory of Multiple Intelligences.* New York: Basic Books, 1983.

———. *The Unschooled Mind: How Children Think and How Schools Should Teach.* New York: Basic Books, 1991.

Ginsburg, Herbert. *Piaget's Theory of Intellectual Development.* 3d ed. Englewood Cliffs, NJ: Prentice-Hall, 1988.

Healy, Jane. *Endangered Minds: Why Our Children Don't Think.* New York: Simon & Schuster, 1990. Offers much to parents regarding their children's reading and critical thinking.

Kohl, Herbert. *Growing Minds on Becoming a Teacher.* New York: Harper & Row, 1989.

Glasser, William. *Schools without Failure.* New York: Harper & Row, 1969.

*———. *The Quality School: Managing Students without Coercion.* New York: Perennial Library, 1990.

Gorman, Richard. *Discovering Piaget: A Guide for Teachers.* Columbus, OH: Charles E. Merrill, 1972.

*Holt, John C. *How Children Fail.* Revised ed. New York: Seymour Lawrence/Delacorte, 1988.

Montessori, Maria. *The Montessori Method.* Cambridge, MA: Schocken, 1988.

*———. *The Secret of Childhood.* New York: Ballantine Books, 1982.

Piaget, Jean. *The Language and Thought of the Child.* New York: Meridian Books, 1955.

*Pulaski, Mary Ann Spencer. *Understanding Piaget: An Introduction to Children's Cognitive Development.* Revised and expanded. New York: Harper & Row, 1980. Very good presentation of Piaget's maturational stages.

*Sizer, Theodore. *Horace's Compromise: The Dilemma of the American High School.* Boston: Houghton Mifflin, 1992.

————. *Horace's School: Redesigning the American High School.* Boston: Houghton Mifflin, 1992.

ARTS

Allen, Anne, and George Allen. *Everyone Can Win.* McLean, VA: EPM Publications, 1988.

Ames, K. "Why Jane Can't Draw (or Sing or Dance . . .). Education: A Consumer's Handbook." *Newsweek Special Issues:* Fall/Winter, 1990.

Dewey, John. *Art and Education: A Collection of Essays.* 3d ed. Merion, PA: Barns Foundation Press, 1954.

Di Leo, Joseph H. *Interpreting Children's Drawings.* New York: Brunner/Mazel Publications, 1983.

Edwards, Betty. *Drawing on the Right Side of the Brain: A Course in Enhancing Creativity and Artistic Confidence.* Los Angeles: Jeremy P. Tarcher, 1989.

Gardner, Howard. *Art, Mind and Brain: A Cognitive Approach to Creativity.* New York: Basic Books, 1984.

APPENDIX 3

TAPES AND VIDEOS

"The ABC's of Learning Disabilities" (45 mins.) This film illustrates the case histories of four learning disabled students with various learning difficulties. VHS. Contact: Scott Pryor, American Federation of Teachers, 555 New Jersey Avenue N.W., Washington, DC 20001. (202) 879-4458.

"Adolescence and Learning Disabilities" (40 mins.) Describes the tasks of adolescence and relates them to the learning disabled adolescent. Contact: Lawren Productions, P.O. Box 1542, Burlingame, CA 94010.

"All Children Learn Differently" (30 mins.) Professionals, parents, and students present some innovative approaches to the remediation of learning disabilities, and the need for the right professional team. Contact: Orange County ACLD, P.O. Box 25772, Santa Ana, CA 92799.

"Dyslexia, the Hidden Disability" (60 mins.) This is a documentary that examines the history, symptoms, possible causes, and successful techniques for dealing with this widespread learning disability. It is designed for teachers who feel unprepared to recognize or help the dyslexic student, for parents who suspect dyslexia in their child, and for individuals who work in the field. Contact: Grand Rapids Community College, Media Services, 143 Bostwick N.E., Grand Rapids, MI 49503. (616) 771-3830. Cost: $85 for ½" VHS, $115 for ¾".

"Homework and Learning Disabilities: A Common Sense Approach" (34 mins.) This video will help: clarify responsibility between teachers, parents, and students, establish structure and routine that lead to better study habits, develop abilities and study techniques to maximize learning, and help children make the most of their strengths and abilities. Contact: The Menninger Clinic and Center for Learning Disabilities, (800) 345-6036. $99 purchase, $45 rental.

* "How Difficult Can This Be? Understanding Learning Disabilities Through the F.A.T. City Workshop" (70 mins.) This film features a unique workshop wherein adults have the opportunity to experience learning disabilities firsthand. The participants are professionals (teachers, social workers, psychologists) and parents of learning disabled children. Contact: PBS Video. (800) 328-7271. $39.95 complete with teachers' guide.

"If a Boy Can't Learn" (28 mins.) Deals with a seventeen-year-old high-school student with a learning disability and shows how he was helped to make progress. Contact: Lawren Productions, P.O. Box 1542, Burlingame, CA 94010.

* "I'm Not Stupid" (51 mins.) This video provides an enlightening and heartening introduction to and overview of the nature of learning disabilities. Contact: LDA, 4156 Library Road, Pittsburgh, PA 15234. (412) 341-1515. $22.

---

* Extraordinarily effective

* "L.D. Stories" (7 mins.) Animated film by The Lab School Day School students about what it is like to have learning disabilities. Winner of 1992 Rosebud Award for Animation. Contact: The Lab School of Washington, Products and Services Division, 4759 Reservoir Road N.W., Washington, DC 20007. (202) 965-6600. $12.

* "Learning Disability: A Family Crisis" (45 mins.) This videotape dramatizes what happens in the family of an eight-year-old boy when his learning disability is diagnosed by school staff. The video describes strategies that teachers, special educators, school psychologists, counselors, and other mental-health professionals can employ to reduce stress and enhance the family's ability to cope effectively. Contact: The Menninger Clinic and Center for Learning Disabilities, (800) 345-6036. $165 purchase, $45 rental.

* "Reach for the Stars" (22 mins.) This film tells about The Lab School of Washington and the annual Outstanding Learning Disabled Achievers Awards. It shows celebrities with L.D. talking with children with L.D. Contact: The Lab School of Washington, Products and Services Division, 4759 Reservoir Road N.W., Washington, DC 20007. (202) 965-6600. $22.

"Strengths and Weaknesses: College Students with Learning Disabilities" (28 mins.) Four students share their experiences and feelings and four professionals explore possible adjustment and compensation relative to learning disabilities. The students' emphasis on what they can do provides optimistic prognoses for their academic survival. Contact: Altschul Group, 930 Pitner Avenue, Evanston, IL 60202. (312) 326-6700.

* "We Can Learn." This five-part series clearly outlines the steps critical in helping to determine if a child has learning disabilities and what to do if she/he does. It celebrates the results of good intervention through the eyes of those children and young adults with learning

disabilities who have received this help. Contact: NCLD, 381 Park Avenue South, New York, NY 10016. (212) 687-7211.

The Lab School of Washington is transferring some of its old teaching films on teaching academic skills through the arts onto videotape. Calling them "The Lab School Classics," the following will be available:

"Teaching Academic Skills Through Woodwork"
"Linking Sound and Symbol Through Music"
"Movement in Learning"
"Learning for a Lifetime: The Academic Club Method"

Contact: The Lab School of Washington, Products and Services Division, 4759 Reservoir Road N.W., Washington, DC 20007. (202) 965-6600.

"Issues of Parenting Children with Learning Disabilities," a twelve-part lecture series, is available on audiotape. Contact: The Lab School of Washington, Products and Services Division, 4759 Reservoir Road N.W., Washington, DC 20007. (202) 965-6600.

APPENDIX 4

INFORMATION CENTERS, ORGANIZATIONS, AND RESEARCH CENTERS

ABLEDATA
National Rehabilitation Information Center
The Catholic University of America
4407 Eighth Street NE
Washington, DC 20017
(202) 635-5822

ABLEDATA maintains a computerized database of products for learning disabilities and other disabilities.

AMERICAN COLLEGE TEST (ACT) ADMINISTRATION
Box 168
Iowa City, IA 52243
(319) 337-1332

Those with a documented learning disability are allowed to have special arrangements made when they take this test including untimed tests, tests on cassettes, and readers.

AMERICAN SPEECH-LANGUAGE-HEARING ASSOCIATION
10801 Rockville Pike
Rockville, MD 20852
(301) 897-5700
(800) 638-8255 Consumer Action Line

Provides technical assistance to professionals needing resources for diagnostic services. The Consumer Action Line is available to the public and attempts to answer speech-language-hearing-related questions.

ASSOCIATION ON HANDICAPPED STUDENT SERVICE PROGRAMS IN POSTSECONDARY EDUCATION (AHSSPPEE)
Box 21192
Columbus, OH 43221
(614) 488-4972

A professional organization for educators committed to promoting full college participation for individuals with disabilities, including learning disabilities. AHSSPPEE has materials for teachers and counselors who work with the learning disabled.

*CHILDREN WITH ATTENTION DEFICIT DISORDER (CHADD)
499 70th Avenue N.W. #109
Plantation, FL 33317
(305) 587-3700

---

* Asterisked entries have been described in Chapter 11.

*COUNCIL FOR EXCEPTIONAL CHILDREN (CEC)
1920 Association Drive
Reston, VA 22091
(703) 620-3360

EDUCATIONAL TESTING SERVICE (ETS)
Princeton, NJ 08541
(609) 734-5068

Special accommodations for those with learning disabilities are
offered through ETS for the Scholastic Aptitude Test (SAT),
Graduate Records Exam (GRE), and Graduate Management Test
(GMAT).

ERIC CLEARINGHOUSE ON DISABILITIES AND GIFTED EDUCATION
COUNCIL FOR EXCEPTIONAL CHILDREN
1920 Association Drive
Reston, VA 22091-1589
(703) 620-3660

Makes available two publications: *Digest on Learning Disabilities*
and annotated bibliography called *Digest on Readings about
Learning Disabilities.* Both publications are free.

GED TESTING SERVICE
American Council on Education
1 DuPont Circle
Washington, DC 20036
(202) 939-9490

The GED (General Educational Development) Test can be taken
with special accommodations and adaptations by those with a
documented learning disability. Guidelines and applications are
available upon request.

HIGHER EDUCATION AND ADULT TRAINING FOR PEOPLE WITH
HANDICAPS (HEATH)
HEATH Resource Center
1 DuPont Circle
Washington, DC 20036
(202) 939-9320
(800) 544-3284

A national clearinghouse on postsecondary education for people
with handicaps. Many free publications are available including
information on support services at colleges and universities,
Resources for Adults with Learning Disabilities, and *Getting Ready.*

INSTITUTE FOR RESEARCH ON DISABILITIES
The University of Kansas
3060 Robert J. Dole Human Development Center
Lawrence, KS 66045
(913) 864-4780

The focus of the research is on children, but there is also
information on adult issues.

INTERNATIONAL READING ASSOCIATION
Dept. TE, Box 8139
Newark, DE 19714
(302) 731-1600

This association holds reading conferences and works with issues of
the learning disabled.

*LEARNING DISABILITIES ASSOCIATION OF AMERICA (LDA)
4156 Library Road
Pittsburgh, PA 15234
(412) 341-1515 or 8077

NATIONAL ATTENTION DEFICIT ASSOCIATION (NADA)
Membership: P.O. Box 488
                 West Newbury, MA 01985
                 (800) 487-2282

Support Groups: 1962 Jamboree Road
                 Irvine, CA 92715
                 (800) 487-2282

This organization provides referrals and information to parents and
parent support groups.

*NATIONAL CENTER FOR LEARNING DISABILITIES (NCLD)
381 Park Avenue South, 14th Floor
New York, New York 10016
(212) 687-7211

NATIONAL INFORMATION CENTER FOR CHILDREN AND YOUTHS WITH
DISABILITIES ACADEMY FOR EDUCATIONAL DEVELOPMENT
Box 1492
Washington, DC 20013-1492
(202) 884-8200
(800) 695-0285

Provides parents with information about special education and the
rights children and youth with disabilities have under the law. State
resource sheets are also available to parents and give information
about state agencies, disability organizations, and parent groups.
Many publications are available at no cost.

NATIONAL NETWORK OF LEARNING DISABLED ADULTS
808 North 82nd Street, Suite F2
Scottsdale, AZ 85257
(602) 941-5112

The purpose of this organization is to increase communication among adults with learning disabilities. There is a quarterly newsletter and a list of support and self-help groups.

OFFICE OF VOCATIONAL REHABILITATION SERVICES
330 C Street S.W.
Switzer Building
Washington, DC 20202
(202) 205-9404

A federal agency that helps disabled people prepare for and keep jobs. It is interested in adults with learning disabilities and how their disability affects their job.

*ORTON DYSLEXIA SOCIETY
Chester Building, Suite 382
8600 La Salle Road
Towson, MD 21204
(410) 296-0232
(800) 222-3123

PROJECT LITERACY U.S. (PLUS)
4802 Fifth Avenue
Pittsburgh, PA 15213
(412) 622-1491

PLUS focuses on adult literacy problems in the United States and works with the National Center for Learning Disabilities.

RECORDING FOR THE BLIND (RFB)
20 Rozel Road
Princeton, NJ 08540
(609) 452-0606

Those individuals with learning disabilities who meet eligibility requirements can have educational textbooks recorded on tapes.

SENSORY INTEGRATION INTERNATIONAL
1402 Cravens Avenue
Torrance, CA 90501
(310) 533-8338

Provides general information about sensory integration or
information on a specific subject, such as treatment efficacy.
Maintains a list of occupational and physical therapists trained in
the field.

SERVICES FOR THE BLIND AND PHYSICALLY HANDICAPPED
Library of Congress
1291 Taylor Street N.W.
Washington, DC 20542
(202) 707-5100
(800) 424-8567

Current books and magazines are on tapes and records for
individuals who cannot use printed material. Applicants must have
a documented disability to receive this service.

SPECIALIZED TRAINING PROGRAMS OF MILITARY PARENTS (STOMP)
12208 Pacific Highway S.W.
Tacoma, WA 98499
(206) 588-1741

A training and information center that provides workshops on the
special needs of children in military families. An excellent referral
system for military families is provided.

LEARNING DISABILITY RESEARCH CENTERS AND RESEARCH PROGRAMS

As of 1994, the National Institute of Child Health and Human Development (NICHD) is funding three multidisciplinary research centers
to develop new knowledge about the definition, classification, preven-

tion, identification, etiologies, developmental courses, and most effective interventions for children with learning disabilities and related disorders, such as ADHD. The three centers are:

> Yale University of the Study of Learning and Attention Disorders
> Johns Hopkins Learning Disability Research Center
> University of Colorado Learning Disability Research Center

The NICHD also funds two Program Project grants to undertake detailed studies of the neurophysiology, developmental course, and treatment of dyslexia. The projects are located at:

> The Bowman Gray School of Medicine
> Beth Israel Hospital/Harvard University

The NICHD is also funding two large longitudinal studies to identify which interventions are most effective with well-defined groups of reading-disabled children. These studies are located at:

> Florida State University
> The University of Houston

The research carried out at these sites has greatly enhanced our knowledge about learning disabilities. For detailed information contact:

Dr. Reid Lyon
HLB/CRMC/NICHD/NIH
6100 Building, Room 4B05
9000 Rockville Pike
Bethesda, MD 20892
(301) 496-6591

SOME NATIONAL LEGAL, ADVOCACY, AND SERVICE ORGANIZATIONS

Center for Law and Education
955 Massachusetts Avenue, Suite 3A
Cambridge, MA 02139
(617) 876-6611

Children's Defense Fund
122 C Street N.W.
Washington, DC 20001
(202) 628-8787

Commission on Mental and Physical Disability Law
American Bar Association
1800 M Street N.W.
Washington, DC 20036
(202) 331-2240

Developmental Disabilities Law Center
2510 St. Paul Street
Baltimore, MD 21218
(410) 235-4700

Learning Disabilities Association of America (LDA)
4156 Library Road
Pittsburgh, PA 15234
(412) 341-1515 or 8077

For parents, teachers, and other professionals. Provides needed
information and support, follows the latest educational and medical
research, and supports legislation for special classes and trained
teachers in the field.

Mental Health Law Project
1101 15th Street N.W., Suite 1212
Washington, DC 20005
(202) 467-5730

Mexican-American Legal Defense Fund
182 2nd Street, 2nd Floor
San Francisco, CA 94105
(415) 543-5598

While IDEA (PL 101-476) is not a specialization, they will offer consultation on the law as it affects Mexican Americans.

National Association of Protection and Advocacy Systems
900 2nd Street N.E., Suite 211
Washington, DC 20002
(202) 408-9514

Clients can receive information for contacting a state office and/or a referral for assistance from other agencies or individuals. Eligibility criteria must be met to receive services.

National Education Association
1201 16th Street N.W.
Washington, DC 20036
(202) 833-4000

Teachers' organization.

Native American Rights Fund
1506 Broadway
Boulder, CO 80302
(303) 447-8760

Has education specialists and information on IDEA (PL 101-476) and Section 504 as they affect Native Americans.

Public Interest Law Center of Philadelphia
125 South 9th Street, Suite 700
Philadelphia, PA 19107
(215) 627-7100

Youth Advocacy Clinic
T. C. Williams School of Law
University of Richmond
Richmond, VA 23173
(804) 287-6093

National Center for Youth Law
114 Sansome Street, Suite 900
San Francisco, CA 94104
(415) 543-3307

APPENDIX 5

RECOMMENDED PROFESSIONAL JOURNALS

ANNALS
Orton Dyslexia Society
P.O. Box 9888
Baltimore, MD 21284-9888
(410) 296-0232

Official bulletin of the Orton Society, a nonprofit scientific and educational organization for the study and treatment of children with specific language disability (dyslexia). All ages, international scope. Many useful reprints.

EDUCATIONAL LEADERSHIP
Association for Supervision and Curriculum Development (ASCD)
1250 North Pitt Street
Alexandria, VA 22314-1403
(703) 549-9110

Official journal of ASCD, offering information on curriculum instruction, supervision, and leadership in education. Articles are by leading educators, including reports of programs and practices and interpretations of research as well as book reviews and columns.

THE EXCEPTIONAL CHILD
.1920 Association Drive
Reston, VA 22091-1589
(703) 620-3660

Covers all of the areas of exceptionalities in children. It presents a variety of articles, including many on reading and language for different types of children.

THE EXCEPTIONAL PARENT
Psy-Ed Corporation
209 Harvard Street
Brookline, MA 02146
(617) 730-5800
(800) 852-2884

A reassuring journal for parents; information and detailed articles.

INTERVENTION IN SCHOOL AND CLINIC (FORMERLY: ACADEMIC THERAPY)
Pro-Ed
8700 Shoal Creek Boulevard
Austin, TX 78757-6897
(512) 451-3246

Interdisciplinary journal directed to an international audience of teachers, parents, and specialists working in the fields of reading, learning, and communication disabilities. All ages. Methods, identification, diagnosis, and remediation emphasized.

THE JOURNAL OF LEARNING DISABILITIES
Pro-Ed
8700 Shoal Creek Boulevard
Austin, TX 78757-6897
(512) 451-3246

Multidisciplinary; primarily concerned with learning disabilities
(diagnosis and treatment). All ages. International scope. Theoretical
and practical contributions.

JOURNAL OF READING
International Reading Association
800 Barksdale Road
Newark, DE 19711-3269
(302) 731-1600

Primarily directed to secondary teachers, the journal also concerns
itself with older remedial readers and motivational techniques.
Its purpose is to exchange information and opinions on reading
skills.

THE JOURNAL OF SPECIAL EDUCATION
Pro-Ed
8700 Shoal Creek Boulevard
Austin, TX 78757-6897
(512) 451-3246

Primarily devoted to all types of children in a special setting, the
journal contains relevant material for remedial reading approaches.

LDA NEWSBRIEFS
4156 Library Road
Pittsburgh, PA 15234
(412) 341-1515

Bimonthly newsletter for parents, professionals, and adults that includes up-to-date research findings, information on current publications, and a list of scheduled conferences.

LEARNING DISABILITIES: A MULTIDISCIPLINARY JOURNAL
4156 Library Road
Pittsburgh, PA 15234
(412) 341-1515

Biannual publication put out by LDA and directed to parents and professionals. A scholarly journal representing the major disciplines concerned with learning disabilities.

LEARNING DISABILITIES RESEARCH PRACTICES
1920 Reston Drive
Reston, VA 22091
(703) 620-3660

Journal providing a forum for current research in the field of learning disabilities and for the dissemination of information important to practitioners in the field.

LEARNING DISABILITY QUARTERLY
Council for Learning Disabilities
Box 40303
Overland Park, KS 66204
(913) 492-8755

Primarily contains research studies in learning disabilities directed to professionals.

PERSPECTIVES ON DYSLEXIA
Chester Building, Suite 382
8600 La Salle Road
Towson, MD 21204
(410) 296-0232

Quarterly newsletter developed by the Orton Dyslexia Society that has articles on people, education, and medical research. It also gives information about meetings, seminars, workshops, and conferences on the subject of dyslexia.

TEACHING EXCEPTIONAL CHILDREN
Publication of the Council for Exceptional Children
1920 Association Drive
Reston, VA 22091-1589
(703) 620-3660

Directed to the special class practitioner in both elementary school and high school.

APPENDIX 6

DESCRIPTION AND LIST OF TESTS ORDINARILY USED TO DIAGNOSE LEARNING DISABLED STUDENTS

At this time, the various specialists concerned with learning disabilities do not agree which test battery should be used for diagnosis. Even when only one specific aspect of learning disabilities (such as language or visual perception) is under consideration, there is no consensus among professionals as to which tests are appropriate.

A typical diagnostic battery includes tests of general intelligence or academic aptitude and tests of academic performance in reading, writing, spelling, composition, and arithmetic. Depending upon the age of the child and the nature of the problem, tests of auditory and visual perception, sensory motor integration, motor development, and language may be given. Tests of information-processing capacities including memory, attention, processing speed, and other abilities necessary for learning can yield valuable information. Young children may have tests designed to measure their general developmental level and academic readiness. Tests or rating scales to measure social and emotional adjustment may also be used.

The purpose of testing is to seek out the youngster's academic potential, identify his academic strengths and weaknesses, and determine how he or she learns best.

Some of the most frequently used tests are listed here. All of these tests would never be used for one child, and other instruments not mentioned here may be included in an evaluation. Tests that may be used for more than one purpose are listed in several categories. The examiner will select those that are most suited to each child's situation. Group administered aptitude and achievement tests primarily designed to monitor the school progress of nonhandicapped children are not included.

TESTS OF COGNITIVE OR INTELLECTUAL ABILITY

These tests are used to indicate a youngster's intellectual functions. They measure general intelligence and/or academic aptitude.

Arthur Adaptation of the Leiter Performance Scale. (1949) Adaptation of the *Leiter Performance Scale* for 3- to 8-year-olds that assesses nonverbal reasoning skills.

Bayley Scales of Infant Development—II. (1993) The Bayley II is a norm-referenced, three-part evaluation of the developmental status of children from one month to 42 months (3½ years) of age. The three areas of development assessed are mental abilities, motor skills, and behavior.

Extended Merrill-Palmer Scale. (1978) Individually administered test of cognitive ability for children between the ages of 3 years and 5 years 11 months. Evaluates both the content and the process of thinking in young children.

Goodenough-Harris Drawing Test. (1963) A brief, nonverbal test of intelligence. A child's human figure drawing is scored for number and proportion of body parts. For ages 3 to 15. The purpose is to assess intellectual maturity—the ability to form concepts of an abstract nature.

Hiskey-Nebraska Test of Learning Aptitude. (1966) A nonverbal intelligence test that can be used with children who have a language handicap or hearing impairment. Can be administered entirely through pantomimed instructions and does not require verbal responses. Norms are available for 2½- to 17-year-olds.

Kaufman Adolescent and Adult Intelligence Test (KAIT). (1993) The KAIT is a multisubtest battery for measuring the mental abilities of individuals ages 11 years to 85+. The battery yields three global scores of fluid, crystallized, and composite intelligence. Fine motor coordination and motor speed are deemphasized, providing a more meaningful measure of the intelligence of individuals with problems in that domain.

Kaufman Assessment Battery for Children. (1983) Measures intelligence and achievement for children ages 2½ to 12½. Provides scores for sequential and simultaneous processing along with achievement and nonverbal ability.

Leiter International Performance Scale. (1948) This is a nonverbal measure designed to assess the intelligence of children 2 to 12 years of age. Appropriate for children who are deaf, hard of hearing, bilingual, nonfluent in English, or language-impaired.

McCarthy Scales of Children's Abilities. (1972) Assesses the general intelligence of children ages 2½ to 8½. Includes verbal, perceptual, motor, memory, and quantitative scales.

Raven's Progressive Matrices and Colored Matrices. (1986) A nonverbal test (colored matrices) of reasoning abilities suitable for children ages 5 to 11 years. Older children can take the standard matrices and adults can take the advanced matrices. The subject is asked to select a pattern to complete a design. It is a test of perception and spatial relations, useful for children with language difficulties.

Slosson Intelligence Test (SIT). (1983) Measures primarily verbal ability, preschool through high-school level. Useful for screening since it is short and easy to administer. All questions are presented verbally and require spoken responses.

System of Multicultural Pluralistic Assessment (SOMPA). (1978) Not a test but a series of assessment devices incorporating medical, social, and pluralistic information attempting to arrive at a culture-fair evaluation of learning potential.

Stanford-Binet Intelligence Scale—Fourth Edition. (1986) One of the most widely used tests of cognitive ability for 2-year-olds through young adults. Yields scores for verbal reasoning, abstract/visual reasoning, quantitative reasoning, and short-term memory.

Test of Nonverbal Intelligence—Second Edition (TONI-2). (1990) A language-free measure of cognitive ability for 5- to 85-year-olds. Entails abstract/figural problem solving.

Test of Variables of Attention Computer Program (TOVA). (1989) The TOVA is a 22½-minute computerized assessment of attention used as a screening tool for attention disorders. Norms are available for 5 years and up.

Wechsler Adult Intelligence Scale—Revised (WAIS-R). (1981) Tests general intelligence, including verbal and nonverbal abilities, of adults and older adolescents ages 16 and up.

Wechsler Intelligence Scale for Children—Third Edition (WISC III). (1991) Designed to test general intelligence, ages 6 to 16. This test has established itself as one of the most useful tools for diagnosing learning disabilities. Verbal, performance (nonverbal), and full scale scores are available. Also yields factor indices for freedom from distractibility and processing speed in addition to verbal reasoning and perceptual organization.

Wechsler Pre-School and Primary Scale of Intelligence—Revised (WPPSI-R). (1989) For ages 3 to 7. This test measures verbal and nonverbal reasoning and perceptual motor abilities. This is one of the major instruments for assessing the cognitive ability of young children.

TESTS OF INFORMATION PROCESSING

These tests are designed to give diagnostic information about the kinds of perceptual and communication deficits often found in learning disabled students.

Detroit Tests of Learning Aptitude-3 (DTLA-3). (1992) Measures various reasoning memory and perceptual abilities from age 6 to 18 years. The DTLA-P is an abbreviated version for 3- to 9-year-olds.

Jordan Left-Right Reversal Test. (1974) Designed to measure letter and number reversals in the area of children's visual receptive functioning for ages 5 to 12 years.

Meeting Street School Screening Test. (1969) Screens kindergartners and first-graders for possible learning disabilities in language and sensory-motor areas. A preschool version is available for prekindergartners.

Slingerland Screening Tests for Identifying Children with Specific Language Disability. (1970) Screens for learning disabilities that relate to reading, writing, spelling, speaking, and listening. Emphasis is given to written, as opposed to oral, processes. Includes visual and auditory memory sequencing and discrimination. Available from preschool through junior-high level (Malcomesius test is for grades 6 to 8).

Visual-Aural Digit-Span Test (VADS). (1978) Assesses sensory integration skills, using both auditory and visual reception and oral and written expression. Permits assessment of the best channels of modalities for learning.

Woodcock-Johnson Psychoeducational Battery—Revised—Tests of Cognitive Ability. (1989) A battery of cognitive tests from preschool to adult level, measuring learning and memory skills, short-term memory, processing speed, auditory processing, visual processing, comprehension-knowledge, and fluid reasoning.

DEVELOPMENTAL OR READINESS TESTS

These tests are used to determine maturational lag in young children, evaluate academic readiness, and screen for children who may need special help upon entering school.

Boehm Test of Basic Concepts—Revised and Preschool Version. (1986) Measures mastery of concepts needed for academic work: space, quantity, time, opposites, etc. Provides norms for kindergarten through second grade at three socioeconomic levels. Preschool version is appropriate for 3- to 5-year-olds.

Columbia Mental Maturity Scale. (1972) Age range 3½ to 9 years. Measures general reasoning. May be used to assess children who have difficulty reasoning verbally.

Denver Developmental Screening Test—Revised. (1975) Detects delayed development in children aged 2 weeks to 6 years 4 months. The test consists of four sections: personal-social, fine motor, language, and gross motor. Can be used to screen for children with learning and behavior problems.

Evanston Early Identification Scale. (1967) Identifies children aged 5 years to 6 years 3 months who are at low, middle, or high risk for learning problems in school. The child is asked to draw a human figure, which is scored on a scale of point values for missing body parts.

McCarthy Scales of Children's Abilities. (1972) Assesses the general intelligence of children ages 2½ to 8½ and includes cognitive, verbal, memory, and gross and fine motor development.

Meeting Street School Screening Test. (1969) Screens kindergarten and first-grade children for risk of learning disabilities. A prekindergarten level is available.

Pre-School Attainment Record (PAR). (1967) Assesses social, physical, and intellectual functions of children, aged 6 months to 7 years. The parent is interviewed concerning the child's developmental behavior.

The Scales of Independent Behavior. (1989) Individually administered scales of skills needed to function independently in community and home settings. Infants to mature adults.

Slingerland Pre-Reading Screening Procedures. (1977) May be given individually or in a group to kindergarten and first-grade students. Assesses visual perception, auditory perception, and both auditory and visual memory as applied to reading readiness tasks.

Test of Basic Experience (TOBE). (1972) This test is designed to assess the preschool, kindergarten, and first-grade child's conceptual understanding of language, social studies, science, and math. The test is group-administered.

ADAPTIVE FUNCTIONING

Vineland Adaptive Behavior. (1984) Assesses the social competence of disabled and nondisabled individuals, through 19 years of age.

GENERAL ACHIEVEMENT TESTS

These tests provide an overview of a student's academic skills and establish the degree of aptitude-achievement discrepancy.

Brigance Diagnostic Inventory of Basic Skills. (1977) Assesses basic readiness and academic skills from kindergarten to sixth-grade level in reading, math, and language arts. A criterion-referenced test designed to assist the teacher in developing instructional objectives for the classroom.

Kaufman Test of Educational Achievement (K-TEA). (1985) Individually administered measure of school achievement of students in grades 1 through 12. Yields measures of skill level in reading, decoding and comprehension, mathematics, computation and applications, and spelling.

Metropolitan Instructional Achievement Tests. (1978) A battery of tests in mathematics, reading, and language arts for grades 1 to 12. May be given in a group or individually. Assesses a variety of component skills in math, reading, and language arts and provides instructional objectives and suggestions for teaching.

Norris Educational Achievement Test (NEAT). (1992) The NEAT is a set of individually administered tests of educational ability for use with students from age 4 to 17 years 11 months. Tests composing the battery are: word recognition, spelling, arithmetic, oral reading, and comprehension, written language, and three readiness tests assessing fine motor coordination, math concepts, and letters.

Peabody Individual Achievement Test (PIAT). (1989) Measures general academic achievement in reading mechanics and comprehension, spelling, math, and general knowledge. For ages 5 to adult, with a variety of scores available that can be used in diagnostic profile with data from aptitude tests such as WISC-R.

Stanford Diagnostic Achievement Tests. (1976) A battery of tests in mathematics and reading for grades 1 to 12. May be given in a group or individually. Assesses a variety of component skills in math and reading and provides instructional objectives and suggestions for teaching. Similar to the Metropolitan tests but with somewhat more emphasis on listening skills and oral vocabulary.

Wide Range Achievement Test—Third Edition (WRAT-3). (1993) The WRAT-3 assesses word recognition, spelling, and arithmetic computation skills for individuals aged 5 to 75 years.

Weschler Individual Achievement Test (WIAT). (1992) For 5- to 19-year-olds.

Woodcock-Johnson Psychoeducational Battery, Tests of Academic Achievement—Revised. (1989) For preschool through adult level, these tests measure achievement in reading, math, written language, and general knowledge.

DIAGNOSTIC ARITHMETIC TESTS

There are few standardized diagnostic arithmetic tests, so a math education specialist must use informal inventories and evaluations to assess a child. One-to-one interviewing and observing is necessary to diagnose the child's thinking process with numbers.

Key Math—Revised. (1988) An individual test, designed for children from kindergarten up, the Key Math provides a comprehensive assessment of a student's understanding and application of mathematic concepts and skills. Now available for K to ninth grade. Provides valuable, detailed information on a student's strengths and weaknesses in basic concepts, operations, and applications. The test assesses skills in numeration, fractions, geometry, symbols, addition, subtraction, multiplication, division, mental computation, numerical reasoning, word problems, missing elements, money, measurement, and time.

Inventory of Error Patterns in Basic Mathematics. (1979) A test designed to be administered individually to children experiencing difficulties in addition, subtraction, multiplication, fractions, and decimals.

The Math Teaching Handbook, Informal Diagnostic Testing. (1978) A criterion-referenced, informal diagnostic test is included in this handbook with many suggestions for diagnostic teaching.

Stanford Diagnostic Mathematics Test. (1976) This test may be given individually or in a group and is suitable for students from the end of grade 1 through grade 8. It may also be used with high-school students who are below the level of algebra. Skills in numeration, computation, and applications (problem solving, tables and graphs, geometry, and measurement) are assessed.

TESTS OF SOCIAL AND EMOTIONAL ADJUSTMENT

These tests measure a child's emotional development and his or her ability to relate to others in social situations. In addition to tests, informal observations by teachers and parents are important.

1. Projective Tests: These tests provide an in-depth assessment of personality and emotional functioning. They should be administered only by a trained clinical psychologist.

Children's Apperception Test (CAT). (1955) Children are asked to look at animal pictures and respond with a story. For younger children but similar to the TAT test.

Rorschach Inkblot Test. (1966) Subjects, from preschool to adult, are asked to look at ink blots and respond by telling what they see.

Minnesota Multiphasic Personality Inventory—Adolescent (MMPI-A). (1991) The MMPI-A is an empirically based test of adolescent adjustment and psychopathology. Derived from the MMPI, the MMPI-A is designed specifically for identifying personal, social, or behavioral problems in 14- to 18-year-olds.

Personality Inventory for Children—Revised (PIC). (1984) Parents indicate whether 600 inventory items are true or false in regard to their child. Scoring yields clinically relevant descriptions of child behavior affect and cognitive status as well as family characteristics, for children and adolescents ages 3 to 16 years.

Tasks of Emotional Development (TED). (1975) Projective storytelling technique similar to CAT but uses pictures designed for both latency and adolescent boys and girls. Assesses social, developmental, and family issues.

Thematic Apperception Test (TAT). (1943) Older children and adults are asked to look at pictures and respond with stories. Themes and topics chosen by the subject can reveal inner drives and fantasies.

Roberts Apperception Test for Children. (1982) 6- to 15-year-olds are asked to tell stories in response to pictures of children and adults in everyday interaction. It measures both adaptive and maladaptive functioning vis-à-vis an objective scoring system and norms.

House-Tree-Person Technique. (1964) The child is asked to draw a house, tree, and person. These drawings may reveal the child's view of himself and his world.

Children's Depression Inventory (CDI). (1981) A self-report measure of childhood depression with norms for second- to eighth-graders. The child reports emotions and thoughts experienced in the past two weeks.

Piers Harris Children's Self-Concept Scale. (1984) A brief self-report measure designed to aid in the assessment of self-concept in children and adolescents, ages 8 to 18 years. Includes a scale for intellectual and school status that can be very valuable in assessing the impact of learning disabilities on social-emotional development.

2. *Rating Scales:* Teachers, parents, or other persons acquainted with the child answer questions regarding his behavior and development. Established norms enable the examiner to interpret the results.

AAMD Adaptive Behavior Scales. (1969) A behavior rating scale for ages 3 to adult and suitable for emotionally maladjusted, mentally handicapped, and developmentally disabled persons.

Burk's Behavior Rating Scales. (1969) Identifies children in grades 1 to 8 with pathological behavior.

Child Behavior Checklist. (1989) A checklist for evaluating behavior problems and symptoms of emotional disturbance in 4- to 18-year-olds. The respondent is the parent.

Conners Parent Rating Scale. (1985) Parents rate their children in terms of a variety of symptoms on a four-point scale. Norms are available for 3- to 17-year-olds.

Conners Teacher Rating Scale. (1985) Elicits teacher ratings on a variety of potential problematic classroom behaviors. Used for identifying behavior problems in 4- to 12-year-olds.

Deveraux Behavior Rating Scale. (1967) Provides a profile to measure fifteen behavior dimensions for children and adolescents.

Social Skills Rating System (SSRS). (1990) Multirater assessment of student social behaviors that can affect teacher-student relations, peer acceptance, and academic performance. May be used with preschool, elementary, and secondary students with parent, student, and teacher as respondents.

Teacher's Report Form. (1986) Obtains teachers' ratings of a student's classroom behavior problems and competencies as well as school performance.

Vineland Social Maturity Scale. (1967) Assesses personal and social competence.

Walker Problem Behavior Checklist. (1970) Provides a profile for elementary-school children of behaviors that interfere with successful achievement. Measures acting out, withdrawal, distractibility, peer relations, and immaturity.

TESTS OF ORAL LANGUAGE

These tests are used to assess a child's strengths and weaknesses in understanding and using oral and written language. The tests measure a child's perception and use of various linguistic systems. These systems include sound patterns of the language (phonology); grammar rules on a word and phrase level (syntax); meaning of word labels and word relationships (semantics); topic development using appropriate linguistic form and manner (pragmatics); and rate, rhythm, and intonation patterns of language (prosody).

Bankson Language Test-2. (Bankson, Pro-Ed, 1991) This test for 3- to 7-year-olds measures semantic knowledge for various categories of word labels; various syntactical rules, such as verb forms and comparatives; and pragmatic conventions such as informing, controlling, and imagining. Scores provide standardized norms for comparison to age peers.

Carrow Elicited Language Inventory. (Carrow, Learning Concepts, 1974) This oral sentence imitation task measures word and phrase level syntax and is sensitive to problems with short-term auditory memory. It is available in English and Spanish forms. Scores allow informal comparison to age peers.

Clinical Evaluation of Language Fundamentals—Revised. (Semel, Wiig, and Secord, Psychological Corporation, 1987) This widely used, broad measure assesses understanding and use of word and phrase grammar, meaning, and organization in oral and written language. Results allow standardized comparison to age peers. Guided analysis of subtest item allows targeting of intervention for problematic linguistic rules. *Clinical Evaluation of Language Fundamentals— Preschool* (1992) allows similar assessment tasks for 3- to 6-year-olds.

Detroit Tests of Learning Aptitude-3. (Hammill, Pro-Ed, 1991) This test measures receptive and expressive oral and written language on picture, letter, word, and phrase levels, by having the child perform tasks such as naming opposite words, arranging pictures in a meaningful sequence, writing a sequence of letters backward, and telling a story about a picture. The test is particularly sensitive to short-term memory problems, attention deficit, and difficulty with tasks involving motor expression. Scores provide standardized comparison to age peers. The *Detroit Test of Learning Aptitude—Primary* provides similar tasks and scores for children aged 3½ to 10 years.

Dysarthria Profile. (Robinson, Communication Skill Builders, 1982) This assessment protocol provides a systematic format for reviewing breath support for speech, voice quality, nasal resonance, and oral structures at rest and in motion.

Expressive One-Word Picture Vocabulary Test—Revised. (Gardner, Academic Therapy Publications, 1990) This test measures expressive semantic skills by asking the child to name pictures that represent increasingly difficult words. This test tends to be sensitive to word-finding problems. Scores provide standardized comparison to age peers.

Fletcher Time-by-Count Test of Diadochokinetic Syllable Rate. (Fletcher, Pro-Ed, 1979) This test measures the ability to produce rapid, patterned movements of the mouth in various syllable patterns. Accuracy, rate, quality, and ease of motion are rated and compared to average rates for age peers.

Gray Oral Reading Tests-3. (Wiederhold and Bryant, Pro-Ed, 1992) This test measures oral reading speed and accuracy and passage comprehension. It allows comparison of factors that affect reading success such as coding sounds for letter symbols, fluency and rate of reading, and passage comprehension. Results allow standardized comparison to age and grade peers.

Khan-Lewis Phonological Analysis. (Khan and Lewis, American Guidance Service, 1986) For use with the *Goldman-Fristoe Test of Articulation.* (Goldman and Fristoe, American Guidance Service, 1972) After administering and recording phonetically the responses on the picture-naming articulation test, the *Analysis* facilitates detection of which distinctive features of phonemes and which phoneme syllable positions give the child difficulty. The profile prescribes a tailored articulation therapy program.

Language Processing Test. (Richard and Hanner, LinguiSystems, 1985) This listening/talking test measures the child's ability to make associations and categorize words, state similarities and differences between words, provide multiple meanings for words, and describe attributes of words. Scores provide standardized comparison to age peers.

Lindamood Auditory Conceptualization Test. (Lindamood and Lindamood, DLM, 1979) This test measures ability to listen to sound sequences and code them using colored blocks. The child must be able to rearrange block sequences to match changing patterns spoken by the examiner. Scores allow informal comparison to grade peers and provide a starting point for an intensive auditory training program that the Lindamoods have developed.

Oral Speech Mechanism Screening Examination—Revised. (Louis and Ruscello, Pro-Ed, 1981) This test measures structure and range of motion for speech and nonspeech movements. The test presents a model for systematic review of structures and movement.

Peabody Picture Vocabulary Test—Revised. (Dunn and Dunn, American Guidance Service, 1985) This widely used test measures receptive, one-word, semantic skills by asking the child to point to one picture in four that matches a word spoken by the examiner. Scores provide standardized comparison to age peers.

Preschool Language Scale-3. (Zimmerman et al., Psychological Corporation, 1992) This test measures receptive understanding and expression with focus on syntax (word and phrase level) and semantics (vocabulary, concept development, and cognitive skills). Items are ordered to evaluate a child's development of sequential milestones in language. Scores allow standardized comparison to age peers from birth to 7 years.

Receptive One-Word Picture Vocabulary Test—Revised. (Gardner, Academic Therapy Publications, 1985) This test measures understanding of word meaning by asking the child to point to the picture that matches a word spoken by the examiner. Scores provide standardized comparison to age peers.

SCAN: A Screening Test for Auditory Processing Disorders. (Keith, Psychological Corporation, 1986) This test measures ability to listen to and repeat words heard under earphones in three obstacle listening tasks. Results allow standardized comparison to age peers. A variety of score patterns signal auditory processing problems.

Screening Test for Developmental Apraxia. (Blakeley, Pro-Ed, 1980) This test measures oral motor movement, production of complex words to pronounce, transpositions of sounds, and fluency of speech. Performance is compared to generally agreed-upon symptoms of dyspraxia.

Slosson Oral Reading Test—Revised. (Slosson [revised by Nicholson], Pro-Ed, 1992) This brief test measures word-calling skills by having the child read lists of increasingly difficult words. Scores provide standardized comparison to age and grade peers.

Test of Adolescent/Adult Word Finding. (German, DLM, 1990) This test measures the speed and accuracy of picture naming for different types of words, sentence completion, naming target words described by their attributes, and naming the category described by its components. Results allow standardized comparison to age and grade peers.

Test of Adolescent Language-2. (Hammill et al., Pro-Ed, 1987) This test measures receptive and expressive word and sentence level syntactic, semantic, and pragmatic skills. Scores allow standardized comparison to age peers with quotients for listening, speaking, reading, and writing.

Test of Auditory Comprehension of Language—Revised. (Carrow-Woolfolk, DLM, 1985) This test measures understanding of word and sentence level semantic and syntactic rules by asking a child to match pictures to words or sentences spoken by the examiner. Scores allow comparison to age and grade peers.

Test of Auditory Perceptual Skills. (Gardner, Children's Hospital, San Francisco, 1985) This test measures auditory memory for digits, words, and sentences, auditory discrimination of similar word pairs, ability to paraphrase directions, and ability to provide short answers to spoken questions. Scores allow informal comparison to age peers.

Test of Early Language Development. (Hresko et al., Pro-Ed, 1991) This test measures form (syntax) and content (semantics) of receptive and expressive language by asking the child to listen to instructions and give oral responses that show understanding and use of vocabulary, word relationships, and grammar. Toys and pictures are used to structure responses. Parents provide answers to some of the questions, especially for younger children, based on how the child understands and uses language at home. Standardized age norms are provided to compare performance of other 2- to 8-year-olds.

Test of Early Reading Ability-2. (Reid et al., Pro-Ed, 1981) This test measures general orientation to reading such as pointing to the top of a book, as well as understanding nonletter symbols such as store signs, and oral and silent reading of alphabet letters, words, and paragraphs. Results allow standardized comparison to age peers.

Test of Early Written Language. (Hresko, Pro-Ed, 1988) This test measures understanding of nonletter symbols such as McDonald's Golden Arches, letters, words, and passages as well as ability to copy print and write letters and words. Results allow standardized comparison to age peers.

Test of Language Development—Primary-2. (Hammill and Newcomer, Pro-Ed, 1988) This widely used test measures receptive and expressive linguistic systems, resulting in standardized scores for listening, speaking, semantics, syntax, and phonology, all of which can be compared to age peers between 4 and 9 years. The *Test of Language Development—Intermediate-2* provides the same type of tasks and scores for children ages 8½ to 13 years.

Test of Language Competence—Expanded Edition. (Wiig and Secord, Psychological Corporation, 1989) This test, which focuses on semantic, pragmatic, and syntactic skills, measures the child's ability to clarify meaning of ambiguous sentences, infer missing information in a short paragraph, make up sentences for targeted words, and interpret idiomatic or figurative expressions. Level I of the test is for 5- to 10-year-olds and uses pictures as stimulus probes, whereas Level II is for 9- to 19-year-olds and probes with written sentences that are read silently and heard at the same time. Both levels of the test provide standardized norms for comparison to age peers.

Test of Minimal Articulation Competence. This test measures how sounds are produced as the child names pictures, reads sentences, or imitates utterances of the examiner. Error scores allow informal assessment of severity of the articulation problem.

Test of Pragmatic Language. (Phelps-Terasaki and Phelps-Gunn, Pro-Ed, 1992) This test, for 5- to 14-year-olds, measures six core components of pragmatic language, including physical setting, audience, topic, purpose, visual-gesture cues, and abstraction. Scores allow standardized comparison to age peers.

Test of Oral Structures and Functions. (Vitali, Slosson Educational Publications, 1986) This diagnostic protocol provides a systematic format for assessing speech and nonspeech patterns, including vegetative functions such as chewing and swallowing.

Test of Problem Solving. (Zachman et al., LinguiSystems, 1984) This test measures a child's ability to understand various types of *wh* questions (e.g., who, what, where) and provide salient responses to these questions with reference to pictures depicting problem situations. Scores provide standardized comparison to age peers.

Test of Reading Comprehension. (Brown et al., Pro-Ed, 1986) This test measures several aspects of silent reading, including paragraph comprehension; sentence grammar; understanding of word meaning with focus on math, social studies, and science vocabulary; and ability to sequence sentences for meaning. Scores allow standardized comparison to age peers.

Test of Word Finding. (German, DLM, 1986) This test, for 6½- to 13-year-olds, measures the speed and accuracy of picture naming for different types of words, sentence completion, naming a target word described by its attributes, and naming the category described by its components. Results allow standardized comparison to age and grade peers.

Test of Word Finding in Discourse. (German, DLM, 1991) This test measures word substitutions, reformulations, insertions, repetitions, empty words, time fillers, and delays in a transcribed, recorded conversation, using probe pictures and questions to elicit responses. Results provide informal severity descriptors of word-finding behaviors.

Test of Written Language-2. (Hammill and Larsen, Pro-Ed, 1988) This test measures vocabulary usage, spelling, grammar, capitalization, and punctuation in structured writing tasks and in a spontaneous writing sample. Ability to develop a topic is also measured in the spontaneous sample. Results allow standardized comparison to age peers.

Test of Written Spelling-2. (Larsen and Hammill, Pro-Ed, 1986) This test measures spelling of words, with regular and irregular spelling rules, as dictated in isolation and in sentence context. Scores allow standardized comparison to age peers.

Token Test for Children. (DiSimoni, 1978, DLM) This test measures a child's ability to follow oral directions that specify color, size, shape, and relative position with an increasing number of elements to recall. The test is sensitive to confusion with temporal and spatial terms. Scores allow comparison to age peers between 3 and 12½ years and grade peers between kindergarten and grade 6.

Utah Test of Language Development-3. (Mecham and Jones, Pro-Ed, 1989) This test measures receptive and expressive language with focus on semantic, syntactic, and pragmatic linguistic systems by asking the child to repeat sentences, answer questions, and identify pictures that match targeted words and sentences. Scores allow standardized comparison to age peers between three and ten years.

TESTS OF MOTOR DEVELOPMENT

These tests are used to assess a child's gross and fine motor coordination. Much can be learned from watching how a child moves as well.

Bruininks-Oseretzky Test of Motor Proficiency. (R. H. Bruininks, American Guidance Service, 1977) A recent modification of the Lincoln-Oseretzky tests. For children from 4 to 18 years. Subtests include running speed and agility, balance, bilateral coordination, strength, response speed, visual motor control and upper-limb coordination, speed, and dexterity.

Sensory Integration and Praxis Tests (SIPT). (A. J. Ayres, Western Psychological Services, 1989) A series of seventeen tests that assess sensory integration, sensory motor skills, perceptual skills, and praxis (motor planning) in children ages 4 through 8 years, the SIPT is specifically designed to be used with learning disabled children. This is a revised and updated version of the original Southern California Sensory Integration Tests.

Peabody Developmental Motor Scales. (M. Rhonda Folio and Rebecca R. Fewell, DLM Teaching Resources, 1983) This provides measures of fine and gross motor skills from birth through 83 months. The test was developed for handicapped as well as nonhandicapped children and can be used for children older than 7 with developmental delays.

Quick Neurological Screening Test. (Margaret Mutti, Harold M. Sterling, and Norma V. Spalding, Western Psychological Services, 1978) The QNST is a screening device for early detection of children with learning disabilities that looks at neurological integration as it relates to learning. Can be used for children ages 5 to 17.

TESTS OF VISUAL PERCEPTION AND VISUAL-MOTOR INTEGRATION

Test of Visual-Motor Skills (TVMS). (Morrison F. Gardner, Children's Hospital of San Francisco, 1986) Measures visual-motor functioning by having the child copy designs with a pencil. Can be used for children 2 through 12, either individually or in a group.

Test of Visual Perceptual Skills (nonmotor) (TVPS). (Morrison F. Gardner, Children's Hospital of San Francisco, 1982, 1988) This test assesses visual-perceptual skills without requiring a motor response. Seven areas of visual perception are addressed: visual discrimination, spatial relationships, form constancy, sequential memory. Can be used for children ages 4 through 12.

Jordan Left-Right Reversal Test. (Brian T. Jordan, Academic Therapy Publications, 1990) Used as a screening instrument for children with reading problems and learning disabilities including reversals. Designed for ages 5 through 12.

APPENDIX 7

THE LAB SCHOOL OF WASHINGTON

Founded in a basement in 1967 by current director Sally L. Smith, The Lab School of Washington is now internationally recognized as a leading force in the field of learning disabilities. With a day school, a night school, a clinic for testing and tutoring, and a full range of support services and products, the school serves the diverse needs of children and adults with learning disabilities and the parents and professionals who care for them.

The Day School has two hundred fifty students in grades K–12. Students are intelligent, often gifted school-age children who have learning disabilities that hinder their academic success in regular classrooms. Approximately 83 percent of student tuitions are paid by local school systems under Public Law 101-476. The average student-teacher ratio is four or five to one, depending on the division level. Since each child's problems are different, The Lab School carefully tailors its activities and programs to meet the special needs of each individual student.

Within the Day School there are five divisions:

Primary Program: for five- to six-year-olds who are at high risk for learning disabilities and need two years of intensive remediation before returning to regular school

Elementary Program: ungraded groups II through VI

Intermediate Program: ungraded groups VII through XI

Junior High School: grades 7–8

High School: grades 9–12

The success of The Lab School approach is evident in the success of the school's alumni and graduates. Almost every former student has completed high school; most have gone to college, many to graduate or law school. Graduates now lead productive lives in fields as diverse as art, engineering, business, law, and computer programming.

Colleges that Lab School students have attended include The American University, the University of Arizona, Bard, Brown, Florida A & M, Guilford, Howard, James Madison, Misericordia, Oberlin, Rhode Island School of Design, Rochester Institute of Technology, Savannah School of Art and Design, Southern Vermont, Western Maryland, and West Virginia Wesleyan.

THE LAB SCHOOL NIGHT SCHOOL

Established in 1984, The Lab School Night School helps adults strengthen academic, communications, and employment skills. Some students are working to pass the G.E.D., others want to enter or reenter college, and still others are working to overcome problems with a particular college course. Enrollment ranges from seventy-five to ninety students each quarter. With a student-teacher ratio of five to one, courses are taught on an individual basis; students act as coinvestigators and planners in their programs. Courses offered include reading, math, phonics/spelling, English and composition, literature, computer, study skills, life skills, and job-seeking skills, as well as a guided study course supporting students currently enrolled in college classes. In addition to academic growth, students also enjoy social and emotional support. They are able to meet other learning disabled adults, share experiences, and problem-solve together. They are able to dispel feelings of isolation and become motivated for achievement and success.

THE LAB SCHOOL SUMMER SCHOOL

Each summer a six-week program is available to students in grades K–12. Many children who do not attend The Lab School during the year come from around the country and overseas to brush up on their skills and participate in the Art, Science, and Club programs. A different theme is developed for the summer program each year and the Art, Science, and Club curricula vary accordingly. Past summer themes have included Magic, Riverboat Summer, Explorers, and Treasure Island. Intensive remedial instruction focuses on each student's deficit areas.

CLINICAL AND SUPPORT SERVICES

A full range of support services is available to members of the community as well as to Lab School families. Clinical services offered include diagnostic testing and psychological services, occupational therapy, and speech and language therapy. Tutoring is provided for all age groups, primarily for reading, spelling, study skills, and math, but also to teach specific content areas (i.e., history and chemistry) and academic-readiness skills. More than one hundred tutors have been trained at The Lab School. They learn diagnostic/prescriptive techniques while spending an academic year in practicums under master teachers, culminating in a certificate declaring them competent to tutor any age group under the aegis of The Lab School. Tutors are matched with appropriate clients and carefully supervised. Career and college counseling focuses on helping high school students and adults with learning disabilities to reach their academic and career goals. Student profiles are matched with appropriate colleges. Special attention is given to determine specific accommodations needed for success.

OUTREACH PROGRAMS

In addition to serving the Washington community, The Lab School is an international resource for children and adults with learning disabilities, as well as for parents, educators, and medical professionals.

Through national media coverage and speeches to parent and education organizations, school administrators hope to increase public awareness and understanding of learning disabilities.

The American University graduate program in Special Education: Learning Disabilities has trained thousands of teachers. Each year most of the graduate students serve their practicums under master teachers at The Lab School. Howard University, George Washington University, and Mount Vernon College also use the school as a training site.

The Lab School International Training Center offers products and training in Lab School methods. The Lab School Lecture-Discussion Series provides a popular forum for the community, parents, teachers, and mental-health and medical professionals.

In 1994 The Lab School was identified as an exemplary educational program by the National Diffusion Network (NDN) of the U.S. Department of Education. Through NDN, The Lab School approach (or parts of the school such as the Arts and Academic Clubs Advisory Service) can be made available to all U.S. public and private schools.

The Lab School believes that although people with learning disabilities are exceptional in their disabilities, frequently they prove to be as exceptional in their abilities.

INDEX

Abstract thinking, 68, 170, 171, 192, 200
  definition of, 311
  and language/reading skills, 102, 103,
    110
  and mathematics, 115, 116
  and social skills, 277
  teaching, 157, 158–59, 164, 167
  and thinking patterns, 116–17, 118,
    119
  and time, 87, 88–90
Academic clubs, 177, 182–92
Academic programs, 170, 182, 189, 190,
    230–31. *See also* Three Rs; *specific
    subject matter.*
Acceptance, need for, 278–80
Achievement tests, 368–69
ACLD. *See* Learning Disabilities.
  Association of America
ADD (attention deficit disorder), 30, 34,
    42, 44
ADHD (attention-deficit/hyperactivity
    disorder), 28, 199. *See also* ADD.
  books about, 328–29
  causes of, 37
  Combined Type of, 35, 47
  definition of, 34–35, 43
  and development, 38, 41
  diagnosing, 43, 45–48
  and direct observation, 45–48

and learning disabilities, 35–37, 53
  legal provisions for, 36–37
  and medication, 35, 48–51
  as an official term, 35
  and parents, 44, 199, 302, 303
  Predominantly Hyperactive-Impulsive
    Type of, 35, 38–43, 46–47, 48, 49
  Predominantly Inattentive Type of, 35,
    37–38, 47
  rating scales for, 44–45
  symptoms of, 34–35, 37–43, 53
  treatment of, 39–40, 48–51, 52–53
Adolescence, 28, 38, 186
  and acceptance, 278–80
  and anxiety, 263–66
  and chronological age, 265–66
  and competency, 263–66, 269
  and daily living skills, 269–70
  and development, 265–66, 269
  and language, 272–73
  and organization, 266–71
  overview of, 260–63
  and parents, 261–62, 303, 304
  and social skills, 261, 273–75
  and special talents, 280–82
  and survival strategies, 271–72
Adopted children, 197–98
Adults. *See also* Parents; Professionals;
    Teachers.

with ADHD, 38
failures of, 294–95
responsibilities of, 293–95
vulnerability of, 295
Advocacy. *See also* Organizations.
    organizations for, 254, 257
    and parents, 224, 297, 302
    and school systems, 253
    and self-advocacy, 258, 297, 302
    and teachers, 134–35, 224
Age. *See* Chronological age;
    Developmental age.
Ambidextrousness, 79
American Psychiatric Association, 43,
    313
Americans with Disabilities Act (ADA,
    1990), 183–85, 258, 308
Analogies, 117–18
Anger, 204, 212, 213–14, 294
Animism, 17
Anxiety
    of children, 48, 63–64, 260–61, 263–
    66
    and parents, 196, 198–201, 262
    of teachers, 127
"Appropriate education," 224–25, 252,
    254, 259
Arithmetic. *See* Mathematics.
Artists, 179–82, 190, 192
Arts, 73, 169–82, 188, 192, 341. *See also*
    Artists.
Association for Children with Learning
    Disabilities (ACLD). *See* Learning
    Disabilities Association of America
    (LDA).
Attention Deficit Disorder. *See* ADD.
Attention, paying, 18, 33, 100. *See also*
    ADD; ADHD; Attention span;
    Distractibility.
Attention span, 97, 135, 165, 229. *See also*
    Distractibility.
Attention-getting behavior, 138
Auditory skills. *See* Hearing; Listening.
Automation, 298–99. *See also* Computers.

Body, 99, 175, 316, 319. *See also* Motor
    skills.
    awareness of, 80–86, 92–93, 312
    development of, 78
    image of, 82, 312, 314

as information-gathering tool, 77–78
learning about, 80–86
and space, 76–86, 92–93, 191
and time, 92–93
Brain injury, 22, 26–27, 37
Brainstorming, 145, 147, 212
Buddy system, 138, 267

Case managers, 243, 259
Categorization. *See* Classification.
CHADD. *See* Children with Attention
    Deficit Disorder (CHADD).
Challenging students, 71, 166–68
Checklists, importance of, 268–69
Child Attention Problems Scale, 44
Child Behavior Checklist, 44
Children with Attention Deficit Disorder
    (CHADD), 52, 208, 347
Choices, making, 62–63, 86, 210, 277
Chronological age
    and adolescence, 265–66
    and developmental age, 11–12, 18–19,
        67–68, 228–29, 265–66, 312, 316
    and evaluations, 228–29
    and teaching materials, 159–60
Classes. *See also* Groups.
    overcrowded, 301
    size of, 189, 250, 300
Classification, 97, 117, 119, 120, 165. *See
    also* Organization.
Clumsiness, 83–85, 95, 173, 279
College education/students, 281–82, 283–
    85, 308, 347, 349
College Entrance Examination Board, 156
Comparisons, learning, 117, 118, 166
Computers, 68, 243, 297, 298–99
Concentration. *See* Distractibility.
Concrete Child, 58–60, 64, 88
Concreteness, 115, 170, 277. *See also*
    Concrete Child.
    definition of, 312
    and language, 101, 102, 103
    and learning, 67, 68
    and teachers' feelings/concerns, 130–31
    and teaching approaches, 155, 158–59,
        164
    and thinking patterns, 118, 119
Costs. *See* Financing/costs.
Council for Exceptional Children (CEC),
    207, 348

Counseling. *See* Therapists/therapy.
Counting, 114, 116
Critical thinking, 304, 305–6
Culture, 28, 29, 75–76, 297–98, 337

Daily living skills, 269–70, 287
Dance, 174–75, 179–80, 181–82
Daydreaming, 30, 42–43, 94, 97, 124
Decision making, 307–8
Decoding skills, 109, 110, 312
Denial of disabilities, 31–32, 202, 203,
    253, 271, 278
Depression, 48, 205, 214–15
Development, human, 78, 92, 269, 312,
    316, 317. *See also* Developmental age.
    overview of, 66–71
    tests for determining level of, 366–67
Development. *See* Development, human;
    Developmental age; Personnel
    development.
Developmental age, 32–33, 58, 60, 154
    and ADHD, 38, 41
    and adolescence, 265–66
    and chronological age, 11–12, 18–19,
        67–68, 228–29, 265–66, 312, 316
    and multidisciplinary evaluations, 228–
        29
    and stages in human development, 66–
        71
*Diagnostic and Statistical Manual of
    Mental Disorders,* 4th Edition (DSM
    IV), 35, 42, 43, 313
Differentiation, 13–15, 97, 110
Directions
    following, 41–42, 80, 100, 103, 129, 227,
        230, 318
    giving, 140–43, 211
    hearing, 100
    oral, 140–41
    repeating, 140–41
    and teaching, 155
    understanding, 278
Discipline, 41–42, 128, 137–38, 191, 250
Discrimination, against learning disabled,
    283–85
Disoriented Child, 63–64
Distractibility, 83, 91, 173, 191
    and ADHD, 39, 48, 49
    and causes of learning disabilities, 27
    definition of, 312

and language, 101, 103
and organization/structure, 12–15, 137
and teaching, 156
and transitions, 139
Drama class, 12, 68–69, 176, 179, 181
Dressing of self, 80, 210–11
DSM. See *Diagnostic and Statistical
    Manual of Mental Disorders.*
Due process, 224, 242, 252–57
Dyslexia, 297, 313, 353

Education. *See also* Educators; Learning;
    Teachers; Teaching
    books about theory of, 339–41
    and causes of learning disabilities, 28
    definition of, 133
    for the future, 296–309
    progressive, 133
    purpose of, 299
Education for All Handicapped Children
    Act (1975), 179–82, 221–22
Educational Testing Service (ETS), 156,
    348
Educators. *See also* Teachers.
    goals of, 181
    organizations for, 347
    as parents, 200
    support/help for, 208
Egocentricism, 17–19, 58, 118, 176, 277
Elementary schools
    and academic clubs, 186–87
    and the arts, 169, 171–72
Emotions. *See also specific emotion.*
    tests concerning, 370–73
Employment. *See* Jobs.
Encoding skills, 110, 314
Environment
    and academic clubs, 191
    and causes of learning disabilities, 24,
        28, 30, 31
    confusing, 15–17
    and dispelling tension, 137–39
    least restrictive, 224, 245–48, 254, 255
    and need for organization, 15–17
    teachers' role in establishing, 122, 137–
        39
Evaluations, of teachers, 147
Evaluations, multidisciplinary
    and academic programs, 230–31
    components of, 232

delays in doing, 226–27
and due process, 252, 253
and evaluation team, 227, 231–32, 236–37, 238
and financing/costs, 226, 232
and groups, 227
hearings about, 253–56, 259
and IDEA, 223, 224, 225–34
and IEP, 235–44
and other handicapping factors, 229
and parents, 215–16, 226, 227–28, 235–44, 252–53
permissions for, 226, 253
questions concerning, 216, 227–28
reports of, 231–32, 238
and school systems, 232
and second opinions, 232
and seeking professional help, 215–16
and "severe discrepancy" factor, 228–29
sources of information about, 227, 232–33
teachers' role in, 225–26, 227, 253
and testing, 227–28, 229–31, 233
Eye tracking difficulty, 314
Eye-hand coordination, 112, 113, 114, 314

FAD (Focused Attention Disorder), 22, 42
Failure. See also Success.
and academic clubs, 191
of adults, 294–95
and learning, 61, 71, 74, 300
and Perfectionist, 61
and social skills, 278
and Three Rs, 104, 120–21
Family relationships, 200–206. See also Siblings.
Fatigue, 156, 268, 272
Feedback, 77–78, 93, 275, 295, 308. See also Praise/recognition.
Filmmaking, 176–77, 181–82, 183
Films, 166, 342–45
Financing/costs
of evaluations, 226, 232
and IDEA, 222, 225
and IEP, 242
and inclusion, 249
and private schools, 255, 257
and school systems, 223
statistics about, 225
of support/transition services, 282

Focused Attention Disorder. See FAD.
Focusing, 16, 141, 191, 314. See also Distractibility; FAD
and the arts, 172, 176–77, 179
and survival strategies, 272
and teaching, 155, 165
and thinking patterns, 119

Games, 158, 166, 177, 270–71, 306. See also Play.
Gender issues, 30
Goals
of artists, 181
attainable/reasonable, 18, 295, 307
of educators, 181
and IEP, 236, 242
of learning disabled, 307
and organization, 307
of parents, 307
of teachers, 123
of teaching, 121, 151
Graphic arts, 175–76, 181–82
Group homes, 287–88
Guilt
and adolescence, 263–66
and parents, 23–24, 25, 32, 126, 196, 198, 210, 262
of siblings, 202, 203–4
and teachers, 124, 126

Halfway houses, 287–88
Handwriting, 112–13, 313, 316
Hearing, 99, 100, 102, 108–9, 111, 170, 182, 311. See also Listening.
Heredity, 25
Home management, 209–11, 242–43
Human development. See Development.
Humor, sense of, 8, 59, 103, 137–38, 143, 217, 278 ·
Hyperactivity, 27, 31, 41–42, 44, 49–50, 70, 101, 124, 229, 315. See also ADHD.
Hyperkinesis, 37, 315
Hypoactivity, 30, 42–43, 70, 229, 315

IDEA (Individuals with Disabilities Education Act). See also IEP.
and academic programs, 230–31

IDEA (Individuals with Disabilities
    Education Act) (*continued*)
    and ADHD, 36–37
    and an appropriate education, 224–25,
        252, 254, 259
    and case managers, 243, 259
    and confidentiality of records, 224,
        234–35
    and definition of learning disabled, 20
    and due process, 224, 252–57
    and financing/costs, 222, 225
    and inclusion, 248–50
    and the "least restrictive environment,"
        224, 245–48
    and multidisciplinary evaluations, 224,
        225–34
    overview of, 221–24
    and parent-teacher relationships, 220–
        59
    and personnel development, 224, 250–
        52
    purpose/intent of, 222, 259
    and transition services, 257–58, 282
IEP (Individualized Educational
    Program), 223, 224, 245, 251, 252,
        254, 256, 258, 282
    for home, 242–43
    overview of, 235–44
Impulsivity, 27, 71, 91, 101, 174, 231, 277,
        314, 315. *See also* ADHD.
Inclusion, principle of, 248–50
Individual Transition Plan (ITP), 258
Individualized Educational Program. *See*
    IEP.
Individuals with Disabilities Education
    Act. *See* IDEA.
Information centers, 346–53
Information processing
    difficulty with, 317
    tests for, 365–66
Instruction. *See* Teaching.
Instructions. *See* Directions.
Integration, 314
    and the arts, 176, 179
    and learning, 69, 70, 71
    and motor skills, 82, 83
    and organization/structure, 13–15, 136–
        37
    sensory, 82, 318, 352
    and space, 76, 82, 83, 86
    tests concerning, 282

and Three Rs, 97, 110, 115
    and time, 86
    visual-motor, 282
Intellectuals, as parents, 200
Intelligence, 104, 120, 166–68, 362–65
Inter Agency Committee on Learning
    Disabilities, 20
Irritability, 27, 40, 48, 53
ITP. *See* Individual Transition Plan.

Jobs, 273, 282, 283–88, 308, 351
Journals, professional, 354–58

Lab School of Washington
    and academic clubs, 182–92
    and ADHD, 35, 37, 49, 52
    arts as central to teaching at, 170, 172–
        79, 180, 182, 188, 192
    clinical and support services of, 167,
        174, 177, 285, 286
    and creating/reinforcing organization,
        177–78
    drama classes at, 12
    and FAD, 42
    and IEP, 243
    and medication for students, 49
    night school of, 284–85
    overview of, 283–84
    social science curriculum at, 189
    summer sessions at, 187, 189, 285
    and teachers' feelings/concerns, 126
    and teaching, 157, 158, 159, 166–67
    and time, 88–89
Language
    and academic clubs, 189, 191, 192
    and adolescence, 272–73
    and the arts, 177, 181, 182
    body, 99
    evolution of, 102
    expressive, 314
    and gender issues, 30
    and motor skills, 82
    receptive, 317
    and school readiness, 99
    and social skills, 273
    and teaching, 155, 165, 167
    tests for oral, 375–80
    and Three Rs, 101–4
    typical problems concerning, 102–3

Laterality, 78–80, 81, 108–9, 315
LDA. *See* Learning Disabilities Association
   of America.
Learning. *See also* Abstract thinking;
   Transfer of learnings.
   and anxiety, 63–64
   and body awareness, 80–86
   and concreteness, 58–60, 64, 67, 68
   definition of, 73
   and developmental age, 66–71
   and Disoriented Child, 63–64
   and failure, 61, 71, 74
   in future, 297, 299–301
   and group size, 189
   individualized, 299–301
   and integration, 69, 70, 71
   and mistakes, 71
   and Naive Child, 65–66
   and Now Child, 57–58
   and One-Way Kid, 55–57, 64, 71
   and organization, 71
   and Perfectionist, 60–62
   and perseveration, 56, 62–63, 71
   and play, 189
   and space, 76–80
   and starting tasks, 54–56, 71–72
   student involvement in, 153, 191–92
   teachers' role in, 71–72
   the Three Rs, 94–121
Learning disabilities. *See also* Denial of
   disabilities.
   and ADHD, 35–37, 53
   books about, 320–25
   and causes of disabilities, 20–33, 198,
      229, 318
   definition of, 223
   diagnosing, 206–9
   and hypoactivity, 42–43
   as learning disorders, 35
   pervasiveness of, 26
   and range of disabilities, 21
   and recognizing problem, 28–32
   second opinions about, 208
Learning Disabilities Association of
   America (LDA), 20, 30, 52, 207, 208,
   215, 240, 249, 253, 254, 349
Learning disabled
   as achievers, 206
   as adopted, 197–98
   adult reactions to, 3, 4
   civil rights of, 248

common school characteristics of, 96–
   97
definition of, 20, 21
examples of, 1–9, 206
feelings of, 4–5, 125–27, 262–63
in future, 296–309
identification of, 94–97
"instant remediation" for, 31–32
and other handicapping conditions, 21
severely, 248
special talents of, 71, 280–82, 286–87
statistics about, 20
strengths of, 19
support/help for, 263, 286–87, 297, 303
symptoms of, 1–9, 27, 32–33, 229–30,
   273–74, 277–78, 318
terms used to refer to, 21–23
as twins, 200–201
victimization of, 214–15
Learning disorders, 35
Learning profile, 151, 154
"Least restrictive environment," 224, 245–
   48, 254, 255
Left-handedness, 79
Left-right confusion, 27
Legal assistance, 254–55
Life situations. *See* Daily living skills;
   Social skills.
Listening, 99, 103, 109, 165, 167, 277

Mainstreaming, 23, 144, 146, 236, 245–50
Mathematics, 35, 73, 113–16, 189, 192, 296,
   313, 333–35, 369–70
Medications, 35, 48–51
Memory, 42, 171, 191, 313
   and concreteness, 158
   and language, 103
   and mathematics, 114, 115, 116
   and reading, 108, 109, 110
   and school readiness, 98, 100
   and social skills, 277
   and space, 86
   and survival strategies, 271–72
   and teaching, 158
   and thinking patterns, 119
   and Three Rs, 97
   and time, 86, 91
   and writing, 110, 111, 113
Mental retardation, 28
Military families, 352

Mistakes, 71, 131–32, 143, 218–19, 295
Mixed dominance, 79–80
Models, teachers as, 131–34, 137, 145–46, 162
Moodiness, 8, 40, 48, 277, 313
Motivation, 120, 154, 167
Motor planning, 81–86
Motor skills, 112, 113, 170, 311, 313, 314, 316
   and body awareness, 81–86, 92–93
   books about, 336–37
   tests about, 281, 282
Multidisciplinary evaluations. *See* Evaluations, multidisciplinary.
Music, 180, 181–82

Naive Child, 65–66
National Center for Learning Disabilities (NCLD), 208, 350
National Institute of Mental Health, 37
National Joint Committee on Learning Disabilities (NJCLD), 21
Now Child, 40, 57–58, 88

One-Way Kid, 55–57, 64, 71, 115, 132, 231, 275
Order. *See* Organization; Sequencing; Structure.
Organization, 39, 229, 317. *See also* Sequencing; Structure; Tasks, analysis of.
   and adolescence, 266–71
   and the arts, 171, 172, 173, 175, 176, 177–79, 180, 181
   and the body, 76–80, 92–93
   creating/reinforcing, 177–79
   and distractibility, 12–15
   and egocentricism, 17–19
   and environment, 15–17
   and focusing on symptoms rather than causes, 32–33
   and goals, 307
   importance of, 10, 289, 290–95, 306–7
   and language, 101, 103
   and learning, 55, 70–71
   and motor skills, 81–86
   need for, 10–19
   and parents, 209–11
   and school readiness, 100
   and social skills, 277, 278, 295
   of space, 73–86, 90–93
   and survival strategies, 271
   and task analysis, 82–83
   and teachers, 16, 70–71, 122–23, 130
   and teaching, 19, 163, 165–66, 267–68, 306
   and thinking patterns, 117, 118, 119
   and Three Rs, 97, 110–12, 114, 120, 267
   of time, 73–74, 83, 86–93
Organizations, 207–8, 346–53, 358–60. *See also specific organization*
Orton Dyslexia Society, 207, 208, 351
Other handicapping conditions, 21, 229, 248

Parents, 41–42, 192, 307. *See also* Adults.
   and ADHD, 34, 35–36, 44, 49, 52, 53
   as advocates, 224, 297, 302
   and anxiety, 196, 198–201, 262
   and causes of learning disabilities, 23–24, 25, 32
   concerns/feelings of, 3, 126, 127, 193–219, 261–62, 302–5
   and diagnosing learning disabilities, 206–9
   and due process, 242, 252–57
   failures of, 294–95
   and family relationships, 200–206
   and guilt, 23–24, 25, 32, 126, 196, 198, 210, 262
   and IDEA, 220–59
   and IEP, 235–44, 252–57
   as intellectuals, 200
   and least restrictive environment, 247–48
   marriage relationships between, 195, 196
   and multidisciplinary evaluations, 215–16, 225–34, 235–44, 252–53
   and Now Child, 58
   and organizing child's life, 17, 209–11
   overreaction by, 198–201
   and parent-teacher relationships, 95–96, 127, 220–59, 301
   problems of, 217–19
   professional help for, 214–17
   responsibilities of, 293–94, 297, 302–5
   rights of, 223, 242

and structuring child's behavior, 211–14

and support for children, 28, 233

support/help for, 206–9, 212, 214–17, 219, 254–55, 257, 305, 350

and teaching, 163–64

and testing, 208

Part-whole difficulty, 316. See also Abstract thinking.

Peer relationships, 261, 287

Perception
    auditory, 311
    definition of, 97, 316
    figure-ground, 314
    kinesthetic, 315
    and mathematics, 115
    and motor skills, 92–93
    about other people's feelings, 70
    and perceptual deficits, 316–17
    and perceptual handicaps, 316–17
    and reading, 104–10
    and school readiness, 99
    tactile, 318–19
    tests about, 282
    and thinking patterns, 119
    and Three Rs, 97, 120
    visual, 319

Perfectionism, 60–62, 113, 143

Perseveration, 27, 139, 264
    definition of, 317
    examples of, 16
    and learning, 56, 62–63, 71
    and social skills, 273, 277

Personnel development, 144–45, 224, 250–52

Phonics, 109, 111

Physical education, 139, 281

Piaget, Jean, 58, 68, 295

Play, 14, 188, 189, 211–12, 214. See also Games.

Praise/recognition, 53, 160–62, 214, 286–87, 303, 304

Private schools, 255, 257

Problem solving, 162, 190, 265, 297

Professionals
    seeking help from, 214–17
    support/help for, 207, 208, 347

Public Law 94–142. See IDEA.

Public Law 101–336. See Americans with Disabilities Act (ADA, 1990).

Public Law 104–476. See IDEA.

Readiness, 92, 120
    and academic clubs, 187, 189, 192
    and the arts, 171, 174, 192
    reading, 98, 171, 174, 187, 189
    school, 98–100, 120, 171
    and teaching, 151–52, 165
    tests about, 366–67

Reading, 35, 79, 267, 313
    and academic clubs, 187, 189, 192
    and the arts, 171, 173, 174, 179
    and automation, 298–99
    as decoding, 109, 110, 313
    definition of, 73
    in future, 296
    and intelligence, 104, 168
    and language, 103
    and learning to read, 104–10
    and mixed dominance, 79–80
    organizations concerned with, 349
    readiness, 98, 171, 174, 187, 189
    research about, 353
    teaching of, 108–9, 166–68, 267
    tests about, 375–80
    typical problems concerning, 109–10

"Reasonable accomodations," 283, 284–85

Reasoning, 109, 110, 114, 115, 119, 177, 271

Records, confidentiality of, 224, 234–35

Rehabilitation Act (1973), 36–37, 283

Relationships. See Abstract thinking.

Research centers, 352–53

Rigidity, 103, 113, 115, 119, 136, 278, 318

Routine, 136, 210. See also Structure.

School. See also School systems.
    coming to, 139
    readiness for, 98–100, 120, 171

School systems. See also Evaluations, multidisciplinary; IEP.
    as advocates, 253
    and due process, 252–57
    and financing/costs, 223
    and parents, 223, 252–57
    support/help from, 208

Second opinions, 208, 232

Section 504 (Rehabilitation Act, 1973), 36–37, 283

Self-advocacy, 297, 302

Self-image, of learning disabled, 42, 53, 71, 92, 214, 262–63, 293, 304

Self-monitoring, 161–62

Sensory defensiveness, 317
Sensory input, 317
Sensory integration, 82, 318
Sensory-motor skills, 66, 336–37
Sequencing. *See also* Organization; Tasks:
  analysis of.
  and the arts, 171
  definition of, 318
  and school readiness, 100
  and social skills, 277
  and space/time, 86
  and teaching, 165–66
  and Three Rs, 100, 103, 110, 111, 114, 116, 120
"Severe discrepancy" factor, 228–29
Sharing, 273, 275, 277. *See also*
  Egocentricism.
Siblings, 9, 192, 195, 200–206, 262
Social skills, 7, 27, 39, 42
  and acceptance, 278–80
  and adolescence, 273–75
  and characteristics of learning disabled, 18, 273–74, 277–78
  and human qualities, 288–89
  and humor, 278
  importance of, 289, 308–9
  and independent living skills, 287
  and language, 102, 273
  and learning, 69–70, 308–9
  and motor skills, 84–85
  and organization, 277, 278, 295
  and teaching social behavior, 275–78
  tests about, 370–73
  and winning and losing, 278
Sorting out. *See* Classification;
  Organization.
Space. *See also* Motor skills.
  adult's use of, 74–76
  and ambidextrousness, 79
  and the arts, 174–75
  and the body, 76–77, 80–86, 92–93, 191
  child as lost in, 74–76
  and culture, 75–76
  and handwriting, 112, 113
  judging, 90–93
  and laterality, 78–80, 81
  learning about, 76–80
  and memory, 86
  and mixed dominance, 79–80
  organization of, 73–86, 90–93
  and readiness, 92

and safety/security, 86–87
and self concept, 92
and social skills, 277
and structure, 86–87, 88
teaching about, 92–93
and Three Rs, 104–10, 112, 113, 116, 120
and time, 83
visualization of, 80
Special talents, 280–82, 286–87
Speech, 27, 30, 91, 99, 101, 103. *See also*
  Language.
Spelling, 110–12, 113, 119, 192, 375–80
Sports, 139, 281
Sportsmanship, 61–62
Staff development. *See* Personnel
  development.
Structure, 49, 178, 190–91, 215. *See also*
  Organization.
  and behavior, 211–14
  definition of, 318
  parents' role in providing, 211–14
  and rigidity, 136, 318
  and safety/security, 210–11
  and space/time, 86–87, 88
  teachers' role in providing, 130, 135–37
  and teaching, 154–56
Success, 120–21, 151, 153, 155, 212, 303, 304. *See also* Failure.
Supplemental services. *See* Support/
  supplementary services.
Support. *See also* Organizations.
  for learning disabled, 263, 286–87, 297, 303
  for parents, 206–9, 212, 214–17, 219, 254–55, 257, 305, 350
  for professionals, 347
  for teachers, 123, 126–27, 143–45, 250
Support/supplementary services, 160, 236, 282, 285, 349. *See also* Transition
  services.
Survival strategies, 271–72
Systems approach, 306–7

Tactile, 76, 82, 108, 170, 318–19
Tasks
  analysis of, 82–83, 152–54, 252, 268–69, 319
  developmental, 312
  starting, 16, 54–56, 71–72, 154–56

Teacher rating scales, 45
Teachers, 25–26, 181, 190, 192, 298. *See also* Adults; Educators; Teaching.
  accountability of, 243
  and ADHD, 40, 41–43, 52–53
  as advocates, 134–35, 224
  as ally of child, 135–37
  attitudes/feelings of, 3, 42–43, 122–49
  checklist for helping, 148–49
  competency of, 3, 126
  demands on, 123–24
  and dispelling tension, 137–39
  ego of, 127–31
  evaluation of, 147
  failures of, 294–95
  and focusing on symptoms instead of causes, 32–33
  and giving instructions, 140–43
  goals of, 123
  and IDEA, 220–59
  idealization of, 129
  and IEP, 235–44
  and learning, 70–72, 299–300
  and manipulation by children, 132–33
  and medications, 50, 51
  militancy of, 133–34
  as models, 131–34, 137, 145–46, 162
  and multidisciplinary evaluations, 225–26, 227, 233–34, 253
  and organization/structure, 16, 70–71, 130, 135–37
  and parent-teacher relationships, 95–96, 127, 220–59, 301
  and records of children, 235
  respect for, 301
  responsibilities of, 293–95
  selection of, 146
  self-esteem of, 127–31
  and staff development, 144–45
  supervisors of, 143–45, 147
  and support for learning disabled, 28
  support/help for, 123, 126–27, 143–45, 147–49, 207, 250
  training of, 145–46, 250–52, 300
  written reports of, 44
Teaching. *See also* Learning; *specific subject matter.*
  and abstract thinking, 158–59
  and academic clubs, 177, 182–92
  and alternate plans/back-up materials, 156

  and alternative forms of instruction, 299–301
  approaches to, 150–68
  basic questions about, 150–51
  and buddy system, 267
  and challenging the intellect, 166–68
  and computers, 68
  and concreteness, 155, 158–59
  and developmental vs chronological ages, 19, 154, 159–60
  as diagnostic, 178–79
  in future, 299–301
  and games, 158, 177
  goals of, 121, 151
  and human development, 66–71
  and humor, 137–38
  and intelligence, 167–68
  keys to high-quality, 159–62
  and learning, 66–71, 151, 154
  materials for, 154, 159–60, 252
  and motivation, 154
  multisensory approach to, 68, 156–57, 190
  need for multiple approaches to, 32–33
  objectives of, 151
  and organization/structure, 19, 154–56, 163, 165–66, 267–68, 306
  pace of, 156
  and parents, 163–64
  and praise/recognition, 160–62
  and preparation for the task, 154–56
  problem-solving approach to, 162
  and readiness, 151–52
  and repetition of lessons, 157
  and self-monitoring, 161–62
  social behavior, 275–78
  sources for determining approach to, 150–52
  about space, 92–93
  and starting tasks, 54–56, 154–56
  step-by-step, 190
  and supplemental services, 160
  and task analysis, 152–54
  of teachers, 145–46, 250–52, 300
  and television, 163–66
  about time, 92–93
  total-immersion, 157
Television, 163–66, 217
Tension, dispelling, 137–39
Testing. *See also specific organization.*
  and academic programs, 230–31

Testing (*continued*)
  books about, 338–39
  diagnostic, 227, 338–39, 361–82
  GED, 348
  and IEP, 237
  intelligence, 227
  interpretation of, 233
  job, 284
  and multidisciplinary evaluations, 227–28, 229–31, 233
  questions parents should ask about, 208
  and time limits for tests, 156
  and typical battery of tests, 361–62
Therapists/therapy, 52, 81–83, 214–17, 352
Thinking patterns, 116–20, 312
Three Rs. *See also* Mathematics; Reading; Writing.
  and characteristics of learning disabled, 96–97
  and intelligence, 104, 120
  and language, 101–4
  and organization, 97, 120
  and perception, 97, 120
  and programming for success, 120–21
  and school readiness, 98–100, 120
  and sequencing, 100, 103, 110, 111, 114, 116, 120
  and space, 104–10, 112, 113, 116, 120
  and thinking patterns, 116–20
  and time, 97, 104–10, 120
Time
  judging, 90–93
  and motor skills, 92–93
  organization of, 73–74, 86–93
  teaching about, 92–93
  and Three Rs, 97, 104–10, 120
Total-immersion teaching, 157
Transition services, 257–58, 282
Transitions, 16–17, 39–40, 70–71, 138–39, 155, 277
Twins, 200–201

Videotapes, 342–45
Visualization, 80, 282, 319
  and the arts, 170, 180, 182
  and hand-writing, 112
  and learning, 68, 69–70, 297
  and mathematics, 114
  and motor skills, 112, 113
  and reading, 108–9, 110
  and school readiness, 98
  and social skills, 277
  of space, 80
  and writing, 111
Vocabulary, 165, 166, 182, 183

Winning and losing, 61–62, 143, 278. *See also* Failure; Success.
Withdrawal, 42, 203
Words, 105, 108, 110
Writing, 35, 80–81, 179, 192
  as encoding, 110, 314
  in the future, 296
  and handwriting, 112–13
  the IEP, 243–44, 251
  importance of, 104, 296
  and intelligence, 104
  and mathematics, 113–14
  and motor skills, 314
  and multidisciplinary evaluations, 231
  and organization, 267
  teaching, 267
  tests concerning, 375–80
  and the Three Rs, 104, 110–13
  typical problems concerned with, 111–12

Yale University, 30, 353

ABOUT THE AUTHOR

SALLY L. SMITH founded The Lab School of Washington in 1967 to provide an education for her bright but severely learning disabled son. Her innovative teaching methods have earned international recognition. The teaching approaches of the school emphasize the arts, using hands-on experiential learning activities to teach very specific academic skills. In 1993 she received the LDA Award, the highest honor given by the Learning Disabilities Association of America, for outstanding leadership in the field of learning disabilities. Under her directorship, in 1994 The Lab School of Washington was singled out as a National Diffusion Network (NDN) Model Education Program by the Department of Education. This honor marked the first time the Department of Education's NDN validated a private, nonprofit special school for the learning disabled.

In 1975 Professor Smith began her affiliation with The American University in Washington, D.C., first as adjunct professor, and in 1976 becoming professor and head of the graduate program in Special Education: Learning Disabilities. Professor Smith has thirty-five to forty graduate students in her program each year, most of whom go on to teach in the public schools.

A tireless advocate for the learning disabled, Professor Smith has authored many articles and frequently speaks to parent, teacher, and educational organizations. Her previous books include the original *No Easy Answers* (1981) and *Succeeding Against the Odds* (1991), which focuses on adults with learning disabilities. She has also written a book for children, *Different Is Not Bad; Different Is the World*.

Professor Smith, a graduate of Bennington College, was honored by the college in 1980 with an award for her outstanding contributions to education. She earned her graduate degree in Human Relations at New York University's School of Education. She is the mother of three sons.

Different Is Not Bad; Different Is the World
A Book About Disabilities

by Sally L. Smith; illustrated by Ben Booz

A colorful, humorous book about learning and physical disabilities for children grades 2 to 6.
For classroom use, special educators, school counselors, or for parents to share with their children.

To order, please contact the publisher:
Sopris West
1140 Boston Avenue
Longmont, CO 80501
(303) 651-2829
or (800) 547-6747